Nice To See It, To See It, Nice

The 1970s In Front of the Telly

BRIAN VINER

SIMON &
SCHUSTER

London · New York · Sydney · Toronto

A CBS COMPANY

First published in Great Britain in 2009 by Simon & Schuster UK Ltd
A CBS COMPANY

1 3 5 7 9 10 8 6 4 2

Simon & Schuster UK Ltd
1st Floor
222 Gray's Inn Road
London
WC1X 8HB

www.simonsays.co.uk

Simon & Schuster Australia
Sydney

A CIP catalogue for this book is available
from the British Library.

ISBN: 978-0-74329-585-7

Typeset by M Rules
Printed in the UK by
CPI Mackays, Chatham ME5 8TD

For my mother, with love, respect and gratitude.

*And in affectionate memory of my childhood
friend Chris Sykes (1959–2007)*

Contents

1

Me, My Dad, The Sundance Kid, Quentin Crisp, and Mother Made Five . . .

It isn't everyone who, more than thirty-three years later, can remember what was on ITV shortly after 8.15 p.m. on Wednesday 4 February 1976. There might not be anyone, in fact. Except me.

I was fourteen years, three months and eleven days old, and I can remember that date and precise time because they became woven into my very psyche, insofar as you can weave anything into a psyche. Moreover, what happened to be showing on telly just after 8.15 p.m. that evening is no less important than the time and date, for television exerted an extraordinarily powerful influence on my adolescence.

That rented box in the corner of our lounge was where I found love (Debbie Harry; Evonne Goolagong; Jenny Hanley from *Magpie*; the blonde one from Abba; Alexandra Bastedo from *The Champions*). It was where I found my male role models (Hannibal Heyes from *Alias*

Smith and Jones; John Noakes from *Blue Peter*; the geeky-looking but courageous England cricketer David Steele; George Carter from *The Sweeney*; the cartoon D'Artagnan from *The Banana Splits Show*). It was where, as an only child, I found escapism in ways too many to enumerate. This book will strive to explain just how large television loomed over my late childhood and burgeoning adolescence, a period of my life which coincided with that unfairly maligned decade, the 1970s. It will celebrate the TV heroes of that decade, find out what happened next for them, explode some myths, and I hope stir a few memories for those of you who, like me, remember with affection a world of only three channels, no remote-control units, and Reginald Bosanquet reading the news with a crooked smile and a dangerous glint in his eye.

So, what *was* on ITV shortly after 8.15 p.m. on Wednesday 4 February 1976? It was *And Mother Makes Five*, starring Wendy Craig as dizzy, harassed housewife Sally Redway. The series was a sequel to *And Mother Makes Three*, in which Craig's character, then called Sally Harrison, was a widow bringing up her sons Simon and Peter. In the 1970s almost all boys were called Simon, Peter or perhaps Andrew, just as almost all boys now are called Zack, Jack or perhaps Josh. The changing fashions of names never fail to intrigue me, and here's an irresistible thought: should the current vogue for Victorian girls' names continue, there will come a time when the nation's old people's homes are full of sparky young women called Edith, Agnes, Mabel and Betty, visiting their arthritic, liver-spotted grandmothers, Kylie, Shania, Britney and Elle.

Anyway, in the final series of *And Mother Makes Three*, in the 'See My Baby Jive', 'Can the Can' and 'Rubber Bullets' early summer of 1973, Sally married an antiquarian bookseller and father-of-one called David Redway, played by Richard Coleman. Their genteel union was a world apart from the alarming face paint worn on *Top of the Pops* by Roy Wood of Wizzard – whose 'See My Baby Jive' reached number one in the charts on 19 May, putting us all out of the misery of yet again having to listen to Tony Orlando and Dawn exhorting us to 'Tie a Yellow Ribbon Round the Old Oak Tree' – but in those days of only three television channels, anything offered in the name of entertainment was gratefully received. We watched the lot, and as an unworldly 11-year-old I garnered almost as much pleasure from Sally Harrison marrying David Redway on *And Mother Makes Three* as I did from a leather-jacketed Suzi Quatro thrusting her loins during 'Can the Can'.

Almost. I had felt my own loins stirring for the first time a year or so earlier, on the afternoon my dad took me to the ABC in Lord Street, Southport, to see *Butch Cassidy and the Sundance Kid*: rather worryingly, the part of my body to which my parents and I had hitherto cheerfully referred as my winkle enjoyed its first stiffening during the scene in which Robert Redford pretended to force the preternaturally beautiful Katharine Ross to undress at gunpoint. Later, in a sense more wholesomely, a leather-clad Suzi Quattro had a similar effect.

Suzi wouldn't have done for fuddy-duddy David Redway, who, inevitably, had been a widower before he married the widowed Sally Harrison. Circa 1973, widowhood was the only means of bringing together two previously married people in the respectable world of British situation comedy, where divorce loomed about as large as it did in Pope Paul VI's Vatican. Moreover, David was a father of one, a girl called not Edith, Agnes, Mabel, Betty, Kylie, Shania, Britney or Elle, but, this being 1973, Jane. Which made five altogether, and set the story up nicely for a few more series of Craig doing her finely tuned turn as a dizzily harassed housewife.

It was her manifest strength. A few years earlier, in a BBC sitcom called *Not in Front of the Children*, she had played dizzy, harassed housewife Jennifer Corner. A couple of years later, in the more memorable or at least less forgettable *Butterflies*, she was to play dizzy, harassed housewife Ria Parkinson, dizzily harassed almost into an affair with a chauffeur-driven smoothie called Leonard, although their relationship was never quite consummated, unlike the real-life affair, I might add, between Wendy Craig and Sir John Mortimer, creator of the semi-autobiographical *Rumpole of the Bailey*, which in August 2004 was revealed to have produced, forty-two years earlier, a son. To Rumpole and Ria, a son! For those of us who grew up no more able to imagine snub-nosed Miss Craig having sex than our own mothers, this revelation of what the tabloid press like to call a love-child came as a shock. To Sir John Mortimer it reportedly came as an even bigger shock, but that's by the by.

Let me get back to Wednesday 4 February 1976, and the penultimate episode in what was to be the final series of *And Mother Makes Five*, an episode called 'Sally's Diary'. Even at fourteen I was scarcely more worldly than I had been at eleven, and, with my Latin homework done, I was more than happy to sit in the lounge with my mum watching telly. My dad had that afternoon gone to London on business, taking the train from Lime Street station in Liverpool.

My dad was in the job business, meaning not that he ran an employment agency, but that he bought ends-of-ranges from manufacturers of women's underwear, so-called job lots of 50,000 bras, say, or 30,000 pantyhose or 20,000 camiknickers, and sold them on to shops or market traders.

That this was known as the job business greatly appealed to me as a child for no more sophisticated reason than that my parents and I, as well as calling my penis a winkle, habitually referred to human waste excreted from the bowels as a 'business' – as in 'have you done a business today, Brian?' This euphemism for the bowel movement varied from household to household. For example, my friends Kay and Alison Taylor, who lived round the corner from us in Clovelly Drive, were brought up calling it a 'job' or a 'jobbie'. But at my house – 58 Lynton Road, Hillside, Southport – it was always a business, and, looked at in a childlike way, this made the job business the poo-poo, which I thought was side-splittingly, roll-around-the-floor-worthy, hilarious. Winkle, business, jobbie: the coy euphemism was something else in which the 1970s specialized. My own children, less equivocally and doubtless more healthily, have grown up talking about poos, wees and willies.

I digress, and not a moment too soon. Shortly after the commercial break in *And Mother Makes Five* that Wednesday evening, with Wendy Craig flapping about something or other, our front doorbell rang. I went to answer it, and was shocked to see, through the swirly-patterned frosted glass, what looked like two police officers. It was: a man and a woman. Looking sombre, they asked if my mother was at home. I led them to the lounge and they suggested that I might want to leave the room, which I did, but only until a terrible wail lured me back in. The two officers had come to convey the devastating news that my father had suffered a fatal heart attack shortly after leaving Lime Street. The train had been stopped at Edge Hill station, from where an ambulance had taken him to hospital, but he was, as lollipop-sucking Lieutenant Theo Kojak of the New York Police Department would have expressed it in Manhattan South's 13th precinct, DOA.

Some years later, incidentally, I learnt from someone or other that the Scouse slang for coitus interruptus is 'to gerroff at Edge Hill', on the basis that Edge Hill is the station just before the terminus at Lime Street. Indeed, it occurs to me now that there is much in this book already to keep a Freudian psychotherapist gainfully occupied, not least that my father's death evokes coitus interruptus and that my first sensation of sexual arousal came while watching the Sundance Kid seemingly about to rape the luscious Etta Place. All I can add is that I consider myself, possibly against the odds, to be fairly well adjusted.

As a teenager, however, I did go through some challenging if not exactly maladjusted phases, and it is tempting to date them from that

Wednesday evening about ten minutes before the end of *And Mother Makes Five*. Although I had plenty of friends, as an only child my sense of security stemmed entirely from my place in our small family unit. Yet now my dad was gone, leaving me as the solitary male. And mother made two.

The police officers left about half an hour later, having waited until a neighbour came round to make the tea. I wonder how long it takes, on average, for news of a death in a British family to be followed by a cup of tea? Do other countries have a similar reliance on a national palliative? I can't quite remember which sympathetic neighbour was drafted in but it was probably Mrs Taylor, mother of Kay and Alison of jobbie fame. Meanwhile, my mother had shakily picked up the telephone and broken the dreadful news to my dad's older sister, Leah, who lived in Liverpool. Her son David, my cousin, was going to drive her through to Southport, and the plan was that David would then take my mum to Walton Hospital to see and I suppose formally identify my dad, while heartbroken Auntie Leah would stay with me.

I didn't have an especially close relationship with Auntie Leah, and was duly horrified when my mum told me tearfully that I would have to share the spare bedroom with her because cousin David would be taking my room that night. At fourteen it didn't exactly fit my game plan for the first woman to spend all night with me in a double bed to be a 68-year-old with a twitch, even though Auntie Leah's twitch had been the source of some fascination to me when I was smaller. I used to think she was winking at me and, to the appalled amusement of my parents, made strenuous efforts to wink back.

While Auntie Leah bustled around our house sobbing, I, not least to defer the worrying going-to-bed moment, watched in a state of numb disbelief the BBC's highlights of Austrian President Dr Rudolf Kirchschlager opening the 1976 Winter Olympics earlier that day in Innsbruck. For the next fortnight, the Winter Olympics provided a

6

decidedly surreal backdrop to the beginning of my life as a fatherless child, the excited paroxysms of the commentators as they watched Britain's John Curry leap and pirouette his way to a figure-skating gold medal synchronizing with my mother's paroxysms of grief as she reflected on a mostly secure, contented past and contemplated a bleak, uncertain future.

Curry was interviewed repeatedly during the Olympic coverage, and was the first gay man – the first really, really gay man – I had ever seen on television, or for that matter anywhere else. There was John Inman on *Are You Being Served?*, of course, but at my school he was widely known to be married with kids. It's a classic brand of school-yard rumour: think of the things least likely to be true and present them as fact. In 1976, as far as the boys of King George V Grammar School, Southport, were concerned, Mr Wilberforce Claybourne Humphries of the menswear department at Grace Brothers was played by the unequivocally heterosexual John Inman, while Clint Eastwood of *The Eiger Sanction* was a raving woofter. It is true that less than two months earlier I had watched the first half-hour of *The Naked Civil Servant*, director Jack Gold's brilliant ninety-minute drama starring John Hurt as Quentin Crisp – a role which he was to reprise fully thirty-two years later – but I knew that Hurt was only acting, and assumed that he was hamming it up, that nobody in real life could possibly be as riotously camp, even the man on whose auto-biography the thing was based.

Curry was hardly any less camp than Crisp, and in a way it was his misfortune to become famous in the mid-1970s, when homosexuality even between consenting adults had been legal for less than ten years, and homophobia, like racism, was still practically state-sanctioned. Nevertheless, I was astounded to find, when researching this book, that at a sporting awards dinner later in 1976, the main guest speaker, lavishly sideburned ventriloquist Roger de Courcy, referred to Curry in his speech as a 'fairy'. And got a big laugh, despite the fact that

Curry was a) in attendance and b) in attendance as the main guest of honour, as that year's BBC Sports Personality of the Year.

As for Quentin Crisp, fifteen years after watching *The Naked Civil Servant* I bought him brunch in New York. I was there on holiday, but someone told me that Crisp's number was in the Manhattan phonebook and that in return for a free meal he would cheerfully give an interview to just about anyone. By then I was on the first rung of my career as a journalist and it would have seemed a dereliction of duty not at least to give him a call in his rooming-house, famously thick with dust. He agreed to have brunch with me in a bar on Second Avenue, and arrived, impressively spry at eighty-one, wearing copious amounts of mascara, a flowery cravat and a pink velvet fedora. Inevitably, even in Manhattan, heads turned, and I confess to my shame that at first I found myself more than a little embarrassed to be seen in his company. 'Englishmen do not even like effeminate women, let alone men,' he mused between mouthfuls of blueberry muffin in that strange rasping voice that Hurt had reproduced so exactly. He had doubtless recognized my discomfort. 'A woman constantly fiddling with her pins, dressing daringly, or asking if you love her as much as you loved her in Vienna. That is very embarrassing to any Englishman.'

It was in the summer of 1976, six months after my father died and eight months after the transmission of *The Naked Civil Servant*, that Quentin Crisp had become a star, with a successful one-man stage show at the Edinburgh Festival. *The Naked Civil Servant* had caused a sensation, by presenting an effeminate homosexual, for the first time on British television, as brave, funny and resourceful, in fact in many ways downright heroic. Unsurprisingly, getting Crisp's shocking autobiography dramatized for television in the first place had been less than straightforward. The BBC were offered it but turned it down flat, and even when Thames Television bravely decided to go ahead, the Independent Broadcasting Authority was terribly jittery about the project, and insisted on removing some of the more daring lines in Philip Mackie's excellent script. 'Sexual intercourse is a poor substitute for masturbation' was deleted with one firm stroke of the censor's pen, and solemnly replaced with 'Wasn't it fun in the bath tonight?'

Despite such prudish surgery, *The Naked Civil Servant* was still pretty racy stuff for 1975, and after half an hour my parents decided that it was not suitable viewing for an impressionable 14-year-old. My father had a habit of watching television with his hands pressed together, with the tips of both forefingers resting against his lips, and the tips of both middle fingers touching his nose. I always knew when he was slightly agitated because his forefingers, instead of resting, would drum against one another, the beat becoming ever more frantic depending on his level of agitation. Half an hour into *The Naked Civil Servant* he was at it like Cozy Powell (whose instrumental tour de force 'Dance With the Devil' had reached number three in the charts in January 1974, and whose name I still cite when I hear impressive drumming, not that I'm stuck in the 1970s or anything), which I knew was the cue for me to go to bed, especially once my parents had exchanged The Look.

The Look was a signal that something had gone awry in the parental universe. In a televisual context it usually concerned robust language or some kind of spectacle deemed inappropriate for my keen young eyes. My father was much more sensitive to this sort of thing than my mother, which was odd, because for a few years in the 1960s, I suppose when the job business was in a trough, he had opened a betting shop in Liverpool city centre, patronized by dockers and builders whose response to losing bets was almost certainly not 'Oh, fiddlesticks!'

Moreover, he played poker most nights and took an endless supply of ribald jokes to the table, which I know only because, after he died, his old poker buddies told me and my mum that their sessions wouldn't be half as much fun without Allen Viner's latest joke. Yet he thought I should be protected from anything remotely lewd. I remember sitting in the car with him one day – I must have been ten or eleven – and boldly asking him what the expression 'rubber johnny' meant. I'd heard it from my friends Jez and Chris Sykes and was too self-conscious to admit to them that I didn't know what they were on about. It was a perfect opportunity for my dad to raise the birds and the bees. But instead he told me that it was a very rude expression and I shouldn't use it again. It was several more years before I knew the meaning of rubber johnny – also known in the 1970s as a johnny bag – and several years more before I understood how it was supposed to be deployed. By which I mean inflated, filled with water, and dropped from my friend Gary's bedroom window onto the patio below. Obviously.

2

'I Think We're Just Out of Waldorfs' – Meeting Basil Fawlty

The 1970s encouraged that kind of naïvety. Sauciness was fine – Benny Hill's immortal 'Ernie (The Fastest Milkman in the West)' topped the charts for four weeks in 1971, setting the innuendo-riven tone for the rest of the decade – yet older people continued to talk about the 'permissive society' as though it were some kind of contagious disease. And my dad, drumming his fingertips, doubtless felt that *The Naked Civil Servant* was one permissive step too far. Little could he or I have imagined that I would one day sit across a small table in a cafe on Second Avenue in Manhattan from the man whose life story had inspired John Hurt's remarkable performance. But then my career in journalism has been full of such encounters, with people who in some way or other figured from afar in my childhood.

The most poignant of these encounters was with John Cleese, in a

Greek taverna in Camden Town, north London, in November 1995. Cleese was a hero to me, not because of Monty Python, which I had been slightly too young to appreciate fully (even though like every other 1970s schoolboy I could recite most of the Dead Parrot sketch, and do a passable imitation of the man from the Ministry of Silly Walks), but because of *Fawlty Towers*.

The first episode of *Fawlty Towers*, 'A Touch of Class', was transmitted on BBC2 on Friday 19 September 1975, when, although none of us could possibly have suspected it, my father had less than five months to live. For some reason, watching the misadventures of Sybil and Basil Fawlty over the next six weeks became a Friday-evening ritual that he and I did together while my mum got on with other things, and at least half of the pleasure I derived from the programme came from watching him sitting forward in his green Parker Knoll armchair, laughing so hard that it was noiseless, tears streaming down his cheeks.

In the 'Hotel Inspectors' episode of *Fawlty Towers* broadcast on 10 October 1975, Sybil asked Basil not to shout at her because she'd had a difficult morning. 'Oh dear, what happened?' replied Basil with his trademark scorn. 'Did you get entangled in the eiderdown again . . . Not enough cream in your éclair?'

At that, my dad's laughter almost propelled him off his Parker Knoll armchair, while I practically hugged myself with delight at the sight of him so emphatically a prisoner of his own mirth. To this day one of the main reasons I so regret him succumbing to life's off-button in February 1976 is that it denied him the chance to enjoy the second six episodes of *Fawlty Towers*, which began almost exactly three years after his death in February 1979, and were unbelievably, triumphantly, even funnier than the first six episodes. It seems downright cruel to me that my dad never lived to hear Basil asking irascible, deaf Mrs Richards – so deliciously played by Joan Sanderson whom I hitherto knew only as the stern headmistress in

Please Sir! – precisely what she expected to see out of a Torquay bedroom window: 'Sydney Opera House, perhaps? The Hanging Gardens of Babylon? Herds of wildebeest sweeping majestically . . .' Or Basil flummoxed by the American guest Mr Hamilton's demand for a Waldorf salad: 'I think we're just out of Waldorfs.'

All these thoughts cluttered my mind as I made my way to Camden Town to meet Cleese in the Greek taverna, wondering whether, were I to order a Greek salad, the waiter might perhaps play the game and declare the kitchen fresh out of Greeks. I also wondered whether I should mention my dad or not. Would it seem overly personal to thank Cleese for the most vivid memories I had of my dead father, or mawkish, or just plain obsequious? I wasn't at all sure. But barely had we shaken hands and exchanged pleasantries, than it all came tumbling out. As the waiter, regrettably oblivious to this unusually tall man's fame, placed some little dishes of complimentary starters on the table, I said to Cleese that I would forever owe him a debt of gratitude, and explained why. At which, to my absolute horror, his eyes filled with tears and he half-rose from his chair making a sort of gesture towards me, though whether he intended to hug me, embrace me or shake my hand I didn't know and I don't think he did, either. In the end we ended up doing a kind of clumsy high-five over the table, and I got a little blob of vibrant pink taramasalata on the elbow of my jacket.

Once we'd got that awfully unEnglish business of emoting out of the way, we started discussing *Fawlty Towers*, which had recently been repeated on BBC2. I wondered whether Cleese had watched it? 'I watched the German episode,' he said, grimacing, 'and I spotted three absolutely terrible bits of slapstick. There was a bit of business with a fire extinguisher, a bit of business when Manuel hit his head on a saucepan, and the thing with the moose's head falling off the wall. Basil was crouching there waiting for it to fall. It was embarrassingly awful. All these years and nobody's ever said anything. Are they being polite, or haven't they noticed?'

I liked the idea of John Cleese groaning at Basil's antics while the rest of the nation cracked up. Moreover, he had been out of step with his fans before, he told me. 'I never liked the silly walk sketch much,' he said, which was considered such a newsworthy revelation even twenty-five years after the last episode of *Monty Python's Flying Circus* that it quickly reached Los Angeles, where the *LA Times* ran a story beginning: 'The comedian John Cleese yesterday admitted in an interview with a British newspaper [i.e. me] that he was never amused by Monty Python's silly walks.'

Cleese explained that he was forced into doing the silly walks against his own better judgement. 'We went on tour with Python and I did it in Southampton to almost complete silence. Afterwards I said to the other Pythons, "You see!" They said, "If it doesn't work in Brighton tomorrow night then we'll drop it." Of course, it did work in Brighton. But that's comedy, you see. It's an extraordinarily fragile thing.'

'Are you sure,' I said, 'that it's not more that Southampton is a peculiarly humourless place?' A hoarse bark seemed to rise from under the table and echoed round the taverna. It was Cleese doing me the honour of laughing.

He was right, though. Comedy is extraordinarily fragile, its genesis, if this is not too fanciful, as arbitrary as that of a tree which grows from a tiny seed carried by the wind. There is no better example of this phenomenon than *Fawlty Towers* itself, which was famously based on an actual hotel in Torquay, the Gleneagles, run by a bad-tempered ex-naval commander called Donald Sinclair with his acidic – one might even say Sybilline – wife Betty. You or I might have stayed there and been merely annoyed by Mr Sinclair's rudeness; Cleese stayed there and was inspired by the experience to create a television masterpiece.

A few years after I had met Cleese in the taverna and expressed my very personal debt of gratitude, *Fawlty Towers* was voted the greatest programme of all time in a poll of TV industry folk conducted by the British Film Institute. I contacted Cleese's office in London asking if he would talk to me about this, and a couple of days later he rang me from his home in Santa Barbara, California. This time, he said, if I didn't mind, he would rather not say any more on the subject of Basil. I understood, but I persevered. Could he remember anything about Donald Sinclair, on whom Basil was based? 'Was his name really Donald?' asked Cleese. 'I only knew him as Mr Sinclair. My God, I am making a film at the moment called *Rat Race*, in which I play a casino owner whose name is Donald Sinclair. Extraordinary.'

Extraordinary indeed. As for the real Donald Sinclair, having failed to jog Cleese's memory any further, I called the ever-obliging Michael Palin. 'Oh yes, I remember the Gleneagles,' he said, chuckling. He told me that the Python team had stayed there in the summer of 1970 when they were filming in nearby Paignton, and that he had recorded the stay in his diary: 'Got in at 12.30 a.m. after night filming . . . owner stood and looked at us . . . Graham (Chapman) asked if he could have a brandy . . . idea dismissed out of hand.'

Palin explained that Sinclair had run the place like 'a high-security prison. I remember asking for a wake-up call and his eyebrows went skywards. "Why?" he said. We also had a meal there, and Terry Gilliam, who as you know is American, left his knife and fork at an angle. Sinclair leant over him while Terry was in full flow, put his knife and fork together, and muttered, "This is how we do it in England."

'It's funny now, but it really did seem like the worst hotel in the world. Everything we asked for seemed to be the most unforgivable imposition; in fact Terry Gilliam, Graham Chapman, Terry Jones and myself checked out after just one night. But John and Eric Idle stayed, which I couldn't understand at the time, especially as Mr Sinclair had taken Eric's suitcase and put it outside, by the gate, apparently because he thought it might contain a bomb. John is not a uniquely tolerant person, either. I suppose this is one of the best examples of tolerance being rewarded.'

Cleese's sudden decision to quit the Pythons in 1973 was poorly received by the others; for some years afterwards relations between them, according to Palin, were 'a bit prickly'. As a consequence, Cleese did not tell the others that he had written a sitcom based on the hotel they'd stayed at in Torquay. But when *Fawlty Towers* was transmitted, even though the exterior shots were of a hotel in Buckinghamshire, there was no doubting its origins. In fact, in episode two, 'The Builders', the source of inspiration was actually mentioned, when Basil condescendingly told resident spinsters Miss Tibbs and Miss Gatsby that because of building work they would have to get their 'din-dins' at the Gleneagles.

In September 2000 I was inspired by all this to make the long journey from London down to Torquay to see for myself the Gleneagles Hotel – in fact restyled the Hotel Gleneagles after legal pressure from its grander Scottish namesake, the big bully – and to write a story for the *Independent* pegged to the twenty-fifth anniversary of the first episode of *Fawlty Towers*. I also had my father, deceased now for more than twenty-four years, in mind. He'd have loved to have known that there was a template for Basil and his disastrous hotel.

Before I went I contacted the proprietor, one Ray Marks, and explained what I was doing. Rather disappointingly, Ray could hardly have been more obliging, meeting me at Torquay station and even helping me to trace Trixie, a jolly northerner who had worked for the Sinclairs – exactly as Connie Booth's Polly worked for the Fawltys – as a waitress and chambermaid.

'John Cleese only scraped the top of the iceberg as far as Torquay hotel owners are concerned,' Trixie informed me. 'And Donald Sinclair was worse than Basil Fawlty, much worse. Betty used to lock him in their flat because he upset the staff so much. If he went into the kitchens in the morning, she'd sometimes be three staff short by the evening. She'd lock him in, and say to us, "If Donald starts knocking, girls, don't let him out."

'The funny thing is that he didn't like the guests being unpleasant to the staff — that was *his* job. I remember a humungous woman checking in one evening, with a weedy little husband, and they complained that we were giving them nasty looks, which we were, because we had to stay on to give them a late supper. Mr Sinclair said, "How dare you criticize my staff! Get out of my hotel!" He actually threw them into the street, poor things.'

The Sinclairs sold the Gleneagles in the mid-1970s and Donald died not long afterwards. When I went to Torquay, however, the formidable Betty was still very much alive. Thought to be well into her eighties, she was frequently spotted driving round town in an elderly Mercedes convertible. But I was warned that she gave short shrift to anyone who dredged up the *Fawlty Towers* connection, thundering that Cleese was a 'geek' and that her late husband was once a respected lieutenant commander in the Royal Navy. I didn't bother trying to make contact. 'She didn't have much time for him while he was alive, but she is very loyal to his memory,' Ray Marks told me.

Oddly, Marks had associations with another comedy icon; his first cousin was Peter Sellers, to whom he bore a disconcertingly striking resemblance. He was a dapper, genial man of sixty, who agreed, albeit with reservations, to perform the Fawlty goose-step for the *Independent*'s photographer. His reservations were largely related to the hotel's thriving relationship with a German tour operator. Staff were thus expected not to mention the war. And goose-stepping, as a rule, was frowned upon.

From the outside, the Hotel Gleneagles looked much as it had in 1962, when the Sinclairs had the original Victorian stone wrapped in ersatz white clapboard. Inside, it was typical of a certain sort of English seaside hotel, with lots of old couples dozing in wicker chairs, flock wallpaper, a duo calling themselves Pink Champagne advertised under 'Forthcoming Entertainment', and a faint whiff of mint sauce. Children were discouraged, which was another legacy of the Sinclair years – indeed Donald/Basil would certainly have approved of the hotel's listing in that indispensable guidebook, *'No Children, Please'*.

Otherwise, the spirit of *Fawlty Towers* was barely in evidence, although a pair of guests called Shirley and Dennis Cooper, from Bedfordshire, did mention their encounter the previous evening with 'a little waiter, too fast for himself, flying about and forgetting what we'd ordered'. Moreover, Marks admitted that he was thinking of organizing a *Fawlty Towers* theme weekend: 'I've found a Basil impersonator called Ed Wells, who is 6ft 7ins. He's got a Sybil and a Manuel too.'

I don't know whether or not he ever got round to organizing his theme weekend, but I caught the train back to London later that afternoon reflecting on the curiosity of life preparing to imitate art imitating life. Seemingly, art had got the imitation spot-on. Like Basil, Donald even had delusions of gastronomic grandeur, at least according to a Gleneagles Hotel brochure Ray Marks fished out of the archives for me, advertising Christmas Eve Dinner 1969. It featured, exactly as in the wonderful 'Gourmet Night' episode of *Fawlty Towers* (watched by my dad and me on 17 October 1975), roast duckling with orange sauce. Sadly for *Fawlty* purists, however, the brochure did not specify 'no riff-raff'.

My expedition in search of the ghost of Donald Sinclair remains the only time I have ever been to Torquay, self-styled 'jewel' of the English Riviera, but I later discovered that it was also the retirement home of a close business associate of my father's, a charming man, now a sprightly octogenarian, called Roy Dickens.

In 1997, my family and I started spending ten days every summer at a hotel near Padstow in Cornwall, a ritual we continued for the next ten years. Over that time we became friendly with other guests, including a delightful, genteel couple whose son Ross played every year with our three children. By 2004 we felt we knew Ross and his parents well enough (being English, it had only taken us seven years) to invite them for Sunday lunch at our home in Herefordshire. So one April day they drove up from their house in Wiltshire, and we had an extremely convivial time, made especially memorable when Ross's mum, Angela, asked me over the lunch table, out of the blue, whether my father was perchance still alive.

'No,' I said, rather surprised by the question. 'He died when I was fourteen.'

'I know this is going to sound terribly rude,' said Angela, who in all honesty couldn't sound rude if she had a whoopee cushion underneath her, 'but was his name Allen and did he by any chance collapse on a train?'

I was gobsmacked. Or gobstopped, as my dear mother says when she is trying to connect with her grandchildren by using modern expressions. 'Yes, he did,' I said. 'How on earth did you know that?'

'Because,' she said, blushing slightly, 'he was on his way to meet my father, who was waiting for him at Euston.'

It turned out – an astonishing coincidence – that Angela's dad was Roy Dickens, a name I remembered well from my childhood. Roy had been the sales and marketing manager for Triumph International, the ladies underwear manufacturer, and the very man from whom my dad had regularly bought those vast consignments of bras, pantyhose and camiknickers more than thirty years earlier.

I should add here that in the school holidays after my dad died I sometimes used to go into Liverpool with my mum, who heroically tried to keep the job business going on her own, and help her sort thousands and thousands of bras into colours and sizes, before boxing them up and loading them onto lorries. This humdrum activity, which took place on the second floor of a dank, rodent-infested warehouse in a gloomy Victorian back street near the docks, meant that by the age of seventeen I'd had my hands on more bra cups than even 'Knobber' Abbott, my school's most celebrated lothario.

In stark contrast to Knobber, the bra cups I handled were resoundingly empty ones, but I nevertheless studied them with a good deal more diligence than I did my A-level history notes, with the result that while I remained wobbly on the achievements in both domestic and foreign policy of President Woodrow Wilson, I could unfailingly tell bra sizes from up to twenty paces. I duly acquired some respect from my peers for being able to go into Marshall & Snelgrove in Southport town centre on a Saturday afternoon, look a bra-wearing mannequin up and down, and pronounce '36B' or '34A', which a surreptitious peek at the label always confirmed to be accurate. Obviously I'd have preferred to get respect the way Knobber Abbott got it, but that was never likely to happen.

In a roundabout way, Roy Dickens was the man responsible for my adolescent knowledge of bra sizes, and while I was writing this book I phoned him in Torquay, just to see whether I could join the dots even more satisfyingly in terms of my memories of my dad, and connect him with Donald and Betty Sinclair, the Basil and Sybil Fawlty prototypes. Regrettably, Roy didn't know Betty Sinclair, and couldn't tell me whether she was still alive, but he did say that he lived quite near the Hotel Gleneagles, formerly the Gleneagles Hotel. I was delighted.

3

Miss South Africa, Miss Africa South, and My Annual Date with Miss World

The quirk of the Hotel Gleneagles subtly changing its name from the Gleneagles Hotel leads me inexorably to the Miss World contest, which in the 1970s boasted two entrants from South Africa: Miss South Africa, who was white, and Miss Africa South, who was black.

The Miss World contest in those days was a riot of what is now called political incorrectness, an indefensible festival of condescension not only towards women, but also towards racial minorities and developing nations. I loved it. So did my dad. So, even, did my mum. Everyone's parents did, or at least everyone that I knew. As for those I didn't then know, my wife Jane, who is just ten months younger than me, reports that in her home in South Yorkshire – a relatively enlightened, *Guardian*-reading household – all the heats for the Miss United Kingdom contest were watched just as avidly as Miss World itself, with her, her sister and her mum and dad all chiming in with 'she's got a fat bottom' or 'she's got a pointy nose' or 'she looks like a horse'.

In our house Miss World was an unmissable annual treat. 'Oh yes, now she's not bad, not bad at all,' my dad would say from his arm-chair, of Miss Denmark. 'No, she's knock-kneed,' my mum would counter. 'Wait until you see her in a swimsuit.' The three of us would duly wait for the swimwear stage of the proceedings, and usually my mother, who for some reason had an uncanny eye for knock-kneed women, would be proved correct: from the waist down, the bare-legged Miss Denmark resembled the letter X.

The 1970s was the heyday of the Miss World contest, even though, or perhaps because, it coincided with the heyday of the so-called feminist movement, which angrily branded it, not altogether inappropriately I can see with the wisdom of hindsight, 'a disgrace-ful cattle show'. The very first pageant of the decade was one of the most controversial of all, with 'Women's Lib' protesters – with a new bible in the form of Germaine Greer's recently published feminist tract *The Female Eunuch* – suddenly emerging from the audience in the Royal Albert Hall and not setting fire to their bras (had they wanted to, I could have found them 50,000 assorted sizes in black, white, and taupe) but chucking flour bombs at the bewildered host, Bob Hope.

There is something rather sweet and wholesome now about the idea of indignant protesters trying to convey their message with flour bombs, marching furiously into battle, as it were, behind the Pillsbury Dough Man. But at the time it caused a right old hoo-ha. 'Anyone who would try to break up an affair as wonderful as this has got to be on some kind of dope,' Hope later told the press. Never exactly a paragon of progressive thinking, the veteran comedian rather neatly managed to show his disdain for feminists and dope-smokers in the same sentence, showing just how out of step he was with the 1970s.

But feminists were not the only protesters at the Albert Hall for Miss World 1970. It was the first year of the Miss South Africa/Miss Africa South nonsense, which Liberal Party militants (it being also the heyday of the oxymoron) argued was a blatant endorsement of apartheid. At the forefront of the protest were the Young Liberals, led by an angry young man called Peter Hain, an anti-establishment radical who later helped to found the Anti-Nazi League and whose angry anti-establishment radicalism eventually led him to a job as Leader of the House of Commons.

The target of their ire was Eric Morley, the head of Mecca Ltd, the company that owned the Miss World franchise. Every year, keeping my unmissable date with Miss World, I found Morley slightly creepy, and his raven-haired wife Julia creepier still. But in fairness to him he had come up with the Miss South Africa/Miss Africa South idea because that benighted country had, with incontrovertible racism, always chosen a white woman as its representative. I suppose he was trying, however clumsily, to do the right thing. Moreover, he could at least boast that after twenty years the contest yielded its first ever black winner in 1970, the 100–1 shot Miss Grenada. Just for good measure the similarly dark Miss Africa South was runner-up.

Unfortunately for Morley, Miss Grenada's victory proved controversial because Sir Eric Gairy, the Prime Minister of Grenada (who was later deposed in a coup after being charged with corruption and human rights abuses, and also remains notable for his persistent efforts to persuade the United Nations to investigate the dangers of earthly invasion by extraterrestrials in flying saucers), was one of the judges.

Now, I must not myself subscribe to the sexism of the Miss World contest by failing to give Miss Grenada a name. She was 22-year-old Jennifer Josephine Hosten, and I am delighted to relate that although her subsequent career did not at first confound common preconceptions about beauty queens (she became an air stewardess), she was in

1998 appointed Technical Adviser on Trade to the Organisation of Eastern Caribbean States. 'A mind as well as a body,' as members of the watching public might have patronizingly muttered in 1970, a year in which the Miss World contest, believe it or not, garnered higher viewing figures on BBC Television than any other single programme.

I was just nine at the time, and therefore not watching Miss World through a fug of pubertal testosterone, as was indubitably the case five years later. My Letts Schoolboy's Diary 1975 records that on Thursday 20 November I was permitted to stay up until well after my normal bedtime to watch the Miss World contest. Coverage didn't start until 9.25 p.m., and even that was after my bedtime, but the deal on such occasions was that I had to change into my pyjamas before-hand. That might be why I can still remember watching the 1975 Miss World competition: striped, winceyette pyjama bottoms, and a towelling dressing-gown that always rode open no matter how hard I tried to rope it shut, did not mount much of a defence against the rising excitement of a 14-year-old boy watching a parade of scantily clad young women – a 14-year-old boy, I should add, who attended an all-male school and for titillation relied pretty much exclusively on the underwear section of the Littlewoods catalogue. Playing the field, for me at that time, meant switching from Littlewoods to Grattan's.

Anyway, my mum, dad and I all took our usual places in the lounge that November evening, aware that we were about to watch a contest more significant than most, for not only was it Miss World's twenty-fifth anniversary, but the previous two finals had been marred by debilitating scandals just as damaging to the contest's good name as the 1970 protests.

In 1973 Miss United States of America, Marjorie Wallace from Indiana, was crowned Miss World, but fired less than four months later after 'smooching' on television with Tom Jones. You might think that a public smooch with Tom Jones was positively a requirement of every new Miss World, but not in those days it wasn't. And the following year, 1974, Miss United Kingdom, Helen Morgan from the Vale of Glamorgan, had an even shorter reign, abruptly curtailed after just four days of her victory on 25 November when it was discovered – to the horror of right-thinking folk up and down the land – that she was an unwed mother, with an 18-month-old son being cared for by her loyal mum back home in Barry.

Britain was traumatized. Morgan had been crowned barely a fortnight after the wedding of Princess Anne and Captain Mark Phillips – an event deemed worthy of an official day off for the nation's schoolchildren so that we could watch it on television or, less patriotically, go to the rec to play football – and for a country still in the throes of industrial unrest and political upheaval, the second general election of a tempestuous year having just taken place, a royal wedding and a home-grown Miss World inside the same month was almost too much excitement to take. So when Morgan's reign swiftly went the way that Anne and Mark's marriage eventually would, the national sense of shame was almost unendurable. How we coped, I just don't know.

Actually, motherhood did not in fact break any of the Miss World rules. Contestants were obliged only to be unmarried. But of course it was presumed in those days that unmarried meant childless, if not actually virginal. Miss Venezuela, one Alicia Rivas, rather piously chucked in her two bolivars' worth, saying: 'In my country, a girl who has a baby without being married is regarded as a bad girl, not pure and undefiled as we are led to believe Miss World should be.' Middle England, and doubtless Middle Wales, was in full agreement. Runner-up Anneline Kriel, that year's Miss South Africa (as opposed to Miss Africa South), was duly promoted, and the Vale of Glamorgan became a vale of tears.

This, then, was the lively backdrop to the 1975 contest, with Morley determined that the competition's former prestige should be fully restored. One can only guess at his irritation, therefore, when Marjorie Wallace, the floozy dethroned in 1973, arrived uninvited in London and gave a press conference advising the new winner, before doing anything else, to get herself 'a good lawyer'.

To add to Morley's annoyance, the Spanish dictator General Franco most inconsiderately snuffed it on the very morning of the contest, which not only meant relegation further down the day's news agenda, but also caused the 18-year-old contender from Spain, the nubile but sensitive Olga Fernandez Perez, to withdraw, saying she was simply too upset to continue.

Worst of all for Morley, though, was more of that pesky feminism, this time from the beauty queens themselves. During the preliminary judging in the swimsuit event, four of the French-speaking competitors – Misses France, Belgium, Luxembourg and Mauritius – collaborated by refusing to turn round to have their rears inspected. 'It is degrading for a girl to have to show her bottom to the judges,' declared Miss Mauritius. 'We refuse to be treated like slave girls.' Morley at first remonstrated with them – 'Of course the girls must be seen from behind,' he thundered – but when one of the judges, the actress Susan George, suggested that actually they had a point, he climbed down and benevolently agreed that the rear-view inspection would be left out of future contests.

After all, 1975 was also the year in which the Equal Opportunities Act and Sex Discrimination Act came into force, and even by the standards of the 1970s aspects of the Miss World contest were beginning to look just a little anachronistic. Before the contest, bookmakers had pitched up in the foyer of the swanky Britannia Hotel to examine the contestants and set odds accordingly. 'They come right up to you,' Miss Canada complained, 'look at your badge to identify the country you represent, then step back and eye you up and down before scribbling something into a notebook. You feel like a prize cow.'

At least 1975 would be the last year in which the pick of those prize cows, to borrow Miss Canada's irreverent analogy, was crowned wearing her swimsuit. She was the 16–1 shot Miss Puerto Rico, 18-year-old Wilnelia Merced, whose perfect 34–24–36 figure received the cheerful approbation of my mum, my dad and me, raptly watching in Southport, even though we all had a preference for Miss Uruguay, who also spoke slightly less halting English. Young Miss Merced, with a dazzling smile, said 'no entiendo' to almost every question put to her by that year's host, David Vine. That exchange alone was worth staying up for; the three of us greeted every 'no entiendo' with hoots of unenlightened laughter.

These days, the former Miss Merced's command of English has improved considerably, for she has since 1979 been better known in this country as Mrs Bruce Forsyth (while in Puerto Rico, Forsyth, by his own cheerful admission, remains Mr Wilnelia Merced, or on occasion Mr World). Goodness only knows what my mum and dad and I would have said had we known that the beaming young beauty in the Miss World sash was destined to marry, within four years, the host of *The Generation Game*. As everyone knew in 1975, Brucie was married – we assumed happily – to his toothsome game-show assistant, Anthea 'give us a twirl' Redfern.

Despite the 1975 Equal Opportunities Act, despite Eric Morley agreeing that Miss World contestants would no longer have to turn their backsides to the judges, despite *The Female Eunuch*, the role of women on television in the mid-1970s was still, overwhelmingly, to look pretty. Anthea Redfern, like Anne Aston on *The Golden Shot*, filled this role perfectly. And not only was it the heyday of Miss World, it was also the golden age of the female dance troupe, embodied above all by Pan's People on *Top of the Pops*.

4

Beautiful Babs, Do You Take Jesus of Nazareth to Be Your Lawful Wedded Husband?

I was not, I must confess, a huge devotee of *Top of the Pops*. The reason I watched it every Thursday evening was principally so that I wouldn't feel left out in the school corridors on Friday mornings. In science lessons with 'Jaffa' Fairburn – I think thus called on account of his initials J.A., although he also had orangey hair, which made it a peculiarly satisfying nickname – we studied gas pressure, water pressure and air pressure, but none was nearly as powerful in a boys' school as peer pressure.

It was peer pressure that made me throw massive soggies – enormous balls of newspaper soaked overnight in water – from the top deck of the number 15 bus every morning, and peer pressure that made me want my soggy to be bigger and soggier than anyone else's.

The day (Thursday 28 February 1974, my Letts Schoolboy Diary records) that a boy called Robbo from the year above said to his friend, 'Hey, Rushworth, have you seen Viner's soggy?' was one of the proudest days of my school life, easily surpassing the day I was summoned to the headmaster's study to receive his congratulations on being awarded my third merit card that term in French.

It was peer pressure too that made me flick ink from my cartridge pen at the retreating back of our maths teacher 'Etty' Johnson – thus nicknamed with yet more schoolboy ingenuity because his initials were E.T., which in those days did not evoke a wizened extraterrestrial, more's the pity – as he walked along the aisle between our desks. And it was peer pressure that made me join the crowd around somebody's little transistor radio every Tuesday lunchtime to listen to the new top forty countdown on Radio 1, when the truth was that I couldn't really give a toss whether Mott the Hoople's new single had entered the top twenty, entered the Eurovision Song Contest, or entered Parliament.

It wasn't that I didn't like music, just that I couldn't work up as much enthusiasm for the top forty as those of my contemporaries who listened to the countdown every week as attentively and solemnly as folk during the Battle of Britain listened to Winston Churchill exhorting them to defend our island whatever the cost might be. Some of them even wrote every entry down, and started panicking when they missed one. 'Hey, Greenhalgh, did you get number eleven? Was it "Save Your Kisses For Me", Brotherhood of Man, or "Don't Go Breaking My Heart", Elton John and Kiki Dee?'

Still, I could see the appeal of Pan's People, as indeed could Ronnie Barker's immortal character Norman Stanley Fletcher in *Porridge*, Ian La Fresnais and Dick Clement's third TV masterpiece, after *The Likely Lads*, and *Whatever Happened to the Likely Lads?* In one of the earliest and indeed most often repeated episodes of *Porridge*, in 1974, they had Fletch fantasizing: 'I could call up a couple of birds, those darlings who dance on *Top of the Pops*, what are they called? Pan's People. There's one special one, beautiful Babs.' A beat, immaculately timed. 'Don't know what her name is.'

I have ransacked not only my own memories while writing this book; I have also tried to plunder the memories of others. I duly made contact with Beautiful Babs herself, the former Babs Lord, who in 1975, in a marriage of beauty and showbiz almost as noteworthy as the later union of Bruce Forsyth and Wilnelia Merced, became Mrs Robert Powell.

For television viewers of my generation, Robert Powell is and will forever be Jesus of Nazareth, eponymous star of the only ITV drama, so far as I am aware, ever to get a plug from the Pope. On Easter Sunday 1977 Pope Paul VI stood on the balcony overlooking St Peter's Square dispensing the usual blessings, and then exhorted the crowds to 'go home and watch the rest of *Jesus of Nazareth*'. He never did that for *Coronation Street*.

But then *Jesus of Nazareth* had apparently been the Pope's idea in the first place, and it wasn't every day, either, that the inspiration for ITV projects came from the Vatican. There are conflicting stories about the genesis – if you'll pardon me for mixing my testaments – of *Jesus of Nazareth*. Some say that the Pope suggested it to the director Franco Zeffirelli, others that he sounded out the celebrated producer and impresario Lew Grade, who was Jewish but whose wife Kathie was a practising Catholic. According to this version, the Grades had a few years previously had an audience with Pope Paul, and as they were leaving, the pontiff raised the idea of a TV version of the story of Jesus, which Grade agreed to do after relentless nagging from Kathie. Either way, he duly started raising the £9 million – an astonishing budget for a TV drama in the 1970s – required to make what the tabloids inevitably called 'The Most Expensive Story Ever Told'.

To raise the money, Grade visited the head of General Motors in Detroit. He bluntly asked him for £3m, and when the GM chief enquired how soon he needed it, Grade said 'Yesterday will be fine.' Years and years later, I heard for myself some of his colourful aphorisms when I interviewed him for the *Mail on Sunday* in his capacious office just off Grosvenor Square. He was then pushing ninety, a tiny man with a big bald head, toting a cigar the size of a caber behind a desk the size of a family saloon, and I ventured that he was in some ways British television's answer to the legendary Hollywood producer Sam Goldwyn. I asked Grade whether he had ever met Goldwyn. 'I only met him on the telephone,' he said. It was itself as good a Goldwynism as Goldwyn ever uttered.

As it turned out, the suits who ran General Motors insisted on the company's name being removed from the credits once Grade told them that Zeffirelli intended to portray Jesus as 'gentle, fragile and simple'. They were worried that too much fragility might cause offence in the Bible Belt, and that sales of Buicks and Chevrolets might consequently go into freefall south of the Mason–Dixon line. They should have held firm: when *Jesus of Nazareth* was aired in the United States, it was estimated that over a third of all television sets in the country were tuned to it, with Proctor & Gamble (whose financial might dated from the American Civil War, when Mr Proctor and Mr Gamble supplied all soldiers in the Union Army with soap) rather than General Motors raking in the kudos as the principal corporate backer.

Nevertheless, it was easy to see why the GM bosses panicked. Even in Britain those were more sensitive times. Indeed in 1977, the year *Jesus of Nazareth* was aired, the formidable Mary Whitehouse of the National Viewers' and Listeners' Association won the first prosecution for blasphemy since 1921 when the editor of *Gay News*, one Denis Lemon, was fined £500 for publishing James Kirkup's provocative poem 'The Love That Dares to Speak its Name', which described the thoughts of a Roman centurion as he imagined having gay sex with Jesus on the cross.

There was nothing in Grade's production for Mrs Whitehouse to worry about, yet few projects in the entire history of British television have generated quite so many anecdotes as *Jesus of Nazareth*. Alas, Grade told me that one of the most famous ones wasn't true: he'd never suggested cutting the number of apostles to reduce costs.

When *Jesus of Nazareth*, with a full complement of apostles, was eventually transmitted in two epic parts on Palm Sunday and Easter Sunday, I was among the estimated 25 million Britons watching, although possibly one of the relatively few to cite as the most enjoyable moment of the entire six hours and sixteen minutes the fleeting glimpse – among a glittering cast that also included Laurence Olivier, Ralph Richardson, James Mason, Rod Steiger and Anthony Quinn – of Harold Bennett, the actor best known as Young Mr Grace in *Are You Being Served?*, playing a village elder.

I ached for him to tell his fellow villagers that 'You're all doing very well' as he regularly did Mr Humphries and the rest of the Grace Brothers staff, and was most disappointed that he didn't, but there was compensation in the marvellous discovery, via a slightly disapproving item in the fusty *Daily Telegraph*, that Ian McShane, a wonderfully roguish Judas Iscariot, was married to Sylvia Kristel, the saucy Dutch actress who played the title role as the sex siren Emmanuelle in the 1974 X-film to which my friend Andy Boothman and I had unsuccessfully sought entry when it was shown, as part of a double bill with *Confessions of a Driving Instructor*, at the ABC in Lord Street in the autumn of 1976.

Being married to Emmanuelle seemed to me to be entirely in keeping with the character of Judas. And McShane, whose twinkle-eyed roguishness later found an enjoyable outlet as the resourceful Suffolk antiques dealer Lovejoy, was perfectly cast. My own favourite *Jesus of Nazareth* story concerns the scene when Judas creeps out of the room during the Last Supper. With Zeffirelli's cameras rolling, McShane stole out surreptitiously as bidden by the script, then popped his head back through the doorway and said, 'Now have I got this right? Nine cod, four haddock, all with chips and mushy peas?' I would pay good money, perhaps even thirty pieces of silver, to see that out-take.

Whatever, while it made perfect sense to learn that Judas and Emmanuelle were an item, far more surprising was the revelation that Jesus himself was in real life married to Babs from Pan's People.

Unlike many of my friends, I always enjoyed Pan's People's contributions to *Top of the Pops*, mainly I think because even then I recognized the irredeemable cheesiness of many of their routines. Some of the cheesiest pop up on telly even now, generally so they can be tittered at. And Legs & Co, the troupe which succeeded Pan's People on *Top of the Pops* in April 1976, were no less cheesy, once donning masks and carrying swag bags when dancing to 'Bank Robber' by The Clash. If Joe Strummer was watching, it can only have been through his fingers.

Legs & Co continued the tradition of clumsy but impressively strenuous literalism begun by Pan's People, one of the finest examples of which was a routine Babs and co did to 'Get Down' by Gilbert O'Sullivan, which reached the number one spot in March 1973. The girls shared the stage with several Labradors, which, as dear old Gilbert sang 'told you once before / and I won't tell you no more / get down, get down, get down', they admonished with wagging fingers. In fact, the song was about a tempestuous love affair between two human beings and had nothing whatever to do with Labradors, but because the lyrics included the words 'you're a bad dog, baby', the ever-literal choreographer Flick Colby saw an unmissable opportunity for paws and wet noses.

When I reminded Babs Powell of this, she recalled one of the dogs itself getting a bit over-literal, Flick Colby-style, and responding to the words 'get down' by jumping off the stage and trotting out of the studio. But the routine that fully thirty years later still had the power to mortify her, she said, was the one they did to 'Monster Mash' by

Bobby 'Boris' Pickett and the Cryptkickers. The song had been around since 1962, but had been banned by the BBC because, with such deeply disturbing lines as 'the ghouls all came from their humble abodes / to get a jolt from my electrodes', it was deemed 'too morbid'. By 1973, however, the BBC had decided that the nation was strong enough not to be traumatized by 'Monster Mash', and the song, precisely interpreted by Colby who tried to turn Pan's People into the Addams Family for the week, reached number three in the charts.

I also asked Babs about the famous line in *Porridge*. It turned out that she had known about it in advance because Ronnie Barker had come up to her in the BBC canteen, palpably anxious, and told her that they'd used her name and he hoped she wouldn't mind. He then added that they'd changed the script – that originally it was to be 'Big Babs' but the producer, keen not to offend her, had insisted on the change to 'Beautiful Babs'. 'I wouldn't have been offended at all,' she told me. 'It was a huge tribute to be mentioned in *Porridge*. Besides, it was true. I was the most buxom of the group.'

I suppose there must have been some people even in 1974 who were offended by the 'beautiful Babs' line in Porridge, doubtless contending that the female breast should never be a platform, so to speak, for comedy. But in the 1970s, more than any decade before and arguably any decade since, it became just that. Tits, boobs, knockers, whoppers, jugs, melons, torpedoes, bazookas . . . there had always been dozens of schoolboy euphemisms for breasts, but by the time I hit puberty – which I did with a resounding clang sometime in the second half of 1976 – plenty of them, for the first time, had been officially sanctioned in newspapers and even on television.

After all, what chance did those Miss World protesters have in 1970, trying to draw attention to the indignity of a beauty pageant, when just a few weeks earlier the *Sun* had successfully introduced the topless Page Three girl? There are many reasons why 17 November is a significant date in British history – it was the day Queen Elizabeth I acceded to the English throne in 1558, and the day the future Viscount Montgomery of Alamein was born in 1887, not to mention Peter Cook exactly fifty years later – but not the least of those reasons is that, on 17 November 1970, 20-year-old Stephanie Rahn, from Germany, became the first woman to pose in a national newspaper wth her breasts exposed. Within twelve months, sales had risen by forty per cent, forcing proprietor Rupert Murdoch, who was said to have been furious at the decision by editor Larry Lamb to feature half-naked young women on page three, to reassess his position.

Around the same time that Miss Rahn made British newspaper history, the most popular song in the playground at Farnborough Road Primary School went as follows: 'Sunshine girl I'm looking down your bra / I see two mountains, I wonder what they are?/ It would delight me / to squeeze them tightly / not bloody likely / my sunshine girl.'

I was nine years old and this was by some distance the rudest song I knew. I certainly knew better than to give it an airing in the presence of my mother and father, yet it was considered fine for me even then to contribute to the debate on Miss World evenings, and four years later when Fletch in *Porridge* said 'there's one special one, beautiful Babs . . . don't know what her name is', my mum and dad roared with laughter and I roared with them. I wasn't entirely sure why, but that never really mattered.

5

'Good God, Elsie Tanner's a Redhead!': The Dawning of Colour

When Ronnie Barker died in October 2005, the 'Beautiful Babs' clip from *Porridge* was used again and again, much to Babs Powell's pleasure. So was the classic *Mastermind* sketch from *The Two Ronnies* in its 1970s heyday, in which Ronnie Corbett's specialist subject was answering the question before last. That sketch was written by David Renwick, later to enjoy great success as the creator of *One Foot in the Grave*, which for my money, and I realize this is an almost treasonable thing to commit to print, was consistently as funny as and often funnier than its near-contemporary *Only Fools and Horses*.

I realize too that I have strayed away from the 1970s, but I mention Renwick because I interviewed him for the *Independent* in Soho in November 2000, a few days before transmission of the final episode of *One Foot in the Grave*. A charming and normally mild-mannered man, Renwick was incandescently angry that day, because a national newspaper had blown the plot of his final episode not only by revealing that Richard Wilson's character Victor Meldrew would be killed in a road accident, but even publishing chunks of the script. Renwick raged at the stupidity and selfishness of the newspaper responsible, which I shouldn't mention – it was the *Daily Express* – while I silently celebrated the fact that I was getting some decidedly Meldrewish anger from Meldrew's creator, perfect fodder for my interview.

Aside from it being a fulfilling afternoon professionally, I was also looking forward to getting home to north London and watching a film with Jane that we had been meaning to see for ages: *The Sixth Sense*, with Bruce Willis. Jane had phoned me earlier to say that she'd finally managed to rent it from Blockbuster Video in Muswell Hill; I said I'd bring home an Indian takeaway and a decent bottle of wine.

But first I had my interview with Renwick to complete. 'I mean, how utterly stupid of these idiots to give away the ending,' he spluttered. 'I mean, what is the bloody point? Why on earth would they spoil it for everyone like that?' I nodded in sympathetic agreement, while he sought a comparable example of an important ending being gratuitously spoilt. 'It's like, it's like telling someone who's about to watch *The Sixth Sense*,' he thundered, 'that Bruce Willis is a ghost!'

All of which brings me back to my father, because his is really the ghost in this book, sitting in his armchair in front of the telly with his palms pressed together and his forefingers touching his nose, as if in silent supplication to the gods. Which, during the ITV Seven on *World of Sport* on Saturday afternoons, he probably was.

My dad was a huge horse-racing enthusiast and an inveterate gambler. When I talked to his old business associate Roy Dickens, I was reminded that in October 1975 they went to Paris together for the Prix de l'Arc de Triomphe at Longchamps, my dad's favourite event of the entire sporting calendar. I don't think Roy was much of a racing man but my dad invited him anyway, doubtless to thank him for putting 25,000 pairs of pantyhose his way.

My father went to lots of race meetings and those he couldn't attend in person, he watched on the box. And what a box it was. In November 1974 my parents did what almost all my friends' parents had done at least a couple of years earlier, and rented a colour television. Renting tellies was what people in their income bracket did in those days. There were even commercials with inane ditties extolling the virtues of this or that rental company. 'It's great service you get renting your TV set from . . . Granada! It means better TV, that's why millions agree . . . that's Granada!'

The reason most families rented their telly was because to buy one outright was prohibitively expensive, especially if you fancied, as my mum and dad did, one of those large faux-cabinet jobs in lacquered wood, with louvre doors that you could shut if you wanted to pretend that the striking piece of furniture in the corner of the room was what you kept cocktails in, not what you watched *The Golden Shot* on.

But the best thing about our new telly was not that it stood magisterially in the corner of our lounge and had folding doors, but that it showed pictures in colour. It wasn't the first time I had seen colour telly. The first major television event I had seen transmitted in colour was the 1970 World Cup final between Brazil and Italy, which we watched at the home of my mum and dad's friends 'Uncle' Ronnie and 'Auntie' Sybil in Hartley Road. That spectacle had an impact on me that in a way has yet to dissipate. The beautiful game at its most beauteous. And names to conjure with, such as Pelé, Rivelino, Jairzinho, Carlos Alberto, Riva, Rivera, Boninsegna. I had already embarked on love affairs with both football and television, but the love found a powerful new intensity that day, in yellows, and greens, and blues.

Yet it was four more years before we made the leap from black-and-white and all shades of grey in-between. The discussions between my mum and dad on whether or not to get a colour telly had dragged on seemingly for longer than the talks aimed at ending the war in Vietnam and were apparently no less intractable. By the summer of 1974 I had become something of a laughing stock among my friends who came round to play and realized that we still watched television in monochrome.

Still, my parents' vacillations at least boosted the pleasure we all felt when one Saturday morning my dad drove us into Southport town centre and we went to Rumbelows on Chapel Street to complete the rental agreement on a handsome new television that, in its cabinet, was about the size of Dr Who's TARDIS. It didn't have to be Rumbelows. It could have been Radio Rentals, Granada, or one of the many shops in Southport specializing in renting out televisions to folk who couldn't afford to buy them.

I can still remember vividly my parents' disbelief on learning that the model they were renting would cost £400 to buy. To put that in perspective, the Right Honourable Jeremy Thorpe, in his Liberal Party manifesto a month earlier, had pledged, in the admittedly some-what unlikely circumstances of the Liberals being voted into power, to increase Britain's minimum wage to £27 for a forty-hour working week. And the average cost of a house in Britain at the time was £10,900. No wonder my parents baulked at forking out £400 for a telly. In proportion to the average cost of a house, which as I write is a whopping £210,578, that would today be about £8,000.

Our new telly was greeted with the sort of excitement with which some households greet new babies. We cooed over it, we stroked it, we gazed at it lovingly even when it was, as it were, asleep. I don't know what experiences my children will have to match the wide-eyed wonder of seeing colour television for the first time. My friend Craig Cash remembers it too. He grew up on a council estate in Heaton Norris, Stockport, and the first family on the estate to get a colour telly were called Hostler. 'It was like they'd brought home the World

Cup,' Craig remembers now. 'Everyone was in awe.' Eventually he got an invitation from the Hostlers to spend an evening in front of their cherished telly. He asked what they'd be watching and was told *The Black and White Minstrel Show*, which was Mr Hostler's favourite. 'I remember thinking it was just my bloody luck to finally get an invite to watch a whole programme in colour, and for it to be the Black and White Minstrels,' says Craig. 'But it was quite a colourful show, actually.'

Much as we cherished the new experience of watching even the Black and White Minstrels on colour television, however, it would not have made much difference to the most memorable broadcasting episode of my boyhood, the *Apollo 11* moon landing, which by some otherworldly stroke of fortune coincided with American television primetime but unfolded here in the early hours of the morning of 21 July 1969. I was only seven years old and consequently unaware of the historic significance of what was going on, especially as it was going on in what appeared, whether one was watching in monochrome or colour, to be a grey blizzard. For my dad, born in 1916 when not even aeroplanes had been around for very long, it was of course a viscerally exciting moment. But it was only in later years that I came to appreciate the fact that he had woken me up in the dead of night, and came to understand the full import of Neil Armstrong's memorable words: 'one small step for man, one giant leap for mankind.'

If, of course, that is what he said. I am told on very good authority that Neil Armstrong was once on a lecture tour of the United States, and wound up at the bar of some motel near Omaha, Nebraska, where a stranger insisted on plying him with drinks, and kept congratulating him on his iconic line 'one small step for man, one giant leap for mankind'.

'You know,' said Armstrong after a while, 'it's very kind of you to compliment me for saying that, but it's not actually what I said. I've been misquoted all these years, and I've been too embarrassed to point it out to anyone.'

The stranger was agog.

'I grew up,' Armstrong continued, 'in an apartment block in Wapakoneta, Ohio, and in the apartment next door lived a Jewish couple, Manny and Gloria Klein. The walls of our apartment were thin and their bedroom was next to mine. I often heard them arguing. And what they argued about in particular was Gloria's refusal to give Manny oral sex. I often heard him pleading with her and I heard her yelling at him, "I'll tell you when you can have a goddamn blow-job, when man walks on the goddamn moon!" So what I actually said up there on the moon was "one small step for man, one giant leap for Manny Klein".'

My dad would have enjoyed that one. He might even have shared it with his late-night poker pals. It remains a source of sadness to me that I never knew him on man-to-man terms; that I was never able to give him a joke he could use at the poker table. He died before he could cast an eye over my first girlfriend, or buy me my first pint of bitter. We never even clinked wine glasses. But at least I was able to share his intoxication with the new colour television, which transformed his beloved horse-racing as a viewing experience, not least because he could now distinguish between the jockeys' silks, making it easier for him to follow the horse on which he had staked his money, although that hapless quadruped could also invariably be identified, it has to be said, by its place at the tail of the field.

Colour had been introduced in 1967, on the first day of the Wimbledon tennis championships transmitted on BBC2, so at 58 Lynton Road it had taken us more than seven years to embrace the new technology. By then, at least, the colours had settled down to something vaguely lifelike. The archivist on *Coronation Street* once told me that viewers had practically needed sunglasses when the first colour episodes were shown, more than two years after that first day of Wimbledon, late in 1969. 'People said "Good God, Elsie Tanner's a redhead!" But it wasn't just red, it was blazing red. And the blues were bright, vivid blue. The corner shop looked like rainbowland.'

It's easy to forget now that colour, for all that it greatly enhanced the viewing experience, brought its own problems. Whenever the weather was stormy, we seemed to suffer a bluish tinge at the top of the screen. As I moved into adolescence, knob-twiddling was by no means confined to my bedroom after dark; plenty of it went on at the back of the TV, and we, like every other household, were on intimate terms with the vertical and horizontal hold buttons.

As for *Coronation Street*'s inaugural colour episode, the intention had been to shoot it in the Lake District, to prove to the nation in glorious technicolour that there was more to the North than milk stout and cobbled back streets. A coach trip from Weatherfield to Windermere was hastily written into the script, and every camera angle was meticulously planned. Unfortunately, however, the colour stock didn't arrive at Granada studios in time. And at the end of that episode, the coach crashed. So the very first colour scene was Hilda Ogden all bloodied up in hospital. It was hardly the desired advert for the north of England.

6

'Is There Any Salad Cream?': My Burgeoning Love for *Coronation Street* and Millicent Earnshaw

I fell in love with *Coronation Street* a few years later. My friend Andy Boothman's mum was addicted to it, and if I was ever at their house at 7.30 p.m. on a Monday or a Wednesday, which I usually seemed to be, viewing of the Street (it was never 'Corrie' in those days) was a near-religious ritual. Coincidentally, the Boothmans were also devout Christians (which didn't stop Andy coming with me to try to bluff our way into the *Emmanuelle/Confessions of a Driving Instructor* double bill at the ABC), and from time to time used to have Bible meetings at their house. I remember thinking that for hushed reverence in their front room, there wasn't much to choose between the Bible meetings and the twice-weekly visits to Weatherfield.

At first, sitting with Andy and his mum, I found the goings-on at the Rovers Return decidedly dull. But gradually, insidiously, the storylines sucked me in. I was studying Shakespeare's *Julius Caesar* at school, but it didn't have a storyline as engrossing as Gail Potter losing her virginity in the stockroom at Sylvia's Separates. By 1976 I was duly hooked, and even had my eyes opened by *Coronation Street* to what was happening in the wider world. In August 1978 the aforementioned and deflowered Gail Potter had the following conversation with her much flightier friend Suzie Birchall, while they were making a salad in the kitchen of number 11.

Gail: 'Do you think there'll be another war?'

Suzie (flatly): 'Do I think there'll be another war?'

Gail: 'Do yer?'

Suzie: 'How should I know?'

Gail: 'They're talkin' about it, aren't they?'

Suzie: 'Are they? Who?!'

Gail: 'The Americans and the Russians.'

Suzie: 'Is that right?'

Gail: 'Don't you even listen when there's *News At Ten* on?'

Suzie: 'Only the interestin' bits . . .'

Gail: 'Sometimes I get quite worried about it, honest I do.'

Suzie '. . . a divorce or someone dyin' and leavin' a load of money.'

Gail: 'Don't you care if there's another war?'

Suzie: 'I don't think about it much – it don't bother me.'

Gail: 'Yeah, but if they do.'

Suzie: 'Well, if they do they wouldn't ask me anyway, would they?'

Gail: 'That's the whole point, innit, they wouldn't bother askin' you, they'd just blow us all up.'

Suzie: 'Well, if they do ask me, I'll tell them not to bother, all right? I'll say they need their heads bangin', they should kiss an' make up.'

Gail: 'I think it's quite scary if you think about it.'

Suzie: 'Then DON'T. Is there any salad cream?'

Fortuitiously, my new-found devotion coincided with one of the Street's golden ages, inspired by a new producer, Bill Podmore. The first golden age had begun with the first episode in November 1960, almost a year before I emerged from the womb, and lasted until 1964. But between 1964 and 1968, when all over the country terraced streets just like Coronation Street were being demolished (including Archie Street, on which Coronation Street was modelled and where the opening titles were filmed, and which coincidentally enjoyed another claim to fame as the birthplace of Eddie Colman, one of the Manchester United players killed in the Munich air crash) and replaced with tower blocks, the programme became over-nostalgic in its bid to recall the good old days.

I know all this because of my conversation with the programme's archivist, Daran Little, which for an aficionado like me seemed far more like pleasure than business. 'It harked back too far, to about 1955,' Little told me. 'Somebody like Lucille Hewitt, the Street's token teenager, would have been on the pill. Instead, she never even had a boyfriend.'

In 1968, a modernizing phase began. Lucille Hewitt was belatedly, at the age of nineteen, turned into a proper teenager, while Emily Nugent (later Emily Bishop, and at the time of writing still going strong) had her virginity taken, as gloriously improbable as it sounds, by a Hungarian demolition expert. Poor old Emily, later to have one husband murdered and another turn out to be a bigamist, got from her Hungarian more of a bang than she had bargained for.

This modernizing drive took some interesting turns. By the time I started watching, Billy Walker and Ray Langton were cracking jokes about 'Pakis', which might have been perfectly realistic for a northern back-street pub in the mid-1970s, although realism went only so far: *Coronation Street* didn't get an Asian-run corner shop, or indeed any Asian residents, until years after it would have happened in an equivalent street in real life. Moreover, modernization was hampered by simple budgetary constraints. The mini skirt dug out of the Granada studio wardrobe and worn by Norma Ford in 1973 had last been worn by Paula Wilcox in *The Lovers*, in 1969. Rather like my quilted anorak, which is where I keep such scintillating facts, it was quite plainly years out of date.

When Podmore became producer, though, *Coronation Street* entered another halcyon period. He had been a director on *Nearest and Dearest* – the sitcom starring Jimmy Jewell and Hylda Baker which relied for most of its laughs on an incontinent octogenarian mute called Walter – but nobody seemed to hold that against him, and he introduced genuine comedy to the Street, the main source of which was the ever-bickering Stan and Hilda Ogden and their splendid foil, the Liverpudlian binman Eddie Yeats.

In 1979, aged seventeen, I went to Liverpool with some mates to see the ska band The Specials. That evening is memorable for various reasons, not least because I begged my mum to lend me her Ford Escort, which eventually she did on the non-negotiable condition that I got it back safely by midnight. This was a Cinderella clause some-what inconsistent with going to see the anarchic Specials, who used to gob at each other on stage and would doubtless have gobbed at me too if they'd known that I had borrowed my mum's car for the occasion and had solemnly pledged, not very anarchically, to have it parked safely in the drive by midnight. Not that my pledge was honoured, alas. I emerged from the gig to find to my absolute horror that the multi-storey car park where I had left the Escort was firmly locked up. Consequently, my mates and I were forced to find a taxi driver willing to take us the eighteen miles or so from Liverpool back to Southport, which cost us an outlandish £14, and I had to wake my mother up with the devastating news that not only was it well past the witching hour, but that her precious car was barricaded into a Liverpool shopping precinct.

So the night ended traumatically, but on the way to the gig, at least, we'd had the inestimable thrill of spotting none other than Eddie Yeats, the actor Geoffrey Hughes, crossing Lime Street. My friend Mike King was beside himself. 'Eddie Yeats, Eddie Yeats,' he screamed. 'It's bloody Eddie Yeats.' The Specials performing 'Too Much Too Young' was downright anticlimactic after that.

Of all my schoolfriends, Mike was the one who most shared my feelings for *Coronation Street*. Every Tuesday and Thursday morning before registration we would stand in the corridor dissecting the previous night's events in Weatherfield, which might seem like a somewhat old-biddyish thing for two schoolboys to do, but Mike, at least, had the saving grace of being cool. He was a good footballer, which I certainly wasn't, and he had a girlfriend, which I definitely didn't. Moreover, she was two years older than he was, and she had her own car, a Mini, in which she picked him up every lunchtime. Occasionally, he prevailed upon her to give a few of his mates a lift, and two, three, sometimes even four of us would squeeze into the back of the Mini, to be driven to the Zetland Arms by the ever-forbearing Ann.

I was immensely impressed, as well as psychotically jealous. At seventeen, a girlfriend and a car were what I coveted most in life, and for a girlfriend with a car I would have very seriously considered exchanging a limb, which, now that I think about it, might have lost me the girlfriend. Whatever, with less than no chance of my impecunious mother buying me a car of my own, I obsessively entered any competition I could find which offered any kind of motor vehicle as the prize. In July 1979 Coca-Cola ran a competition with a Triumph TR7 as the main prize. All you had to do, together with sending in the requisite number of ring-pulls from Coke cans, was make as many words as possible out of the phrase 'All Summer Long', to which end I spent two entire days of my summer holiday in Southport's town library, laboriously but tirelessly poring through the colossal Oxford English Dictionary.

After labouring much more intensively than I ever had on my schoolwork, I found no fewer than 167 words, and sent off my entry so unshakably confident of winning that I had already planned what I was going to put in my TR7's glove compartment. I was mystified, therefore, when a week after the competition's closing date I still had not received a letter telling me when my new car would be delivered. So I wrote to Coca-Cola asking them to send me the results of the competition, which they kindly did. To my utter bemusement and acute disappointment it turned out that a grand total of 1,134 words, or thereabouts, could be formed from 'All Summer Long'. I was almost 1,000 words short. Someone had obviously spent even longer in the library than I had. Probably all summer long, the bastard.

A few weeks after I so comprehensively failed to win the TR7, I began my A-level year. Unfortunately it coincided with a major distraction at my school: a boys' grammar since its foundation in 1926, King George V (known to us all as KGV) was in the process of being converted into a mixed sixth-form college, and a battalion of pulchritudinous pupils from Greenbank High School for Girls crossed the threshold for the first time in September 1979, entering the lower sixth. For those of us in the upper sixth, this was a form of torture. The boys in the year below us not only had the pleasure of sharing classes with these exquisite creatures, but also had the luxury of knowing that their exams were the best part of two years away. We, however, were expected to knuckle down just as our testosterone was in danger of bubbling over. I've always thought that allowances should have been made when our papers were marked the following summer, but of course none were, and KGV's A-level results duly took a wholly explicable nosedive.

By some miracle that I still don't fully understand, my own results were pretty decent; good enough, at any rate, for me to stay on for a term in an attempt, albeit unsuccessful, to win a place to read history at Jesus College, Oxford. My A and two Bs came as a delightful shock because not only had my head been turned, indeed positively spun, by the attractions of the opposite sex, but 1979 and 1980 were also notably fine years for television. Michael Palin's *Ripping Yarns*, and *Minder*, with George Cole and Dennis Waterman, the latter still an icon from his role as George Carter in *The Sweeney*, boosted the repertoire of what we talked about before, after and sometimes during morning registration. And though it wasn't something to discuss with my schoolfriends, I also formed a firm attachment to *To the Manor Born*, with Penelope Keith as the former lady of the manor fallen on hard times, Audrey fforbes-Hamilton, and Peter Bowles as the nouveau riche immigrant grocer, Richard De Vere (formerly Bedrich Poulouvica). It was something I could watch with my mum, and even as a 17-year-old I could appreciate the convenience of that.

About eight years later, it so happened that I went skiing for the first time with a bunch of friends from the University of St Andrews, where I had spent four happy years after Jesus College sensibly rejected me. We went to Borovets in Bulgaria because it was improbably cheap, and one evening took an excursion into a forest on a one-horse open sleigh, jingling all the way to a wooden hut in a clearing where a man and his wife served dinner for westerners in search of the genuine Bulgar experience. As soon as my friends and I set eyes on the man, who had lived all his life in this Bulgarian forest, we were instantly reminded of Peter Bowles. He had the same erect bearing, and wore the same slightly raffish moustache. It was uncanny. We started giggling. Then he brought over some Bulgarian sausage for us to try and, with a huge melancholy sigh, said in fractured English, 'I know. Pitter Bols. To Ze Manor Born.' Clearly, not a single British party ever looked at him without nudging each other and giggling, and he had eventually insisted on being let in on the joke.

That the twin distractions of girls and television did not scupper my A-levels is all the more remarkable considering that television alone had almost done for my O-levels. In February 1978 I had done so disastrously in my mock O-level exams that my mother took the radical step of having the TV removed. It was no longer the huge, faux-cabinet job on which my father had watched the ITV Seven, incidentally. His death two years earlier had forced my mother to make major financial cutbacks, so my cousin James agreed to buy our brown Ford Granada (to which I was devastated to say goodbye, not so much because I associated it with my dad as because it was exactly like the one Regan and Carter used in *The Sweeney*), and my mum arranged for two strapping Rumbelows men to collect the telly. In place of the Granada she bought the Escort that I would later leave overnight in a Liverpool multi-storey, and in place of the handsome telly she rented a bog-standard set on four spindly legs from Radio Rentals. Hardly anything symbolized our new status as a one-parent family, with its attendant economic pressures, quite so eloquently as our ordinary Radio Rentals telly.

It was this set that, at my mother's behest, Mr Williams from number 54 took away and put in his garage. I knew deep down, of course, that he and my mum had my best interests at heart, yet at first I couldn't help seeing him as a collaborator in a particularly heinous crime. Not having a television set in the house was like not having a bed: it was just as fundamental to my lifestyle. And to go into school not having watched *The Sweeney* the night before, or even *Hazell*, was almost like going in not wearing your trousers. It made you feel no less conspicuous.

Of course, there was always the possibility of pretending that you had watched what everyone else had watched, but I knew that this tactic was fraught with danger thanks to a lad who lived down my road to whom I'll give the prosaic pseudonym Martin Earnshaw: I wouldn't want to embarrass him even now, wherever he might be, by naming him.

On Saturday and Sunday afternoons, Martin often used to fall into step with my friend Jez Sykes and me as we made our way along

Clovelly Drive to Waterloo Road Recreation Ground – the rec – to play football. Invariably, Jez and I would be discussing what we had watched the evening before, and whatever we had watched, Martin had always watched it too. Except, of course, that he hadn't. So, realizing this, and demonstrating the kind of cold-blooded, sadistic cruelty otherwise exemplified by Anthony Valentine's character Major Horst Mohn in *Colditz*, Jez and I used to set traps for Martin into which he would obligingly and unfailingly fall.

'Hiya, Mart. Hey, Mart, me and Bri were just talking about that ace film on ITV dead late last night. The one with Oliver Reed. Did you see it?'

'Yeah, it was ace.'

'Mart, me and Jez reckon that the scene when Oliver Reed rode down the steps of that church on his motorbike was one of the best things we've seen on telly for ages. What do you reckon, Mart?'

'Best thing I've seen for ages, Bri. It was probably my favourite scene. Oliver Reed, riding down them steps on his bike. Brilliant.'

'Fuck off, Mart, there wasn't even a film on ITV last night.'

'Yeah, fuck off, Mart. Oliver Reed probably can't even ride a motorbike.'

At which Mart would look ashen, and then try to recover his reputation. 'Yeah, well, I knew that. I never thought there was a film on ITV last night. I was just having you on.'

'Oh, OK, Mart. You fooled us there.'

I'm not sure why Martin wanted to remain friends with me after these episodes, but he did, and I don't suppose either he or I missed the irony when a few years later, unable to watch telly in my own house on account of it sitting on the workbench in Mr Williams' garage, and no longer friends with Andy Boothman at whose house I used to watch *Coronation Street* on account of him forming a band called Oasis (destined never to succeed, I always thought, mainly because of its ineffably crap name) to which he devoted all his time,

I used to ask Martin if he would mind if I spent the odd evening round at his place, watching the little black-and-white portable set he had been given – the jammy get – for his birthday.

My mother, with me round at Mart's house and her compelled to spend yet another evening with her needlework in the absence of a telly, eventually realized that her plan had backfired, and asked Mr Williams to bring the set back. But for at least six weeks I did my viewing sitting on Mart's bed, which sometimes seemed unnervingly intimate, but at least saved me from the discomfort of watching with him and his family downstairs, because he had an older sister called Millicent whose beauty tied my tongue in knots.

7

'Is That a Man Or a Woman?': Dads, and *Top of the Pops*

From a distance, and in fading light, and notwithstanding a broad expanse of chubby, milky-white thigh that her denim hotpants did little to conceal, Millicent Earnshaw looked passably like the blonde one in Abba, whose name was Agnetha Faltskog except to boys of my generation, to whom she was and still is 'the blonde one from Abba'.

Until the former Playboy Bunny Debbie Harry burst onto the scene and into my dreams sometime in 1978, the blonde one from Abba was my idea of utter unblemished beauty, and as the nearest thing to her in Lynton Road, Millicent Earnshaw struck me as pretty gorgeous too. But then, as I say, along came Debbie Harry, not a bona fide blonde, so it was said by those who knew about such things, but certainly a sultrier, less wholesome-looking woman than the blonde one from Abba. From the moment I saw Debbie Harry on *Top of the*

Pops in Martin Earnshaw's bedroom, his sister Millicent began to wane in my affections (not, of course, that she either knew or cared). Moreover, there was more credibility in fancying Debbie Harry, whose picture could be Sellotaped to a teenage boy's bedroom wall in a way that a picture of Abba could not, not without you getting the occasional Chinese burn from your disdainful friends. I also discovered that, like me, she was adopted: she had been born plain Angela Trimble. I felt that in the highly unlikely circumstance of us ever meeting, we'd have plenty to talk about.

Seeing Debbie Harry now, or Deborah Harry as she has restyled herself, I find a slightly unsettling experience. It's not that she hasn't aged well – there can't be many better-looking pensioners – but her slight jowliness, and the care she seems to take to keep her neck covered, reminds me powerfully of my own long-departed youth. I recently pointed her out in a magazine to my teenage daughter, Eleanor, and explained that I'd once considered her the most alluring creature on earth. Eleanor gave me the same slightly pitying look that I remember giving my own father when he told me that Diana Dors, whose blubber seemed almost to fill her little cubbyhole on early editions of *Celebrity Squares*, had in her youth been a regular stunner.

This seems like an appropriate juncture to relate a story that Diana Dors herself swore was true, that she was once asked to open a church fête in her home town of Swindon, and had lunch with the vicar beforehand. He asked her about her early life, and seemed interested when she said that she had been born Diana Fluck (she used to claim that the Rank Organisation advised her to change the Fluck in case she ended up with her name in lights, and one of the bulbs blew).

'In that case,' he said, 'I think I should introduce you by your real name.' Unfortunately, the combination of too much elderflower wine on a warm summer's day, and a growing anxiety that he might forget to insert the all-important letter L, led the vicar to drop a terrible clanger. 'Ladies and gentlemen,' he said. 'We are terribly lucky here at St Ethelred's to have a genuine film star to open our fête, and a locally born one at that. So even though you all know her by the name Dors, it seems apppropriate to introduce her with the name she had as a girl growing up here in Swindon. Please give a warm welcome to . . . Diana Clunt.'

Just to stick with unusual, slightly saucy names for a moment, I might as well share another of my favourite stories, about a group of journalists on the *Daily Mail* who some years ago, doubtless over a few dozen drinks at the end of the working day, struck a bet to see who could be the first to get the words 'moist gusset' into the paper. The bet was won by a resourceful writer on Nigel Dempster's diary page, who made up a story about an imaginary Belgian playboy called Moi St Gusset. I don't know that hack's name, but I salute him here.

To get back to the luscious Debbie Harry, it wasn't only adolescent boys who found her singularly arresting. Their fathers did too. David Morrissey, now an exceptionally fine and powerful actor, told me once that he was sometimes driven to school – St Margaret Mary's secondary modern in Knotty Ash, the district of Liverpool which more notably was also the home of Ken Dodd's Diddymen – in his dad's Ford Cortina Ghia. It was a company car: David's father was regional manager for Mr Minute, the cobbling, engraving and key-cutting company. But far from enjoying his lifts to school, David was decidedly self-conscious about them and used to get his dad to drop him off a safe distance from the school gate. Not many at St Margaret Mary's had parents with cars as fancy as a Ford Cortina Ghia. Which is perhaps why so many decades later some of the exchanges he and his dad had on the way to school are still engraved, Mr Minute-like, on his mind.

On one particular morning Blondie were on the radio, performing their latest hit. 'Denis, Denis, I'm so in love with you,' sang Debbie Harry. 'What a load of rubbish,' responded David's dad. David begged to differ. And then, the evening of that very same day, David was watching Blondie on *Top of the Pops* when his dad came into the room and caught sight of Debbie Harry gazing sensually into the camera as she confessed, 'Denis, Denis, oh with your eyes so blue / Denis, Denis, I've got a crush on you . . .' 'This is good,' said Mr Morrissey with enthusiasm, sitting on the arm of the sofa and making no connection between the vision before him and the earlier noise on the car radio.

It was as hard then to imagine Debbie Harry with sixtysomething wrinkles as it was for Mr Morrissey and his son to imagine that one day far in the future young David would be cast in a Hollywood film as the male lead opposite another sexy American blonde, namely Sharon Stone. The film was *Basic Instinct 2*, the filming of which, regrettably for the male lead, coincided with the 2005 European Cup final. A keen fan of Liverpool FC, David was unable to get to the final, in which Liverpool memorably beat AC Milan in Istanbul after trailing 0–3 at half-time, because he was filming a love scene in a studio somewhere. He was gutted not to be there in person. But how many football fans can claim that they watched their team win the European Cup after spending all day in bed with Sharon Stone? A win double if ever there was one.

All of which is by the by, but returning to Mr Morrissey's dim opinion of Blondie, if only on the radio, it was the prerogative of all fathers in the 1970s to rubbish the musical tastes of their children. These days it is different. We fathers of teenagers consider ourselves a little more enlightened than our parents were, expressing not mere tolerance for the likes of Lily Allen and Franz Ferdinand, but some-times actual admiration. This possibly has the same effect on our children as the resolute fuddy-duddiness of our own parents had on us, making them want to go off and have a quiet puke somewhere, but at least I have the satisfaction of knowing that I have never echoed the father of my schoolfriend Jonny Cook. Jonny reports that he hardly ever got through an edition of *Top of the Pops* without his dad entering the room, saying 'Is that a man or a woman?' with an air of distaste and then walking out. For the father of another of my friends, Chris Taylor, *Top of the Pops* was a weekly exercise in 'jungle music'.

The same did not apply to teachers, who in many cases were only a few years older than we were. My friend Mike King – who took his music so seriously that he became, and as the country music artist Michael Weston King remains, a professional singer-songwriter – still remembers the day when his housemaster Mr Ward came into the house meeting and gloomily announced a minute's silence because of the devastating news that morning – 17 September 1977 – that Marc Bolan had been killed in a car crash. Mike, a devotee of Bolan's TV show *Marc* – 'see you next week, same Marc time, same Marc place' – was impressed. 'I'd previously only thought of Kenny Ward as a slightly intense bloke with dandruff on his velvet jacket,' he says now. 'He went right up in my estimation that day.'

Our parents' generation, meanwhile, was left unmoved by the death of Marc Bolan. 'Probably couldn't see where he was going through all that hair,' was doubtless the verdict of Mr Cook and Mr Taylor, if they even heard about the fatal car crash. As for the glam rock bands, Sweet and Slade foremost among them, I can see now that they must have looked and sounded perfectly horrifying to 1970s dads, who all owned – I think it was a legal requirement of the over-40s – at least one Herb Alpert and the Tijuana Brass LP and another by Acker Bilk. Whatever happened to the bowler-hatted Acker Bilk, by the way? It seems rather a shame that there are now generations of people with no chance of understanding the Neolithic joke about the bank manager's wife who gets her toe stuck fast in the bath tap, necessitating a call to the fire brigade. She is able to put on a blouse to protect her upper dignity, but the only way of protecting her lower dignity is for her husband to position his bowler with strategic care. Then a beefy fireman arrives. 'It shouldn't be a problem getting your wife's toe out of the tap,' he tells the bank manager. 'But I could have more of a problem getting Acker Bilk out of there.'

The one old guy in Southport who shared the musical enthusiasms of the town's teenagers was a bloke called Keith, who ran Discount Discs – used jukebox singles only 20p each, an irresistible bargain even though they were scratched to buggery – just off Tulketh Street. You could feel good about yourself if you walked into Discount Discs and Keith looked up from assembling a roll-up cigarette to nod at you. If he greeted you by name then you were officially cool. On the rare occasions I ventured into Discount Discs, Keith usually looked straight through me. Unless I was with Mike King, in which case Mike would get an 'all right, Mike' from Keith, and I would get a barely discernible raising of an eyebrow. To me that was like being invited to Keith's house for Christmas dinner. It was an acknowledgment I treasured.

Mike, as I have recorded, was by some distance the coolest of my friends. And not only was he good at football, not only did he have a girlfriend two years older than himself with her own car, he also watched *The Old Grey Whistle Test* (the title deriving from the old Tin Pan Alley maxim, that if the grey-haired doorman is heard whistling your tune, you had a hit on your hands). It was one thing to watch *Top of the Pops*, albeit mainly in my case to avoid feeling left out at school the following day, but if you watched *Whistle Test* – which the true cognoscenti never prefixed with 'The Old Grey' – you were unequivocally a hardcore music fan. There was really no point in the rest of us trying to bluff our way through conversations in the school corridor about *Whistle Test*. We'd be exposed in an instant.

Of course, far worse than not being particularly interested in music was embracing the wrong kind of music. And it was easy enough to identify those with crap musical taste. At KGV, swotty boys carried their books in briefcases (and were invariably beaten up for doing so); the rest of us were divided into the Adidas bag brigade and the canvas haversack mob. I carried a blue Adidas bag, the advantage of which was that, when full of textbooks, it could be deployed as a lethal knee-buckling weapon on the school's polished parquet corridors. A full Adidas bag, slid at pace towards the back of Cargill's legs like a great big curling-stone, could bring him crashing down on his backside, and if you timed it right, he would be on his arse just as Mr Rimmer arrived to whisk us all into O-level French: 'What on earth are you doing down there, Cargill? Get up, for heaven's sake!'

The advantage of canvas haversacks, however, was that they could be elaborately painted either with the name of a football team or, more commonly, with the name of a band. To this day I don't think I have admired works of art as much as I admired some of those canvas haversacks, although the unfortunate equation seemed to be that the less cool the band, the more beautifully painted the haversack. The Judas Priest and Black Sabbath haversacks always seemed to be painted with more care than the Rolling Stones and The Who haversacks. And while you could admire the art, it really was impossible to admire the artist.

That's how it was with schoolboys in the 1970s. No matter what the human virtues of other lads your age, you could not consider them as friends if they liked Judas Priest or Black Sabbath, or, to a slightly lesser extent, Thin Lizzy. Oddly enough, the same did not apply to football, about which I had much stronger feelings than I had about music. I was a devoted fan of Everton FC from the age of nine, yet I was perfectly happy for my friends to follow Liverpool, Manchester United and Manchester City. But the same principle most certainly did apply to television. I was prepared to accept that *Coronation Street* was an unorthodox enthusiasm for a teenage boy, but I couldn't be friends with someone who didn't enjoy *The Sweeney*, or *Morecambe and Wise*, or *Fawlty Towers*, or *Alias Smith and Jones*. That would have been downright perverse.

8

'Hannibal Heyes and Kid Curry, the Two Most Successful Outlaws in the History of the West'

Alias Smith and Jones marked the beginning of my love affair with American television. It began in 1971 and starred Pete Duel (pronounced the Yankee way – Dool) and Ben Murphy as Hannibal Heyes and Kid Curry, gallant former bank robbers who operated under the aliases Joshua Smith and Thaddeus Jones and had been promised a pardon by the governor of Kansas if they could go straight for a year.

Maybe I was predisposed to like it having been dealt such pleasure and indeed an early sexual awakening by *Butch Cassidy and the Sundance Kid,* on which it was manifestly based. Whatever, like most of my friends, I knew by heart the opening monologue, which I suppose was designed to appeal to the sensibilities of those who

considered a pair of outlaws inappropriate heroes for primetime network television: 'Hannibal Heyes and Kid Curry: the two most
successful outlaws in the history of the West. And in all the trains
and banks they robbed they never shot anyone. This made our two
latter-day Robin Hoods very popular with everyone but the railroads
and the banks.'

Alias Smith and Jones ran on Mondays at 9 p.m. and I was given
special parental dispensation to watch it. If perchance I missed it then
a shadow was cast over the entire week. My own children are probably fed up with me telling them that there were no means of recording
TV programmes when I was their age: no video recorders or DVD
players or Sky Plus. When I add that until I was thirteen I also
watched everything in black-and-white, they look at me sympatheti-
cally, as if I was telling them that I was brought up in a workhouse on
one bowl of gruel a day. But that's how it was. If circumstances pre-
vented you from watching your favourite programme, circumstances
sometimes as prosaic as your dad wanting to watch whatever was on
the other 'side' (we never said 'channel' in those days), then you were
stuffed. There were programmes I missed in the 1970s that I'm only
catching up on now, thanks to UK Gold and ITV4. Not that it would
have come as much consolation to me had I known in 1974 that it
would take more than thirty years for me to catch the episode of *On
the Buses* I had missed.

Still, the flip-side of missing favourite programmes was that, when
you watched them, you were in the company of tens of millions. The
modern proliferation of channels means that the collective viewing
experience, whereby you just knew that Mrs Watson next door, Mr
and Mrs Abbott at number 62, the Taylor family round the corner in
Clovelly Drive, your primary school teacher Mr Petrie-Brown, your
grandma in London and possibly even the Queen and the Duke of
Edinburgh, were all watching the same programme at the same time,
has gone for ever. But at least there is a collective nostalgia experience;

if nothing else we can get together in pubs and talk about life before the remote-control unit.

'I *was* my dad's remote-control unit,' my mate Chris Taylor recalls, but I don't suppose Chris ever made the short journey from the couch (we never said sofa in those days, either) to the television set with a skip in his step and a song in his heart. Even then, even though we knew no alternative, the act of changing channels seemed like a wearisome business. If I were ever to compose a list of the best inventions of the twentieth century, the TV remote-control unit would be right up there in the top ten as a labour-saving device nonpareil.

With there being only three channels to change, of course, a remote-control unit wasn't quite the essential accessory that it is now, in the 400-channel age. Moreover, in some households the choice was effectively limited to only two channels; the third, ITV, was considered not only downmarket but downright pernicious, what in the north-west of England might have been known as persona non Granada.

I must say that I don't remember my own parents looking down their noses at ITV, but quite a few of my friends' parents did. Jonny Cook's mum and dad thought ITV irredeemably common – 'a bit council house' in Jonny's words – and banned their three children from watching it. *Coronation Street* was a no-no, as was *Man About the House*. No exceptions were made, not even for the irreproachable *World in Action*. My parents were a little less rigid. I considered myself lucky to be able to choose from the full complement of three channels.

This is something else I tell my children and again they look at me with sympathy, mixed with a degree of wonderment that their old dad experienced such privations in his boyhood. Yet my own parents felt that my generation was blessed to have television at all, even though they used to sneer that the American imports, on which I became increasingly hooked as the 1970s wore on, were utter rubbish.

This used to drive me mad – how could any sentient being not appreciate the genius of *Alias Smith and Jones*? – yet I can hear history repeating itself whenever I wander into the kitchen now to find my own kids watching lame sitcoms on the Disney Channel. Few are those parents, I imagine, who have not, in the course of issuing complaints and directives to their children, been strongly and rather disconcertingly reminded of their own parents lecturing them. When I chunter about the influence that American TV seems to be having on my kids, not least in their tendency to utter the word 'like' eight times in every sentence, I can plainly recall my dad's insistence that American TV was altogether inferior to British TV, and somehow more likely to rot the brain.

When a decade or so later I went to live in Atlanta, Georgia, I realized belatedly that he was right. Many if not most American TV programmes are unspeakably awful, so awful that it comes as a relief when they are relentlessly interrupted by commercial breaks, even though the commercials are awful too. But I would also contend that American televison at its best is on the whole cleverer, more imaginative and more daring than our own. In adulthood, nothing has gripped me more than the early series of *NYPD Blue*, and later *Band of Brothers*, *The Sopranos* and *Damages*, or tickled me more than *Frasier*, *Seinfeld*, *The Larry Sanders Show* and *Curb Your Enthusiasm*. And in childhood I felt the same way about *Alias Smith and Jones*. Moreover, it demonstrably enriched my vocabulary. Like many kids of my generation I learnt the meaning of the word 'amnesty' not from reading newspapers or from my parents telling about the work of Amnesty International, but from Pete Duel and Ben Murphy.

In fact I will go even further, and suggest that my ability to remember chunks of speeches, which would later serve me well in exams right up to my Modern History finals at university, was honed on the couch watching the deeds of Hannibal Heyes and Kid Curry. I might never have been able to commit to memory much of President

Franklin D. Roosevelt's rousing inaugural address – 'So, first of all, let me assert my firm belief that the only thing we have to fear is fear itself – nameless, unreasoning, unjustified terror which paralyses needed efforts to convert retreat into advance' – had I not, some years before, made myself word perfect intoning the introductory narration before each episode of *Alias Smith and Jones*: 'Into the West came many men. Some were good men and some were bad men. Some were good men that had some bad in them, and some were bad men that had some good in them. This is the story of two pretty good bad men.'

The actor who narrated these stirring words was Roger Davis, who, I later noted and filed in my anorak pocket, was married to the actress Jaclyn Smith, who would go on to become one of *Charlie's Angels*. More significantly, in February 1972 Davis was handed an unexpected additional role in the series: that of Hannibal Heyes himself. This followed the grisly suicide of Pete Duel, who shot himself in the head with his .38 revolver after watching an episode of *Alias Smith and Jones* on 31 December 1971. Quite what compelled him to take his own life has never been clear, but evidently the contrast between himself and his happy-go-lucky character had something to do with it. Six weeks before he killed himself, Duel had said of Heyes: 'He is hunted by every posse, yet he is still able to laugh. It's something I love him for. I try to be like that, but with so many problems besetting the world, from war to pollution and injustice, I find it difficult to keep smiling.'

There were other celebrity suicides in the 1970s and even more shocking ones – on 15 July 1974, Christine Chubbuck, a 29-year-old presenter on WXLT-TV in Florida, shot herself in the head, also with a .38, live on air – but for me, as for many fans of the series, Duel's death represented the first time that suicide had made an impact on our young lives. Forty miles away in Stockport, Craig Cash was even more shattered than I was at the terrible news. 'I was in our house at 7 Burton Walk and my mum broke it to me. She told me that he'd shot himself under the Christmas tree.'

I wanted to know how he had done it and why, and I suppose at that age I found it mystifying that a character as chirpy and resourceful as Hannibal Heyes could be played by a man as tormented as Duel. Whatever, I could not swallow Davis as the new Heyes and nor, apparently, could anyone else. The series limped on for seventeen more episodes, and was then quietly put out of its misery.

About twenty-five years later, in another fine example of adult life unfolding in a way I could never have anticipated as a child, I was driven slowly in a hearse past the very house in the Hollywood Hills where Duel had killed himself. I was in Los Angeles to attend the taping of the last episode of *Seinfeld*, arranged for me by a good friend and wonderful contact, an ebullient woman called Doree Glaser, who was Sky's PR person in America.

It was while I was in LA to write the *Seinfeld* story that Doree recommended something called the Graveline Tour, a pun on Gray Line, which organizes sightseeing bus journeys round American cities. The Graveline Tour, it turned out, was conducted in a 1968 silver Cadillac hearse by a man dressed as an undertaker, and visited the sites in LA where famous people had come a terrible cropper. Not that the croppers always involved death. One of the early landmarks pointed out to us was a yellow fire hydrant on Sunset Boulevard, the spot where Hugh Grant lost his head with Divine Brown.

Our driver and guide was a man called Steve, who picked up me and my fellow passengers, as arranged, on the corner of Orchid Avenue and Hollywood Boulevard. He introduced himself as our 'sightseeing counsellor' and referred to us all as mourners. Only in Tinseltown. A taped commentary began with the Funeral March, and our first stop was the shabby Highland Gardens Hotel, which was called the Landmark Hotel in October 1970, when Janis Joplin took her final injection of heroin there. With ill-concealed relish, Steve pointed out Room 105 where she was found, 'still clad in her baby-doll pyjamas'.

The level of ghoulishness among my fellow 'mourners' was more than a little unsettling, particularly that of a spectacularly camp gay couple, both of whom talked like Liberace, and whose zoom lenses worked overtime even as we passed the less interesting landmarks, such as the block where David Cassidy's father, the actor Jack Cassidy, burned to death in 1976. When Steve invited each of us to name our favourite dead celebrity – loyal to the memory of Hannibal Heyes, I offered Pete Duel – one of the camp guys said, in his Liberace-like whine: 'It has to be Lee Remick. She was so gracious right to the end.' His partner agreed, but also offered his second-favourite dead celebrity, the singer Karen Carpenter, a victim of anorexia at the age of thirty-two, whose 'open-casket viewing' he described in detail that lives with me still.

We moved on to look at the the garage where Sal Mineo, Oscar-nominated for his role in *Rebel Without a Cause*, was knifed to death in 1976. And we lingered outside the house on North Bedford Drive where, on Good Friday 1958, Lana Turner's 14-year-old daughter, Cheryl, took a kitchen knife to Turner's brutal lover, Johnny Stompanato.

It was faintly worrying to realize that I was beginning to enjoy these macabre sights. I was downright disappointed not to venture by the scenes of arguably the two most notorious crimes in Los Angeles – the 1994 Nicole Brown Simpson–Ronald Goldman killings, and the 1969 Charles Manson massacre. Steve told us that the house where Manson's disciples slaughtered the actress Sharon Tate and others had long since been demolished, but to compensate he drove us by El Coyote, the Mexican restaurant where Tate had her last meal, and merrily informed us that one of his friends once sent out Christmas cards featuring a Manson murder victim lying on a slab in the morgue, 'which was kinda cool'.

Steve was delighted to find that I was British, and indulged me by taking me into the lobby of the Beverly Hills Hotel where Peter Finch dropped dead in 1977. He also told me, with a degree of sympathy as if he were expecting me to take it personally, that the first person to make a suicide plunge from the famous Hollywood sign was a failed English actress, Peg Entwistle, in 1932. I tried to muster some proper patriotic sorrow but the only celebrity suicide that had ever really saddened me, I told him and my fellow 'mourners', was that of Pete Duel. 'Oh, I loved Pete Duel,' said the older half of the camp couple. 'He had such cute ears.' I had to admit I'd never noticed.

9

'Who Loves Ya Baby' – Watching the Detectives

By the time I did the Graveline Tour I had crossed the Atlantic countless times, but even when I made my first visit to the United States, in the summer of 1983, I had formed a firm image of the country based entirely on the imported television shows I had been watching devotedly since childhood. Some of these were westerns – notably *Alias Smith and Jones, The High Chaparral* and *The Virginian* (in which Trampus, played by Doug McLure, was a shining hero to me almost as luminescent as Hannibal Heyes and Kid Curry) – but for obvious reasons it was the shows portraying contemporary America on which my perception of the Land of the Free and Home of the Brave was principally based.

The overwhelming majority of these were detective shows. *The Streets of San Francisco; A Man Called Ironside; The Rockford Files* (a show which introduced to 58 Lynton Road the exciting concept of the telephone answering machine, and also a show immortalized many years later by Jim Royle in *The Royle Family* as rhyming slang for piles); *Starsky and Hutch*; *Macmillan and Wife*; *Hawaii Five-0*; *Kojak*; *Banacek*; *Columbo*; *Madigan*; *Petrocelli*; *McCloud*; *Cannon*; I religiously watched them all from beginning to 'Epilog'.

With the benefit of adult hindsight, I can see now that they were almost all shamelessly formulaic and hopelessly derivative. Most of them were also more than a little implausible. Petrocelli – who was actually a criminal lawyer rather than a detective, but it amounted to the same thing – combined crime-solving with building his own house in a town called San Remo. Hard though he seemed to work on the house every week, it stayed resolutely half-finished for three years.

Then there was Frank Cannon, played by the perpetually perspiring William Conrad. Cannon was an almost completely round Weeble of a man who looked, as Joan Rivers once rudely said of Elizabeth Taylor, as if he spread mayonnaise on his aspirin. Yet hardly an episode of *Cannon* went by without our clinically obese hero legging it down a street, across a basketball court and through a car park, in hot and of course immensely sweaty pursuit of a couple of criminals, whose combined weight was probably less than half of his own, yet with whom he miraculously caught up every time. Still, I don't recall ever questioning the validity of this, perhaps because in my early teens I was myself shaped a little like Frank Cannon, and subliminally appreciated the message that fat guys don't always get left behind.

Besides, it was also a much more naïve age, naïvety on which American detective shows cheerfully traded. My schoolfriend Pete Venables told me once that he had been in his bedroom one Saturday night while his mum was downstairs watching *Parkinson*, whose guest that evening was Raymond Burr, the veteran Canadian actor who played the wheelchair-bound San Francisco police chief Ironside, and that as Burr trotted nimbly down Parky's staircase, Pete heard his mum shouting excitedly from downstairs: 'Peter, quick! Come here! Ironside's on *Parkinson* and . . . he's better!'

So infallible were the policing methods of men such as Ironside, Columbo and Kojak that some of us (Mrs Venables and me, for starters) wondered why there were any crime statistics at all in big American cities. Surely these characters were not complete figments of the fevered imagination of screenwriters; they had to be based on somebody. On the other hand, the fact that America needed so many crimebusters and that they were all so damned busy, with dreadful murders to solve every week, was grist to the mill of those who considered it the most dangerous country on earth. I have another old friend, Roger, whose grandmother was incredulous when she heard that he was planning a trip to New York City. 'Haven't you seen *Kojak?*' she spluttered.

Of all American detectives, with the possible exception of Starsky and Hutch who turned up on our screens a little later, Theo Kojak glittered the brightest. There were some golden opportunities in the 1970s for B-list movie actors to make a name for themselves on television, and Telly Savalas took full, glorious advantage. Even Rock Hudson, unequivocally an A-list movie star, turned up in *Macmillan and Wife*, while George Peppard found gainful employment as *Banacek*, Richard Widmark as *Madigan*, James Garner as Jim Rockford, and Karl Malden, once an Academy Award nominee as Father Barry in *On the Waterfront*, as Detective Lieutenant Mike Stone in *The Streets of San Francisco*, with the future movie star Michael Douglas as his fresh-faced protégé Inspector Steve Keller. It is interesting to reflect, incidentally, that those of us who reached our teens in the 1970s still consider Malden – born Mladen Sekulovic, in case you're interested – to have had the definitive bulbous nose. If you pass a man with a proboscis the size, shape and texture of a medium-sized swede, and hear another passer-by muttering something about Karl Malden, then the odds are that he is a middle-aged male who grew up watching *The Streets of San Francisco*.

But nobody, not even Karl Malden, had a physical feature as distinctive as Savalas's bald head, which had been his trademark feature since he shaved off all his hair to play Pontius Pilate in *The Greatest Story Ever Told* in 1965, and which glistened no less than the lollipops Kojak liked to suck (an affectation which developed because Savalas was trying to quit smoking). Savalas, a Greek-American former lifeguard who was forty-nine and had acted the baddie in over seventy mostly forgettable films by the time he first played Kojak (although in 1963 he had received an Oscar nomination for his supporting role as the sadistic Feto Gomez in *The Birdman of Alcatraz*), is probably most famous these days for having been the actress Jennifer Aniston's godfather.

Yet in the 1970s his was one of the most recognizable faces on the planet. Indeed I can remember going on holiday to the Algarve during the Christmas holidays in 1974 – that there had just been a revolution in Portugal did not put my parents off; in fact it probably increased the country's appeal to my father on the basis that coups d'état tend to keep the cost of package holidays down – and, to my great delight, hearing the stirring opening theme music of *Kojak* on the television in the hotel lounge, followed by an entire badly dubbed episode. I watched it agog, trying but failing to work out the Portuguese for 'who loves ya, baby', the great detective's slightly louche catchphrase, which accompanied his hand-kissing gallantry towards the opposite sex.

Theo Kojak gave the impression that he felt he could charm just about any female into bed. Whether the same was true of Telly Savalas himself I don't know, but as a boost to 49-year-old baldies everywhere, women went nuts over him. In 1975 he recorded the dreary song 'If', which was propelled by his sex appeal to number one in the charts, where it stubbornly remained for nine weeks. For the

Tuesday lunchtime brigade at my school, crowded around the radio to listen to the new top forty, the sustained success of Telly Savalas's 'If', played on *Top of the Pops* over a video almost as cheesy as the soft-focus filmlet that had accompanied Tony Orlando and Dawn singing 'Tie a Yellow Ribbon Round the Old Oak Tree', was a weekly source of loud, indignant and I fear profane disgust.

For *Kojak*, however, we had only admiration, even those of us who preferred other characters in the show, such as the lugubrious Detective Crocker (Kevin Dobson, later to resurface in *Knot's Landing*) and in particular the chubby, shambling Detective Stavros (played by Telly's younger brother George). Stavros was as shabby as Kojak was snazzy, to use a good 1970s word, but the real sartorial antithesis to Kojak plied his trade on the opposite coast: Lieutenant Columbo. As Clive James once wrote: 'That Kojak can dress so well and Columbo so badly on what must basically be the same salary is one of the continuing mysteries of American television.'

In the 1990s, on one of my occasional trips to Los Angeles master-minded by Doree Glaser, I wandered into a slightly down-at-heel art deco hotel on Hollywood Boulevard, interested to know why there were so many people milling about in the lobby. There I found a large banner welcoming 'The Annual Convention of American Morticians', and I congratulated myself on my nose for a good feature story while also wondering what the collective noun for undertakers might be, until I realized that in fact I had stumbled onto a film set. I was reminded of my friend Derek, a neighbour in north London, who at the crack of dawn one morning took his wakeful young sons for a walk through Queen's Wood in Highgate. All was going well until they reached a clearing, where Derek was utterly aghast to see a man hanging from a tree. He gathered his boys to him, hoping against hope that they had not seen this appalling spectacle, only to hear a shout of 'Cut!', whereupon various people emerged from the bushes and some stepladders were produced so that the suicide could climb down and go and get a much-needed cappuccino from the catering truck.

I don't think Derek ever found out what film or telly drama was being made in Queen's Wood, but my morticians' convention in LA turned out to have been set up for a made-for-TV *Columbo* movie, and I loitered for a while in the hope of catching sight of Peter Falk, another B-list movie actor who owed his considerable stardom to 1970s television.

Falk had not been the original choice for Columbo – the producers had first approached Bing Crosby, who took very little time to decide that a TV drama commitment would interfere far too much with his time on the golf course. Falk, happily, grabbed the opportunity with both hands, if not both eyes – his right eye had been removed following the discovery of a malignant tumour when he was just three years old – and with impressive scholarliness decided to base the character on Petrovitch, the detective in Dostoevsky's *Crime and Punishment*. Not having read *Crime and Punishment*, I can't comment on the similarity, but I sincerely hope that at least one unworldly student has read it and concluded that Dostoevsky must have been a fan of *Columbo*.

Whatever, Columbo was a cracking character, beautifully played by Falk, even if the formula – elite member of society commits murder or some other dreadful crime, looks scornfully down on over-respectful, seemingly scatterbrained detective in grubby raincoat, only to be brought to book by said detective, who of course turns out to be smarter than Bamber Gascoigne – was almost risibly rigid. I don't think there was ever an episode of *Columbo* in which the 'loo-tenant' did not trudge over to a door, apparently befuddled by the complexities of the case, before turning, scratching his head, to say 'Just one more thing' before letting the killer question fly. One problem that even Columbo could never solve, however, was that of continuity. Part of the fun now of watching old episodes is to keep an eye on the lootenant's cigar, which seems to get longer the more he smokes. I don't know why we didn't spot that at the time.

Columbo's popularity in Britain in the mid-1970s made the character one of the staples of the impressionist Mike Yarwood's act, and indeed one of the staples of everyone who thought they could do impersonations, including my schoolfriends and me. In the mid-1970s, Columbo was one of the three must-haves in the repertoire of every self-respecting amateur impressionist, together with the intellectually challenged Frank 'ooh Betty' Spencer from *Some Mothers Do 'Ave 'Em*, and the ululating, trilby-hatted rugby league commentator Eddie Waring. But I don't suppose there were many real coppers who adopted Columbo's idiosyncratic style, as was indubitably the case with his fellow detectives *Starsky and Hutch*. According to Kenneth Oxford, the Chief Constable of Merseyside at the time, Dave Starsky (Paul Michael Glaser) and Ken Hutchinson (David Soul) of the Los Angeles Police Department had a manifest influence on the streets of Liverpool. 'Police on duty were adopting sunglasses and wearing their gloves with the cuffs turned down,' he later recalled of the early Starsky and Hutch years. 'They also started driving like bloody maniacs.'

It wasn't only the police. In south-east London a wall had to be lowered by the local council because young fans of the series were using it as a launchpad to jump onto parked vehicles. And far more deleteriously for society, chunky belted cardigans of the kind favoured by Detective Starsky (Hutch preferred brown leather jackets), became hugely fashionable, a terrific and unexpected boost to the profits of British Home Stores.

Without ever jumping off a wall onto a parked car, or wearing a chunky belted cardigan from British Home Stores, and not yet old enough to drive a car even down Lynton Road, let alone through a wall of empty cardboard boxes, which was another habit of theirs, I loved *Starsky and Hutch*. Most boys and not a few girls of my age did. Even when I was old enough to go out on Saturday nights, *Starsky and Hutch*, in concert with *Match of the Day*, seemed like a pretty compelling reason to stay in.

Another, similarly compelling reason to stay in was shortage of money, at least until I was old enough to land a Saturday-night job for 60p an hour plus tips as an enthusiastic but inefficient waiter, at Roundtrees restaurant at the unfashionable northern end of Southport's elegant main shopping thoroughfare, Lord Street. Before that, my only means of supplementing my meagre pocket money was by babysitting, which I did for a girl called Candice who lived at the bottom of Lynton Road. Candice was the granddaughter of some dear old family friends, the Gardners, which was a perfectly good arrangement except for the fact that she was only two years younger than me. Nor were either of us exactly burdened with over-confidence with members of the opposite sex, so aged fifteen and thirteen we used to sit there in resounding silence except for the noise of the television, watching the end of *The Duchess of Duke Street*, followed by *The Two Ronnies* (special guest invariably Barbara Dickson) and *Starsky and Hutch*, until Candice uttered her only sentence of the evening – 'I'm going to bed now' – to which I would respond with my only sentence of the evening: 'OK.'

There was one Saturday night, however, when I challenged this ritual in an extraordinarily daring fashion, by clearing my throat nervously and asking her, in the middle of *Starsky and Hutch*, whether she preferred Starsky or Hutch. She jumped as if I'd fired a pistol shot, which in a sense I had. 'I don't really mind,' she said, once she'd recovered some composure, after which we returned to our Trappist ways until she retired to bed.

Most people did have a favourite, choosing between the wise-cracking Starsky and the more sensitive Hutch. But when Soul did a Savalas and had the temerity to enter the charts, notably with the gruesomely soppy 'Don't Give Up on Us', he surrendered the devotion of many boys, while rising commensurately in the estimation of many girls. Their mothers and even grandmothers still fancied Kojak, but for a while Soul was the number-one pin-up among teenage girls.

In one episode, Hutch had a girlfriend called Gillian, which was a sufficiently uncommon name in 1970s California for her to explain its origin: her father had named her after an old flame in Britain. This gave 15-year-old British Gillians, of whom there were quite a few at the time, an extra reason to fantasise about kissing David Soul. Whatever, between him and Kojak US law enforcement officials suddenly had a disproportionately large claim on the affections of Britain's female population.

Perhaps stung by this, British television executives soon cottoned on to the potential of sexy law enforcers working in pairs: Bodie and Doyle of *The Professionals*, which began in 1977, clearly had their origins in *Starsky and Hutch*. Despite the reverence felt in America towards the BBC in particular, British TV had actually been taking its lead from America since the 1950s. And in 1976 something excitingly new crossed the pond – something called a mini-series.

10

The Rise of the Mini-Series, and the Menacing Evil of Falconetti

The first mini-series was *Rich Man, Poor Man*, based on Irwin Shaw's bestselling 1970 novel about two sons of the immigrant Jordache family, Rudy and Tom, and their divergent fortunes from the end of World War Two to the mid-1960s. I have heard it said that Shaw's theme was philosophical, with each brother representing the good and bad in all of us, but also the ambiguity within that good and bad. After all, to paraphrase the *Alias Smith and Jones* narrator, there are good men that have some bad in them, and bad men that have some good in them. Rudy Jordache was the perfect son, who forged a dazzling career and wound up a senator, but was not true to himself. His brother Tom was a brawler and ne'er-do-well, poorer in most senses but more fundamentally honest. His life ended (violently, of course) with him having become the richer man. I don't suppose I grasped those profound truths at the time, but the story, the acting and the dialogue floored me.

The twelve-part series had already aired on ABC in America, where it was a massive ratings success, by the time it arrived on ITV in the summer of 1976. Partly as a riposte to the BBC's coverage of the Olympic Games in Montreal, it was screened on three consecutive Wednesdays and Fridays, with two episodes shown either side of *News at Ten*. This meant some seriously late nights, but with my dad's passing a few months earlier, my mum had given up trying to impose a bedtime on me.

All these decades on, the very mention of *Rich Man, Poor Man* still has the power to make some folk practically swoon with nostalgia. It still gets discussed in internet chatrooms; indeed I read a paean only recently written by someone who hasn't seen it since it was originally shown, who described it as having a cast – Nick Nolte, Peter Strauss, Susan Blakeley, Ed Asner – that remains unequalled in the history of TV drama. I'm not sure that even I would go that far – after all, as already chronicled in these pages, Laurence Olivier, Ralph Richardson, Donald Pleasence, James Mason, Anne Bancroft and Rod Steiger joined forces for *Jesus of Nazareth*, a cast which might marginally get the nod over *Rich Man, Poor Man* – but it was undoubtedly one of the most compelling dramas of the decade, right up there with *I, Claudius*, which in a sense it resembled. Like Robert Graves's epic tale of imperial Rome, *Rich Man, Poor Man* was a story of ambition, intrigue and redemption, although I can't remember there being any infanticide, incest or, for that matter, stammering.

Tom Jordache was played by Nolte, enjoying his big break, even though he was already well into his thirties. He would soon become better known in the industry for bad breaks – in 1978 he was the first choice to play *Superman*, before Christopher Reeve, and Harrison Ford pipped him to the plum part of Han Solo in *Star Wars* – but *Rich Man, Poor Man* represented his hour in the sun, and he was perfectly cast: a hot-headed bruiser with a soul. As the goody-goody Rudy, Strauss was perfect too.

I do wonder whether *Rich Man, Poor Man* would stand up now as a really top-notch drama – I suppose it might look a little leaden – but at the time it seemed like comfortably the best thing I had ever seen on television, and I can remember being distraught when I jerked awake one night to see a screen crackling with static and full of fuzzy lines. I had committed the unforgivable sin of nodding off, and of course in those days you didn't jerk awake in the small hours to find yourself watching a repeat of Vanessa Feltz's chat show or beach volleyball from Austria, as you do now. Television went to sleep just like we did, in fact for much longer than we did, closing down sometimes well before midnight and waking up only fleetingly during the day.

To pluck at random the BBC2 schedule for Friday 28 November 1975, which I happen to have in front of me, *Play School* was on in the morning at 11 o'clock for twenty-five minutes, and then there was nothing but the test card until 7.05 p.m., when the not very exciting-sounding *Mr Smith's Gardening Programme* kicked off the evening schedule, to be followed by *Newsday* with Robin Day and Ludovic Kennedy, *Pot Black* and *The Money Programme*. It seems incredible now not only that Britain then had just three TV channels, and not only that one of the three should be dormant for practically the entire day, but also that when it did finally splutter into life, it did so with a programme about gardening called *Mr Smith's Gardening Programme*, building up to a programme about money called *The Money Programme*. No wonder my children look at me in puzzlement when I tell them that the 1970s was television's golden era.

It was, though. And *Rich Man, Poor Man* was one of the many programmes that made it so. I was almost inconsolable to have missed that episode, and was forced to rely on a synopsis from Jez and Chris Sykes the following morning. I sat at their kitchen table listening to them enthusing – 'It was fucking great, Bri' – knowing that they at least understood my pain. My mum, still mourning my father's passing less than six months earlier, felt, quite rightly in hindsight, that a missed television programme was no cause for anguish.

Rich Man, Poor Man was compelling for all kinds of reasons, among them the fine performances of Nolte and Strauss, yet it was a supporting character who really captured my imagination. This was Tom Jordache's eye-patched nemesis, the villainous Anthony Falconetti. Not since I had been taken to the Palace Cinema on Lord Street to see *The Wizard of Oz*, and suffered for months afterwards from nightmares featuring the Wicked Witch of the West, had a screen villain worried me as much as Falconetti did.

He was played by an actor called William Smith, who had played genial Joe Riley, one of the Texas Rangers on the western series *Laredo* in the mid-1960s. *Rich Man, Poor Man* made rather a virtue of casting against type: the Jordache boys' boorish, bullish father, Axel, was played by Ed Asner, famous for his performances as the highly principled, warm-hearted newspaper editor whose popularity in *The Mary Tyler Moore Show* led to his own eponymous series, *Lou Grant*.

For me, though, it was impossible to think of Falconetti, and by extension Smith, as anything other than shot through with evil. Physically, Falconetti was extremely menacing, which was no great surprise: Smith had been a successful amateur boxer and was a multiple winner of the world arm-wrestling championship. He was also, I should add, a man of considerable culture. He'd studied at the Sorbonne and for a while even taught Russian at UCLA. Furthermore, he had won a Purple Heart during the Korean War. He was a man to make his country proud. But none of that counted for anything. Smith was the face of Falconetti, and Falconetti was the devil incarnate.

My schoolfriends agreed heartily with this assessment, and even though *Rich Man, Poor Man* had finished at the beginning of the summer holidays, it was still a major topic of conversation by the start of the following term. That autumn I started amusing myself and my friends by drawing caricatures of the teachers, and our Maths teacher E.T. 'Etty' Johnson I drew with an eyepatch, scowlingly working out some sums on the blackboard. This I captioned Falcon-Etty, which met with great approval from my classmates, and I'm pleased to say that I have it still, tucked away safely in a drawer, yellowing like ancient parchment. Although I say it myself, it is a work of near-genius.

So was *Rich Man, Poor Man*, and in America it begat a trend for so-called mini-series based on contemporary novels which continued for at least the next fifteen years. The most celebrated of these was not *Rich Man, Poor Man*, however, but *Roots*, a dramatization of Alex Haley's epic novel about his own African-American ancestry, which was transmitted in Britain in the very same month – April 1977 – as *Jesus of Nazareth*. Oy vey, as Lew Grade, or perhaps even Jesus himself, might have said.

Roots was the biggest television event of the year, possibly of the decade, bigger even than *Jesus of Nazareth* because it imparted powerful racial, social and political messages in, as it were, black-and-white. The actual story, however, didn't always ring precisely true. As Clive James noted in his review in the *Observer*, the African village in the first episode seemed to be inhabited exclusively by philosophers. Nonetheless, he added, 'we got the message we needed to get – that the villagers were the flower of their culture, whereas the slavers were the dregs of theirs.'

In Lynton Road I watched every episode, dutifully rather than devotedly, because there was no overestimating the cultural impor-tance of *Roots*, not with so many adults saying that there was no overestimating its cultural importance. We were told that in America, more than 100 million people – almost half the nation – had watched the final episode, transmitted there a few months earlier. A man called Vernon Jordan, former president of the Urban League, whatever that was, had even gone so far as to call it 'the single most spectacular educational experience in race relations in America'. So the least I could do was sit down in front of it with my chicken and mushroom Pot Noodle, newly invented by Golden Wonder, something else for which the year 1977 deserves to be venerated.

Besides, it was fun to spot familiar faces in the cast, including Doug McClure, my old friend Trampas from *The Virginian*. And, reassuringly, Ed Asner was back playing a man with a conscience after his bullying turn in *Rich Man, Poor Man*, albeit as Captain Thomas Davies, who captured the hero, Kunta Kinte, and against his own better instincts sold him into slavery. I also read somewhere that the actor who played Kadi, one of the West African natives, was in real life the star running back for the Buffalo Bills American Football team, a guy called O.J. Simpson. That seemed immensely impressive to me, a top sportsman acting in a major TV drama. When, I asked my Letts Schoolboy Diary on Wednesday 16 April, was Kevin Keegan ever likely to turn up in a mini-series? I liked the sound of this O.J. Simpson fellow.

11

'Any Time, Any Place, Anywhere': Adverts in the 1970s

Kevin Keegan was possibly the closest thing to O.J. Simpson in British sport in 1977, the transcendent superstar of English football, whose transfer that summer from the European champions Liverpool to Hamburg in the German Bundesliga was one of the biggest stories of the year.

He was also a man of demonstrable character, as we had seen in a 1976 edition of *The Superstars*, when the front wheel of his bike clipped the back wheel of the bike ridden by the Belgian footballer Gilbert Van Binst. Keegan tumbled from the saddle and slithered across the cinder track, in the process removing half the skin from his back. For more details of that dramatic incident, I immodestly refer you to my book *Ali, Pelé, Lillee and Me*. Here, I will merely record that Keegan, with astounding stoicism, got back on his bike and went on to win that week's edition of *Superstars*, all of which was marvellous news for the manufacturers of Brut 33 deodorant, whose sales had already taken a healthy upturn since the appearance of a television commercial starring Keegan and the former British and European heavyweight boxing champion Henry Cooper.

If you're as old and as sad as I am, you will still have an almost perfect mental picture of that commercial (I'm going to call them adverts from now on, which in the 1970s is what everyone called them) which unfolded in the gym where, somewhat improbably, the footballer and the retired boxer were exercising together.

Keegan: 'Good work-out today 'Enry!'
Cooper: 'And after a good work-out . . .'
Keegan: '. . . nothing beats the good smell of Brut . . .'
Cooper: ''Ere, are you trying to muscle in on my act?'
Keegan: 'Yeah, why don't you throw in the towel, 'Enry?'
Cooper: 'Gertcha!'
Voice-over: 'Brut 33 — the deodorant with muscle!'

It doesn't really translate to the written page, and nor in truth was it much cop on the screen, but like so many adverts in the 1970s it wormed its way into the consciousness of a nation in a way that adverts these days simply don't, because a thousand channels means that you can always zap to something else, or fast-forward through them if you're watching something recorded. Like television as a whole in the 1970s, watching the adverts (a delectation, don't forget, offered only by a single channel, ITV) was a communal experience, and it was no surprise in 2006 when a survey of more than 3,000 people conducted by *Good Food* magazine found that of the ten food adverts voted 'the most iconic', most of them originated in the 1970s, including the top one: the 1974 advert for Cadbury's Smash instant mashed potato, and its various sequels, in which an entire family of aliens, including the cat and the dog, laughed uproariously at the earthling habit of going to the trouble of peeling potatoes with our metal knives, boiling them for twenty of our earth minutes, and then smashing them all to bits. We were clearly, they reasoned, a most primitive people. 'For mash . . . get Smash,' went the concluding jingle.

Most of the really memorable adverts in the 1970s came with a jingle attached, and anyone who spent as much time as I did in front of the telly during that excellent decade can still remember every word, offering an easy bonding opportunity with people of roughly the same age. I tried it on my wife just a few minutes ago, sneaking up behind her while she was doing the ironing and saying 'boom boom boom boom', to which, without even turning round, she added 'Esso Blue!'

It must have been a great time to be a jingle-writer; you could knock out any old crap and watch it being more or less instantly clutched to the collective bosom. The most effective ones, naturally, were those which included the name of the product, such as the simple but rather brilliant 'Bring out the Branston!' which helped to make the trade name Branston synonymous with pickle, just as Hoover was with the vacuum cleaner before James Dyson, in more ways than one, started cleaning up. Branston Pickle had been around since 1922 but it was the 'Bring out the Branston!' slogan that turned the product into an enduring institution, to the point that when a fire destroyed most of the Branston Pickle factory in Bury St Edmunds in 2004, the subsequent national shortage forced prices on eBay up to £16 per jar. Also, like all the best advertising slogans, it wormed its way into popular culture. In October 2007, when Darren Ferguson, the manager of Peterborough FC – nicknamed Posh – recalled centre-half Guy Branston from a loan spell at Rochdale, the inevitable headline in the Peterborough *Evening Telegraph* was 'Posh Bring Out Branston'. Not that a man called Phil Wilks would understand such a headline. My friend Craig assures me that Wilks, a schoolmate of his, always thought that the rallying-cry 'Bring out the Branston!' was in fact 'Bring out the Bastard!'

Schoolchildren, of course, very often bastardized – or, if Phil Wilks is reading, Branstonized – these jingles for their own highly immature amusement. This made them even more memorable. Take the Trebor Mints jingle, the frankly unremarkable 'Trebor Mints are a minty bit stronger'. To this the nation's schoolkids added a catchy second line – 'stick 'em up your bum and they last a bit longer'. For that, and the fact that the Yorkshireman's endorsement of the mint – 'e ba gum, Trebor!' – spells Robert Mugabe backwards, Trebor Mints have a special place in my heart. It's nothing to do with the taste.

Now, while I don't want this book to turn into one long reproach to my children for having been born altogether too late to enjoy the cultural references disseminated by television in the 1970s, it does seem a shame that advertising slogans and jingles have had a negligible influence on them, at least by comparison with my generation, who almost without exception think not of America's late-nineteenth century melting-pot society as seen through the eyes of a visiting Czech composer when we hear Dvořák's New World Symphony, but of a young lad pushing a bike loaded with loaves of Hovis up a steep cobbled street somewhere in the north of England.

Everyone with a quilted anorak knows, by the way, that the steep cobbled street in that classic 1973 advert was actually in Shaftesbury in Dorset, and as a proud Northerner I find it most disappointing that the North could not provide such an iconic image of itself. But it's so often the way. I'm told that the unremittingly bleak cityscape of East Berlin, the grim backdrop to the 1965 Cold War thriller *The Spy Who Came in From the Cold*, is actually the unremittingly bleak cityscape of Dundee.

I can also tell you that the young lad in the Hovis advert – and if you're already aware of this then your quilted anorak must have a

piece of elastic strung through both sleeves with mittens on the end –
was 13-year-old Carl Barlow, who landed the part when the other two
boys at the final audition of three were rejected, one because he
couldn't ride a bike (even though, if I recall correctly, he only had to
push it), the other because he adamantly refused to be given a pud-
ding-bowl haircut, a stance which at the age of thirteen I would have
wholeheartedly supported, although I dare say he regrets it now.

It used to be quipped that the definition of an intellectual was
someone who listened to Rossini's William Tell Overture without
thinking of the Lone Ranger. The same can be said about the New
World Symphony and Hovis, and indeed for loads of 1970s adverts
set to classical music, such as Frank Muir's seminal 'Everyone's a
Fruit and Nut Case' set to Tchaikovsky's Dance of the Reed Flutes in
The Nutcracker, or Dance of the Weed Flutes as far as dear old
Fwank was concerned.

But it isn't just jingles that fix 1970s adverts firmly in the mind; it's
also images, one of the most evocative of which had a lovely young
woman reclining by a tropical pool with the breeze in her hair and a
tray of iced drinks at her bronzed elbow. The product being advertised was Martini, and the accompanying ditty was 'Anytime, any
place, anywhere/ there's a wonderful world we can share / It's the
right one / the bright one / It's Martini.' Whether or not the first line
of this ditty was wholly innocent I don't know, but it was certainly
readily interpreted by teenage boys as a reference to sex. By the time
I was old enough to recognize that some girls were more amenable
than others to a snog, or perhaps a little more than a snog, the joke
was that the easy conquests – 'anytime, any place, anywhere' – were
nicknamed Martinis. Not, I should add, that I encountered a Martini
of my own, at least until I was well out of my teens. And when I did
she frightened the life out of me.

Anyway, having given the original Hovis boy a mention, I should
do the same for the original Martini girl, whose name was Erica Wills,

and whose extraordinary life story encapsulates a sad phenomenon about minor celebrity, that it curses as well as blesses those it touches.

At the time of that 1971 Martini ad, Wills, who had changed her name from Deborah, was a 22-year-old former air hostess whose modelling career had begun after she was 'discovered' in a lift at Jenners department store in Edinburgh by the uber-model of the 1960s, Jean Shrimpton. Even before she started modelling, however, she had earned a footnote in history. On her maiden flight with British Airways as a stewardess in the first-class cabin, she was summoned by a passenger, the Duchess of Devonshire, who wished to make a complaint about particularly rum goings-on in an adjacent row, where John Lennon and Yoko Ono, embracing the 'anytime, any place, anywhere' philosophy with gusto, appeared to be engaging in sexual intercourse. Understandably flustered, Wills tapped Lennon on the shoulder and asked him to stop. With the Liverpudlian wit for which he was so famous, he told her to fuck off.

In 1970, apparently in response to the death of her father, Wills became addicted to Valium and also developed claustrophobia, neither of which was altogether compatible with a career as an air hostess. But that fortuitous lift journey propelled her towards another career. With Shrimpton's help, she enrolled at the London Academy of Modelling, financing her education by working, like Debbie Harry, as a Playboy Club bunny girl. She was duly signed up by the Michael Whitaker Agency, where she took the name Erica, and for a while shared a flat with the future Mrs Bruce Forsyth, Anthea Redfern. For students of the 1970s, it is rather satisfying to learn that the women embodying two of the decade's most memorable lines – 'anytime, any place, anywhere' and 'give us a twirl' – should have been flatmates.

Wills also counted the actor and man-about-town Lance Percival among her boyfriends. Hers must have seemed like a gilded life. Yet at the height of her personal and professional success, she impetuously took off for Beirut, evidently to help a friend called Maggie

Sibbering, who had wound up as a result of some difficult personal predicament being forced to dance at a bar called the Crazy Horse saloon.

This is where the Wills story begins to sound like the plot of a Carl Hiassen novel. Waking up after apparently being drugged, she found that her passport had been stolen and that she'd mysteriously signed a contract forcing her, too, to work as a dancer at the bar, which was in fact little more than an upmarket brothel. A few months later, she attracted the admiration of one of the customers, a well-known playboy called Elie Ayache, scion of one of the Lebanon's wealthiest families, who owned the Ferrari franchise for the Middle East, and boasted the impressive address PO Box 1, Beirut. Ayache offered to 'buy' her for $5,000, following negotiations in which the owner of the Crazy Horse generously described her as 'the best whore I ever had'. Enthused rather than discouraged by this recommendation, Ayache persevered. He married her in 1975, and they remained together for fifteen years.

In Beirut Wills revived her modelling career and, having borne Ayache two daughters, stoically remained there even after the outbreak of civil war in 1976. During one shelling attack she ended up rescuing her daughters from school in a Lebanese tank; later, the family's villa was stormed and captured by Hezbollah rebels. Eventually, she and her daughters escaped the benighted country on a hydrofoil operated by Dutch mercenaries, and settled near her mother in – it sounds improbably genteel after being held prisoner in Beirut and escaping with mercenaries on a hydrofoil – the 'auld grey toun' of St Andrews, on the east coast of Scotland, which is benighted only by the weather, and where I myself, after a somewhat less colourful past, arrived as an undergraduate in 1981.

The rest of the Wills story is mercifully less dramatic, but perhaps more at odds with her fleetingly glitzy lifestyle as the Martini girl. Having divorced Ayache, she then married a Scottish publican called

Robert Alexander. They split up a decade or so later, after she bumped into Neil Jackson, a professor of architecture, at a party, and promptly informed him that he was her soulmate. They were married in 2002, but in May 2007, the woman once known as Erica Wills, better known as the Martini girl, and by now using the name Deborah Jackson, died, following a stroke, aged only fifty-seven.

There was a short flurry of press interest following the revelation that the original Martini girl had died, with her widower, Neil Jackson, telling the media that she had been hugely vivacious 'but extremely insecure with it, and maybe that vivaciousness was a way of dealing with it. Her other great character trait was that she didn't think before she did things. She would just see something and do it. Throughout her life, her heart always controlled her mind, and that's why she often got herself involved with unsuitable men.' One can only assume that he was excluding himself. Whatever, it is always poignant to consider those people whose declines took a path as vertiginous as their rises. It was a phenomenon in which the 1970s seemed to specialize.

12

The Spectacular Fall and Rise of Simon Dee

The absolute paradigm of the meteoric rise/headlong fall phenomenon was the talk-show host Simon Dee. And it is fitting that the Simon Dee story should follow a chapter about TV advertising, because, as we shall see, it was an advert he did for Smith's Crisps in the mid-1960s that catapulted him to a level of fame that now seems almost unbelievable, considering the anonymity that would eventually engulf him.

In 1999 I saw a letter in a national newspaper, written by a Nicholas Henty-Dodd. This rang a faint bell. Wasn't Nicholas Henty-Dodd the real name of Simon Dee? It was. So I made contact, and asked if I could interview him for the *Independent*. He agreed, and I reproduce the article here:

Boris Yeltsin's grandson and TV's Philippa Forrester are Winchester's only famous residents, according to a local taxi driver called Dave. What about Simon Dee? 'I ain't never heard of him,' says Dave. In media circles, people had been only slightly more clued up when I told them I was going to Winchester to meet Simon Dee. 'God, I thought he was dead,' said one. 'Didn't he emigrate to New Zealand, or was that the Galloping Gourmet?' said another. 'Ah,' said a third. 'Simon Dee, the locus classicus of the where-are-they-now? feature.' When I reported this exchange, my wife was terribly impressed with the term locus classicus. 'You must drop that into your article,' she said. 'But make sure you use it in the right context. Don't say that Simon Dee pulled up in his Locus Classicus.'

Far from it, as it turns out. Simon Dee is skint. Worse, he is skint and unknown. Imagine if, in 2029, Chris Evans is found living anonymously in a small terraced house in deepest Hampshire. It would represent much the same 30-year fall down the rickety ladder of fortune. For, in 1969, tall, toothy Simon Dee, host of the BBC's hit chat-and-music show, *Dee Time*, was as big a star as there was on television. We meet at Winchester's posh Hotel du Vin. He is still tall and toothy and, physically at least, the years have treated him fairly charitably. Later this year he will be 64. 'Will you still need me, will you still feed me, when I'm 64?' Lennon and McCartney's words have acquired a poignant ring for a fellow golden boy of the Sixties.

Until 1964 he was called Nicholas Henty-Dodd. He was from a well-to-do Lancashire family and went to Shrewsbury School at around the same time as Michael Heseltine and Richard Ingrams. John Peel was there a little later and, of the broadcasters whose careers not only survived the Sixties but continued to thrive, Peel is one of the few for whom Dee admits a grudging admiration.

His own rise to fame began with Radio Caroline, the pirate radio station set up off the coast of Ireland on a retired Baltic ferry. Radio Caroline's founder was an ebullient Irishman, Ronan

O'Rahilly, whose first recruit was his old drama-school pal Henty-Dodd. But Henty-Dodd was no name for a pirate. So he combined his young son's name with the initial letter of Dodd to become Simon Dee.

In the Hotel du Vin – between mock-humble protestations that 'it's all so very, very long ago' – Dee enthusiastically recalls the troubled launch of Radio Caroline. 'We had to test the signal before we left the anchorage, so we played Ray Charles singing "Round Midnight" as a test signal. All seemed to be well, but unknown to us we hadn't quite organised the signals correctly, and on every radio and TV set within a 50-mile radius, Ray Charles suddenly interrupted the main evening news. In Dublin, everyone was crying "My God, what's going on?" and no wonder, because Ray Charles on a Hammond organ was saturating the news.'

Dee roars with laughter. He is very hail-fellow-well-met, joshing loudly with the waitress and later rumbustiously defying her request not to smoke a cigar at the table. But for all the bluster, it is hard not to feel sorry for him. In 1970, following a falling-out with his then-employers London Weekend Television, he took a sabbatical. 'I thought, "I'll have a rest now and take a year off". It became two years off, then five years, then 10 years, then 20 years, then 30 years off.' Again, he roars with laughter. But not, I reckon, because he thinks it's funny. A few weeks ago, Dee wrote to Mike Leggo, BBC TV's head of light entertainment, listing all the guests he interviewed between 1967 and 1970, and suggesting that he meet them again to ask them 'if their dreams came true'. He would, of course, need a medium to make contact with many of them. But he sees no reason why he shouldn't make a comeback.

'After all, if a racing driver stops racing for 20 or 30 years then gets back in the car, he will soon get it together. The control and co-ordination will still be there.' Mike Leggo evidently does not agree.

He has not replied. But let us again wind back the years to Dee's strange sacking from Radio Caroline. 'We finally anchored off the coast of Suffolk,' he recalls. 'One day I was doing Sunday Favourites when the technician on the other side of the glass collapsed. I found him on the floor, dying. I went to the microphone and asked for someone to send a boat. Within an hour there must have been 20 rowing boats, yachts, catamarans, and the local lifeboat. The captain later called me to the bridge and said, "By calling for assistance, you have mutinied. Get off my ship."'

Dee was promptly hired by BBC Radio, but owed his big television break to the mother of Bill Cotton, one of the most illustrious of Leggo's predecessors as head of BBC light entertainment. As Dee tells it, Mrs Cotton – wife of the band leader Billy – saw him on the box advertising Smith's Crisps, liked what she saw, and recommended him to her son. Surprisingly, Bill Cotton confirms this. 'I think my initial reaction was "you do the cooking, let me spot the talent". But on the way home I realised that my mother had seen more performers than I had, and that I ought to take her seriously. So we started *Dee Time*. He was quite difficult in that first year because it went to his head. But by the second year there's no doubt that he was one of the most powerful people on television. He had great influence on the young.'

This influence was channelled partly through the Dee Code, a 1968 version of the Ten Commandments. Youngsters were asked to write in endorsing the Dee Code and, in return, were sent a weekly letter signed by Dee, which amounted to a lecture in moral rectitude. Today, those letters make arresting reading. On the subject of race relations, for instance, one said: 'An intelligent being from outer space might easily decide that the only species of mankind worth preserving was the one with the dark-brown skin, the lustrous eyes, sculpted lips and natural grace in movement, and that all those other pallid, thin-lipped, pale-eyed, lank-haired creatures should be painlessly annihilated before they reduced the physical beauty of humanity any further. Think about this, especially when next you hear someone make disparaging remarks about our coloured fellow-citizens.'

These were worthy enough sentiments, yet not everyone approved of the Dee Code. In the *Daily Mail*, Dee was criticised for 'getting too big for his with-it boots'. But still his career seemed gilded, especially when *Dee Time* replaced the ailing *Juke Box Jury* in the all-important Saturday early evening slot. For Dee, life got better and better. He drove an Aston Martin. At a glitzy party, he danced with Princess Margaret. And no star – not John Lennon, nor Charlton Heston, nor Michael Caine – was too big to appear on his show. Thanks to Caine, he even landed a part in *The Italian Job*. 'Mike had been on the show and thought he'd do me a favour. I played a poofy Savile Row tailor, and I was so good that poofs started chasing me.' This time he laughs so hard that a couple two tables away join in.

In 1970, Dee was poached by LWT, reportedly for the fabulous sum of £100,000 a year. The BBC could not match such a salary, but Cotton wasn't too sorry to see him go. 'It had got to the stage where his ideas of his own importance were actually quite damaging,' says Cotton. 'He thought, as a lot of performers do, that he was bigger than the show. A TV executive has to judge when he has to live with that, and when he doesn't. In his case, I didn't want to. By the way, has he still got those fantasies about MI5?'

Yes, in a word. As lunch at the Hotel du Vin wears on, it becomes increasingly and uncomfortably clear that Dee has what appear to be paranoid delusions. In some ways they are understandable. I don't want to trespass on Anthony Clare territory here, but perhaps they are the only way in which he can make sense of the last 30 years of obscurity, following three years in which he was as famous as anyone in the land. He is convinced, for instance, that he was drummed off television because he opposed Britain's entry into the Common Market. He thinks that the British secret service, and possibly the CIA too, tapped his phone, worried by his interest in the assassination of President Kennedy. Most bizarrely of all, he embarks on a long tale which ends with him firmly at the centre of an international conspiracy. To cut it short, he claims that the Moroccan government commissioned him to design a dome for Casablanca. When he delivered the plans, the Moroccans wouldn't pay up, but a posse of Swiss bankers later took him for dinner at the RAC Club in Pall Mall and said they wanted to build his dome for £100 million.

'I left the RAC Club rather happy. "My God," I thought. "I've found another métier." I wake up the next morning, phone their hotel and they've gone, without leaving any note at all. It was all some vast sting.' By now I can see where this is leading and, sure enough, Dee is certain that he has been denied the recognition he deserves, not to mention the fee, for conceiving the Millennium Dome. But let us again return to 1970. *The Simon Dee Show* on London Weekend was a flop. Ever since, Dee has held on to the notion that it was sabotaged by David Frost, who had a sizeable shareholding in the company.

'He was in New York when I joined, and wasn't very pleased when he found that his biggest rival had signed to his own network.' Certainly, the show was given an unsociable slot. And in due course, Dee's bubble of fame and fortune burst. How, I wonder, does he feel when he sees David Frost on television now? 'I don't see David Frost on television now,' he says bitterly. And what has he done for income for the last 30 years? 'I have had no income,' he says. 'When my father died in 1980 I inherited a vast sum of money, but it was taken from me by death duties.' Financially, Dee depends on his third wife, a teacher, and spends his days looking after their four-year-old son, Cyril George. 'If you have no money,' he adds, 'you have to concentrate on friendships. It's not such a bad thing. You have to dwell in reality.' Actually, I don't think that Simon Dee dwells anywhere near reality, but in his boots, I'm not sure I would, either.

13

'Happiness Is a Cigar Called Hamlet': More Adverts, From a Singularly Hapless Decade

Returning to the life and death of Erica Wills, it was a remarkable tale and for a day or two propelled the slogan 'anytime, any place, anywhere' back into the headlines. Not that you have to look far, among folk of my age, for nods to old advertising slogans. I was recently delighted to find, in a restaurant review in the *Independent* written by Tracey MacLeod, who is just a year older than me, a reference to the Mackeson slogan of years ago. Emerging from a restaurant in London with a warm sense of well-being, she wrote of her dinner that 'it looks good, it tastes good, and by golly it does you good'. Anyone too young to remember the Mackeson advert must have wondered what the hell she was on about.

Actually, that Mackeson slogan had been coined long before Tracey and I started watching telly, way back in the 1950s. There are lots of slogans and jingles like that, much more venerable than we think, some of them born not long after the advent of commercial television in 1955. The very first advert on telly, you might already be aware, was for SR toothpaste. It aired at precisely 8.12 p.m. on 22 September 1955 during a variety show hosted by the long-forgotten Jack Jackson. Viewers saw a tube of toothpaste embedded in a block of ice and a woman called Meg Smith vigorously brushing her teeth 'up and down and round the gums'.

It was purely the luck of the draw that handed Gibbs SR the distinction of becoming the first product to be advertised on British television. The toothpaste was one of twenty-four products advertised in the earliest days of ITV, and numbers were drawn from a hat to determine which of them would take its place in history. It might just as easily have been one of the other twenty-three, which included Guinness, Surf washing powder and Brown & Polson custard. And of course had it been Guinness, the message would effectively have been that a drop of the black stuff was no less good for you than a twice-daily brushing with SR toothpaste. Manufacturers now have to prove that their products are beneficial for health before they can say so in their advertising, but it used to be a free-for-all. By golly, Mackeson did you good, just as Double Diamond worked wonders (to the wholesome tune of 'There's a Hole in My Bucket'), a Mars a day helped you work, rest and play, and Milky Way was the sweet you could eat between meals. It sometimes seems rather a shame, while of course being highly proper, that such slogans should have been regulated into extinction.

Anyway, it swiftly became clear to advertisers in the 1950s that television packed enormous power. That was when Rice Krispies snapped, crackled and popped for the first time, and another slogan minted in 1955, if you'll pardon the pun, was 'Murray Mints, Murray Mints, the too-good-to-hurry mints'. The jingle was recorded by Cliff Adams and the Stargazers, who were doubtless paid handsomely to capitalize on their appearance on *Sunday Night at the London Palladium*, concluding their act by singing the Murray Mints song and chucking packets of Murray Mints to a delighted audience. That was within just a few weeks of the start of commercial television. A monster had been spawned.

It was not until the 1970s, though, that the monster really started making us laugh. I suppose there must have been witty advertising in the 1960s, and I can vaguely remember an advert in which Sid James watched a bus drive off without him and muttered 'What a diabolical liberty!', which as a small and evidently easily amused child I thought was absolutely hilarious; but only from about the mid-1970s did television advertising regularly begin to take the form of mini-narratives, with the advent of colour (and colour licences did not outnumber black-and-white until as late as 1976, so maybe my mum and dad weren't as behind the times as I thought, only succumbing to colour in 1974) offering new opportunities for directors to craft proper little films. This in turn meant rich opportunities for humour.

The funniest adverts, most people agreed, were for Hamlet cigars and the Italian vermouth Cinzano. Both traded on the kind of accident-prone haplessness embodied by Michael Crawford's beret-wearing Frank Spencer in *Some Mothers Do 'Ave 'Em*, whose 'Ooh Betty, I think I done a woopsy' routine was, as I've already mentioned, a staple ingredient in the repertoire of anyone who fancied themselves a half-decent impressionist. My friend Jonny did a particularly fine Frank Spencer, and indeed still does if he's drunk enough but, as he is the first to acknowledge when sober, there isn't much of an audience for it any more. Which didn't stop David Brent having a go in a typically cringe-inducing bid to entertain his colleagues in an episode of *The Office*.

Some Mothers Do 'Ave 'Em ended in 1978 after three series and three Christmas specials (all transmitted at primetime on Christmas Day, which shows how exceptionally popular it was), but by then it had firmly entered the cultural vocabulary, where it would remain. Fully fifteen years later, in 1993, the Leader of the Opposition, John Smith, even cited it in the House of Commons when attacking John Major's government for a series of blunders. 'If we were to offer that tale of events to the BBC light entertainment department as a script for a programme, I think that the producers of *Yes Minister* would have turned it down as hopelessly over the top . . . it might have even been too much for *Some Mothers Do 'Ave 'Em*,' he said. Ten years after that, in 2003, Lord Forsyth of Drumlean was at it again in the House of Lords. 'Would it not be more sensible for the government to get the constitutional changes that they have made right before embarking on another, like the Frank Spencer figure in *Some Mothers Do 'Ave 'Em?*' he asked.

In 2007 a newspaper reported that the *Some Mothers Do 'Ave 'Em* format had been bought by the American television company Fox, much to the delight of the writer, Raymond Allen, who had perhaps thought that his creation would live on only in the pages of the parliamentary record *Hansard*. I'll believe it when I see it, but maybe the time is right in the wake of George W. Bush's presidency. In some ways, Frank was George W. writ small, an accident waiting to happen. He was also an intellectual and emotional retard, slightly incontinent, an incorrigible mummy's boy, and, despite being married to the long-suffering Betty (Michele Dotrice), decidedly effete. I suppose that if Mr Bean can thrive in the twenty-first century, there seems no reason why the profoundly hapless Frank shouldn't make a comeback.

In the 1970s, however, profound haplessness was fairer game than it is now. It was, when you think about it, a singularly hapless decade, in which Richard Milhous Nixon became the first and so far only President of the United States to resign the post, and Britain lurched from crisis to crisis, with power cuts, three-day weeks and strikes in almost every sector of the nation's industry and public services.

The stoical unfortunates in the Hamlet adverts therefore represented the decade perfectly, and although they continued into the 1980s and indeed the 1990s, their heyday was undoubtedly the 1970s. In 1974 we saw a sculptor working on the Venus de Milo, whose arm dropped off with the last tap of his chisel. In 1975, it was the guy in the neck brace and sling, sitting in the crowd at Wimbledon trying in vain to follow the flight of the ball. In 1978 a cowboy with an arrow through his heart turned up at the Pearly Gates where St Peter refused him entrance. And in 1979 it was the turn of the golfer, forlornly hacking away in a bunker. In every case they found solace by lighting up: happiness was a cigar called Hamlet, the mild cigar from Benson & Hedges.

Even if tobacco advertising were allowed on television now, the wording would have to be changed to 'possible lung cancer and subsequent death is a cigar called Hamlet, the mild but potentially deadly cigar from Benson & Hedges'. We inhabit an altogether less joyful world than we did back then, and while I for one am delighted to live in a country where smoking is outlawed in most public places, I rather miss tobacco advertising. It's hard to make a witty advert for Nicotine Replacement Therapy, and I don't suppose there'll ever be a NiQuitin Man to replace the iconic Marlboro Man.

On the other hand, if the advertising industry had been as mighty in those days as it is now, I suspect we'd have seen Nixon himself popping up in a Hamlet advert, lighting up at his desk in the Oval Office moments after tendering his resignation, in return of course for a suitably colossal fee. Who knows, maybe he was approached? Even in the 1970s, VIPs – as they were sweetly known at the time – were not averse to taking the advertising buck. In 1979 no less a personage than Sir Robert Mark, newly retired as Commissioner of the Metropolitan Police, told us he was convinced 'that the Goodyear Grand Prix S is a major contribution to road safety'. A fee of about £50,000 quite possibly helped to convince him.

Nor were even movie stars immune from the persuasive powers of advertising agencies. In 1973 Kenneth More, one of Britain's most admired film actors, who had played a doughty officer on the *Titanic* in *A Night to Remember*, Richard Hannay in *The 39 Steps* and Douglas Bader in the biopic *Reach for the Sky*, and was regarded no less than Bader as the quintessential plucky Englishman, began advertising Mellow Birds instant coffee. For More it was an eye-opener. The set was so full of people, he said later, that one would have thought they were making *Gone With the Wind*. There was a person detailed to make the coffee, another to make sure that the steam wafted up from the cup in the proper manner, and another in charge of the number of bubbles. After thirty-odd takes, the bubble count was still considered unacceptably low, so the bubble lady had to whip up bubbles in a spoon and drop them into the cup just before the director called 'action'. More joked that if the money hadn't been so good, allowing him for at least the rest of that year to be picky about the acting roles he accepted, he would have stuck to tea.

As for his crack about *Gone With the Wind*, it was perhaps more timely than he supposed. Some of the cleverest and most memorable adverts of the 1970s were crafted by directors who would later distinguish themselves making feature films. The Hovis commercial was the work of Ridley Scott, later to make *Alien*, *Thelma and Louise* and *Gladiator*. And the Cinzano adverts, which like those for Hamlet celebrated abject cack-handedness, were conceived by Scott's friend, contemporary and rival Alan Parker, later to bring us *Mississippi Burning* and *The Commitments*.

Parker was already the mastermind behind the series of Bird's Eye commercials that began in 1973 and told mini-stories about a little freckled northern lad called Ben, whose interest in beefburgers was matched by his friend Mary's interest in him. With Cinzano, his masterstroke was to match the glamorous Joan Collins with Leonard Rossiter, already famous as the seedy landlord Rigsby in *Rising*

Damp, and the troubled Sunshine Desserts executive in *The Fall and Rise of Reginald Perrin*. Both played the parts to perfection: Rossiter as the bumbling suitor, Collins as the long-suffering Melissa, who always ended up with Cinzano sloshed down the front of her dress. The pick of the series, for me, was the 1979 advert set on an aeroplane.

Italian air hostess (handing a drink to Melissa): 'Your Cinzano Bianco, signora.'

Rossiter (assuming it's for him): 'Ah yes, gracias.'

Air hostess: 'Due?'

Rossiter: 'No, no, no, no, no, mine was a Cinzano as well . . . Ah, that's better. Oh, can't you just smell those Italian wines, suffused with herbs and spices from four continents!'

Melissa (in unison): '. . . suffused with herbs and spices from four continents!'

Rossiter: 'I'm being boring. [He knocks Melissa's table; she rescues her drink just in time] Oh, sorry. Sorry. [Then he taps the arm of her seat, which goes sharply into recline mode, whereupon, inevitably, she spills her drink down her cleavage] Getting your head down, sweetie? Jolly good idea.'

Suave voiceover: 'From the House of Cinzano . . . Cinzano Bianco.'

It was great stuff, which is more than can be said, in my humble opinion, for Cinzano itself. Nonetheless, that advertising campaign had a predictably dramatic impact on sales, just as Erica Wills had earlier been credited with trebling European sales of Martini. And in 1978 along came Lorraine Chase, wafted not from paradise but Luton Airport, to promote the delights of another alcoholic drink with an Italian name, Campari.

It seems to be the motor industry now which is the most boundlessly inventive in terms of TV advertising, but in those days it was the alcoholic drinks industry, and even the adverts that weren't humorous wormed their way into your head with a catchy tune. There are days even now when 1970s advertising jingles enter my head and resolutely refuse to leave. Just last week it was the jingle for Whitbread (big head) Trophy Bitter, which had '. . . the body, the body, that satisfies / It can't be modest, no matter how it tries / Because it's Whitbread Bitter, Trophy Bitter / The best that you ever bought / Whitbread (big head) Trophy Bitter / The pint that thinks it's a quart!'

This is probably not a phenomenon with which my children will be confronted three decades from now, for all the reasons outlined earlier. In the name of research for this book I recently asked my two older kids whether there were any television commercials that they could recite by heart, and there were only one or two, whereas at their age I knew at least three dozen. I do not present this as a good thing. It's just a thing. Actually, having too many slogans and jingles in your head can be a downright bad thing. Another friend of mine, Chris Barry, tells a story about an old schoolfriend of his who applied to read chemistry at Liverpool University, and at the interview was asked a few simple questions by the head of department, one of which was: 'What does MFI stand for?'

He knew the answer instantly. It was Melt Flow Index (the weight of polymer melt in grams extruded in ten minutes through a standard nozzle under standard load condition at a certain temperature, if you're interested) but just as he opened his mouth to utter it, the jingle advertising MFI furniture entered his brain and Melt Flow Index exited it.

At the same time, he was being pressed for an answer. 'Erm, is it something . . . furniture . . . something,' he said forlornly, after which he scarcely heard another word the professor said because 'M . . . F . . . Iiiiiii' was thumping over and over in his head. The interview was soon terminated, with Chris's friend wondering whether there might be any opportunities to read chemistry at Keele. I don't suppose it came as any consolation to learn that he was right, and that MFI, in the context of the retail giant, does stand for 'something furniture something': to be precise, it's Mullard Furniture Industries, Mullard having been the maiden name of the founder's wife. I know that, you'll be gratified to learn, because I tapped the question 'what does MFI stand for?' into Google, and came across an entire chatroom debate on that very subject. Two of the better suggestions, I might add, were 'Made For Idiots' and 'More Fucking Instructions'.

Whatever, Chris's friend's miserable experience at Liverpool University shows that hardly anything was unleashed on the world in the 1970s that was more powerful than the advertising jingle, with the possible exception of the fifteen-kiloton nuclear bomb exploded by the Indian government on 18 May 1974, with which India became the planet's sixth nuclear power, as gravely reported by Gordon Honeycombe on *News at Ten*.

14

Reggie Bosanquet, Otherwise Known as Reginald Beaujolais, and Other Newsreaders

Gordon Honeycombe. If it seemed like a great name then, and it did, it seems like an even greater name now. Newsreaders in the 1970s, right down to their names, were altogether a more interesting bunch than their modern counterparts. Take Reginald Bosanquet, for example, as the demon drink reportedly quite often did. It would have been a great name even if several of his ITN colleagues had not joined satirists in referring to him as Reginald Beaujolais.

In June 1978, thrillingly, I saw him in the flesh. I had gone with my cousin Daniel to the Wimbledon tennis championships for the first time, and on Centre Court we saw the defending champion Björn Borg almost get knocked out in the first round by the giant American Victor Amaya, which would have been quite exciting enough without the added thrill of almost bumping into Reggie Bosanquet. What a story I took home to Southport to tell my provincial friends.

Danny lived in Winchmore Hill, north London, and was thus much more sophisticated than I was; had he not been with me to tell me exactly when to step off one tube and on to the next one, I might even now be wandering aimlessly along a platform on the Piccadilly Line. Anyway, he steered me successfully that day to the All-England Lawn Tennis and Croquet Club, outside which, as I recall, we queued for three or four months to get in, relying for sustenance on food air-dropped by humanitarian aid charities. In truth it was probably more like three or four hours, and Danny's mum, my Auntie Rose, gave us sandwiches. But it felt like a really, really long time, for which the reward came as soon as we got through the gate. There, right in front of me, was Reggie Bosanquet himself, a crooked grin on his face and a slight hesitancy in his step, doubtless induced by his good friends Messieurs Moet & Chandon. I also recall that he was wearing a huge baggy jumper with a hole in it, which added irresistibly to his characterful image. Not for Reggie a blandly anonymous blazer and tie.

There were no other 1970s newsreaders quite like Reggie, whose exotic surname had in fact been made famous by his father Bernard, a Test cricketer for England around the turn of the twentieth century. It was Bernard who is generally credited with inventing the googly, once actually known as the 'Bosie', the fiendish delivery by a spin bowler which looks to a batsman as if it is going to turn from right to left on hitting the ground, but instead turns from left to right.

In a way, Reggie followed in the family tradition of wrongfooting people. He became famous for his on-air gaffes, the most unfortunate of which concerned Anna Ford, with whom he teamed up on *News at Ten* in the very year that I spotted him at Wimbledon, 1978. Having somehow discovered the date of Ford's mother's birthday, he gallantly wished her a happy birthday at the end of a news bulletin, only for a horrified Anna to pass on the unfortunate but significant information that her mum had expired some years previously.

Reggie's spiritual successor, in my view, was Sir Trevor McDonald, a jolly nice fellow whom I have had the pleasure of meeting, but not, let us be frank, the safest pair of hands with an autocue. As the presenter of *News at Ten*, he often used to conclude the lead story by saying 'and now for the day's other news'. But on more than one occasion I heard the great man get his words mixed up, saying 'and now for the other day's news', which of course means something else entirely.

Still, his transposition of 'day's' and 'other' made me wonder whether viewers would even notice if old news were trotted out? It is a beguiling thought: could an entire bulletin of perennial news items be constructed and brought out from time to time on days when there was simply no news, or when the *News at Ten* team fancied an evening off? Bong! Eight hundred redundancies announced by the Ford motor company! Bong! Her Majesty the Queen admitted to hospital for a minor operation! Bong! French lorry drivers blockade Calais! Bong! Suspected outbreak of foot-and-mouth disease on a Welsh hill farm! Bong! Sporting disappointment for Britain! That could have been the main evening bulletin any night for the last thirty years.

For all Sir Trevor McDonald's slips with the autocue, however, he has generally been better with it than without. In November 1991, when Sir Trev – then plain Trev – was dispatched to RAF Lyneham to report on the homecoming of the Archbishop of Canterbury's luckless envoy Terry Waite after 1,760 days in captivity in Beirut, he explained that Waite was being brought home by the RAC. I confess that in a newspaper column I once had some gentle fun at Trev's expense over this gaffe, which elicited a reproachful letter from a senior ITV executive, defending his man to the hilt and telling me that it had been a completely excusable slip of the tongue in exceedingly trying circumstances. I couldn't argue with that, and I certainly wouldn't want to make light of the suffering endured by those taken hostage by Hezbollah fanatics, but at the same time I was grateful to Trev for unwittingly supplying the image of poor old Waite pacing up and down beside an overheated Ford Sierra at a Lebanese roadside for five years, saying, 'Where on earth is the man from the RAC?'

As for Sir Trevor's spiritual forebear Reggie Bosanquet, he and Anna Ford forged a great on-screen rapport which ended abruptly, not with the embarrassment over Ford's mother, but when Reggie retired, suddenly and with hardly any warning, towards the end of 1979. Before the promotion of Ford, Bosanquet had teamed up with Andrew Gardner, in an attempt by ITN to copy the American model of having two newscasters. But mixing the sexes was racy stuff indeed for British television. Only since 1974 had viewers been used to a regular female newsreader, in the alluring shape (as we would duly find out when she unveiled her excellent legs on the *Morecambe & Wise Christmas Special*) of the BBC's Angela Rippon. It was daring, too, because there was no knowing how Ford and Bosanquet, two forthright characters, would get on. Some years later in America, Connie Chung was brutally dropped as Dan Rather's co-anchor on the CBS evening news because their on-screen chemistry was considered too volatile, and a threat to ratings.

I can add an interesting postscript about Chung, by the way. In the mid-1990s, when I worked for the *Mail on Sunday*, I was sent to New York to write a feature about the famous American chat-show host David Letterman, and in the course of my research I learnt that when CBS were trying to tempt Letterman across from rival network NBC, Chung was persuaded to make a humorous video in which she promised Letterman that if he would only switch networks, she would pant 'Dave, oh Dave' whenever she and her husband Maury Povich, another talk-show host, had sex. It's hard to imagine Fiona Bruce, for example, making the same offer in a BBC bid to attract Ant and Dec, say, over from ITV. Hard, but quite enjoyable.

15

'Oh Bosanquet, Why Did You Leave Me This Way?': The Impact of *Not the Nine O'Clock News*

Whatever the reasons for Reggie Bosanquet's departure, it inspired a song by Pamela Stephenson in the last programme of the first series of the topical, satirical show *Not the Nine O'Clock News*, which by then had become obligatory viewing among teenagers. *Not the Nine O'Clock News* was hugely influential with people of my age, who, notwithstanding our word-perfect mastery of the Dead Parrot sketch, had been a little too young to appreciate fully the scatty irreverence and madcap nonsense of *Monty Python's Flying Circus*.

The series was originally supposed to begin on 2 April 1979, but as the big night drew near, producer John Lloyd began to realize that he only had enough material for the first programme, later admitting that he actually prayed for Prime Minister James Callaghan to call a

general election, on the basis that a comedy series with so much political content would be deemed inappropriate in the middle of an
election campaign, and would have to be postponed. On 28 March
Jim Callaghan obliged. The election was called for 3 May, and *Not the
Nine O'Clock News* was hastily pulled from the schedules. The election therefore helped Lloyd in two ways, giving him more time to
gather material, and indeed giving him more material. On 3 May,
genial Jim Callaghan's unpopular Labour government was booted out
by an electorate still reeling from the so-called Winter of Discontent,
and Britain got its first female Prime Minister: the redoubtable and
eminently satire-worthy Margaret Thatcher.

I was a little under six months short of being old enough to vote in
that 1979 election, which was probably just as well. As an impressionable schoolboy without any coherent political opinions of my
own, and given the intense general dissatisfaction with Labour, I
might well have marked a cross in the Conservative box, and thus
have felt like a fraud when years later I took my place at innumerable
north London dinner parties with liberal intellectuals who wore their
anti-Toryism like badges, and considered Thatcher to have been the
most damaging thing to hit Britain since the Luftwaffe, if not the
Black Death.

But if politics was not my bag at the age of seventeen, comedy definitely was. With my schoolfriends Mark Sutcliffe and Andy
Coughlan I had taken to producing end-of-term revues, which grew
in competence until in 1984 we took a revue to the Edinburgh Fringe,
and were rewarded with full houses, if only because we shamelessly
forged our reviews. The leaflets we dished out on the Royal Mile
boasted that our show had been acclaimed by BBC Radio Scotland as
'the funniest, smartest revue on the Fringe'. The truth was that
nobody at BBC Radio Scotland had said anything of the sort. I hope
we can invoke the statute of limitations if they consider suing us for
misrepresentation. If not, we're very, very sorry.

Anyway, my burgeoning interest in comedy sketches meant that I was practically welded to the first series of *Not the Nine O'Clock News*, which eventually started on 17 October. Victoria Wood, who had been 'discovered' on *New Faces* five years earlier, had turned down the female part, so the little-known Stephenson got the job. Her co-stars in that first series included Chris Langham, whose career almost thirty years later would implode in disgrace when he was found guilty of downloading images of child pornography, and sent to prison. For the second series, Langham gave way to Griff Rhys Jones, producing the quartet for which the show is remembered: Jones, Mel Smith, Rowan Atkinson and Stephenson.

The New Zealand-born, Australia-raised Stephenson, who got her big break after meeting John Lloyd at a party, did not quite supplant Debbie Harry in my affections, but I was immensely impressed that a woman could be quite so attractive and quite so funny. Billy Connolly felt the same, falling for Stephenson when she interviewed him in a sketch as Janet Street-Porter – after she took the alarming false teeth out, presumably – and in due course marrying her.

Connolly's own big break had been his 1975 appearance on Michael Parkinson's chat show, after which, and to this day, Parky habitually described him as 'the funniest man on the planet'. I broadly agreed with that assessment, and considered the story Connolly had famously told on Parkinson – about the Glaswegian who murdered his wife and buried her, but left her bare bum sticking out of the ground because he needed somewhere to park his bike – to be pretty much the perfect joke. So when he married Stephenson in 1989, I loved the idea that the wife of the planet's funniest man was one of the planet's funniest women, and quite irrationally felt a little let down when she gave up showbiz to become a psychotherapist, specializing in, of all unfunny things, anxiety, depression and self-esteem issues.

She set up practice in Los Angeles, where I'm sure she has never wanted for custom, although I've wanted to suggest a new business opportunity to her ever since I went to LA on one of the trips organized by my friend at Sky, Doree Glaser. Doree always recognized that a trip from England to California was a long way for a journalist to travel for only one story, so whenever I went she suggested lots of other things for me to do in the few days I was there, and on one occasion introduced me to a woman in Beverly Hills called Nance Mitchell who specialized in what might be called pubic topiary. Nance was an expert at decorating women's pubic mounds with hearts for Valentine's Day, shamrocks for St Patrick's Day, and, within reason, anything bespoke. She had recently sculpted a Mercedes emblem for a woman who wanted to give her husband – the Mercedes franchise owner for Southern California – a birthday surprise. I ventured to Nance that it was a good job he didn't own the Audi franchise. She was not even slightly amused. But it later occurred to me that Pamela Stevenson Connolly could hook up with her. What better way of raising a woman's flagging self-esteem than carving a shamrock out of her pubic mound?

Returning speedily to *Not the Nine O'Clock News*, Stephenson's song 'Oh, Reginald!' assumed that she, as Ford, had been secretly in love with her fellow newsreader, Bosanquet. Across the Pennines in Yorkshire, some ten years before she had the questionable luck to set eyes on me, my wife-to-be was watching as avidly as I was that Tuesday night in November 1979, and can still remember the words to that song: 'Oh Bosanquet, why did you go away / Oh, Bosanquet, why did you leave me this way?'

It is perhaps stretching a point to say that *Not the Nine O'Clock News* did the same job for Jane's and my generation as *The Goon Show* had done for those twenty years older, and Monty Python for those perhaps five or six years older, but more than Python and the Goons it poked remorseless fun at the solemnity of certain aspects of British life. By the fairly reverent standards of the times, very little was considered sacrosanct. And in some cases, sacred cows were slaughtered that today would be considered beyond parody. Take the footage of thousands of Muslims curled up on their knees praying to Allah, and the accompanying grave commentary: 'The search goes on for the Ayatollah's contact lens.' I doubt whether any sketch-show artists now would be permitted to crack such a gag, or would want to, come to think of it, given the likelihood of needing subsequent round-the-clock protection from Stratford Johns and Frank Windsor, or reassuring people in suits very much like them.

Although British television has become far more liberal in matters of sex, violence and profanity since the 1970s, it has also become far more attuned to racial sensibilities. When in April 2004 the football pundit Ron Atkinson, believing that his microphone was switched off, dropped his terrible, seismic clanger about Chelsea's Marcel Desailly – 'he is what is known in some schools as a fucking lazy, thick nigger,' was Big Ron's ill-chosen half-time assessment of Desailly's performance against AS Monaco – the subsequent fuss concerned his casual use of the word 'nigger', not his casual use of the word 'fucking'. In the 1970s – with Eddie Booth (Jack Smethurst) on *Love Thy Neighbour* habitually referring to his black next-door neighbour Bill Reynolds (Rudolph Walker) as 'nig-nog', 'Sambo' and 'King Kong' – it would have been exactly the other way round.

I don't remember 'fuck', the dreaded F-bomb, ever being dropped on *Not the Nine O'Clock News*. The word had first been uttered on television as early as 1965 by the critic Kenneth Tynan, causing no fewer than 133 outraged MPs to sign motions of censure, and the self-styled guardian of the nation's morals, our old friend Mrs Whitehouse of the National Viewers' and Listeners' Association, to write to the Queen suggesting that Tynan should have his bottom spanked (a blissfully if unwittingly ironic suggestion, given that Tynan was later revealed to have a flagellation fetish).

By the end of the 1970s 'fuck' was still a no-go area even for a show as irreverent as *Not the Nine O'Clock News*, but the series certainly challenged some boundaries. The first programme opened with Kenny Everett, who had been banned by the BBC, announcing that the Corporation had relented and given him his own show, 'as long as I don't say "pubes"'. At this point he was ordered off the set by the floor manager for saying 'pubes', which to those of us unused to hearing the word 'pubes' on the BBC at nine o'clock, or indeed at any other time, was quite snortingly funny. A letter in the *Radio Times* disagreed, the correspondent thundering that 'seldom has so much profanity, vulgarity and sheer lack of inventiveness filled my screen'.

Seldom had so much profanity and vulgarity filled mine, either. I loved it. And very conveniently *Not the Nine O'Clock News* coincided with my transition from King George V School to St Andrews University, where we did not have to watch it worrying that our parents might come into the room and stand by the door, tutting. In my first year at St Andrews my closest undergraduate friend was a guy called Bruce Shearer, who came from Vancouver in Canada, where television was a good deal more conservative than it was here. When Rowan Atkinson, speaking Scandinavian-accented English in the role of a Swedish pharmacist, asked his Swedish customer, played by Mel Smith, what sort of deodorant he wanted, 'ball or aerosol?', and Smith said, 'Neither, I vant it for my armpits,' Bruce laughed for about three weeks solid. I think I remember his stopping once, when his mother phoned from Canada to say that a relative had been run over by a truck, but he soon started again.

16

Vietnam, Watergate and Richard Whitmore's Outdoor Toilet

In the first few weeks of my life at university, the students to avoid were those who watched the *Nine O'Clock News* proper on Tuesday evenings. On the other hand, there was plenty of news to watch. It was 1981, the year in which Britain's inner cities were set alight by race rioters, Egypt's President Sadat was assassinated and Ronald Reagan narrowly avoided the same fate, martial law was declared in Poland, the IRA hunger striker Bobby Sands died, the Prince of Wales married Lady Diana Spencer, and Ian Botham and a few other English cricketers won the Ashes.

For most of that remarkably action-packed year, however, I had been living in Paris. I took myself off there after failing to get into Oxford University, and with the best part of twelve months to wait before I could begin at St Andrews. I got myself a job in a hotel, resolving not to return home until I had learnt fluent French or lost my virginity, or preferably both.

I succeeded in only one of these missions, but thrived in several other ways. The effort of climbing up seven flights of stairs to the attic room I rented on the Rue de Courcelles helped me shed most of the weight that I had carried through my teens, until I no longer looked like Frank Cannon even from a distance. I also parted company with the boy I had been for most of my teens, indeed most of my life, in one other significant respect: for almost a year I watched no telly. Nothing. Three years had passed since my mother had nobly but forlornly attempted to stop me watching television, by recruiting Mr Williams from number 54 to carry the set away, three years in which I had knuckled down and acquired some decent A-levels. There was really no reason at all not to while away my time in front of the box, yet I lacked the opportunity for the first time in my life.

All the big television events of 1981 passed me by. On 29 July, Prince Charles and Lady Diana Spencer somehow managed to tie the knot without me, although I did catch a glimpse of Diana gliding up the aisle of St Paul's Cathedral, her three-mile train in tow, through the net curtains of the Portuguese concierge's ground-floor apartment at 91 Rue de Courcelles. But that was it. Everything else I missed. All the sport, which included not only Ian Botham winning the Ashes but also one of the greatest of all FA Cup final goals, the culmination of Ricky Villa's jinking run for Tottenham Hotspur through the Manchester City penalty area, and every episode of *Coronation Street*.

Alas for me, it was an eventful year in Weatherfield. Ken Barlow and Deirdre Langton beat Charles and Diana to the altar by just two days, and the Rovers barman Fred Gee married Eunice Nuttall, who left him with unseemly haste for Councillor Critchley. I was kept vaguely up to date with all this by Mike King back in Southport, who wrote to me occasionally giving me the Street news.

For a short while, I was even able to phone him, and other friends, at length. There was a faulty public payphone on the Rue de Castiglione, from which international calls could be made for free. To start with, nobody but me had discovered this, so I was able to stand in there for entire evenings, ringing everyone I knew back home. But after a while, the secret got out. Homesick expats like me queued up for hours to use 'my' phone, and when the next few people in the queue felt that you'd been on for long enough, they started banging aggressively on the glass. After a couple of weeks, so long and unruly was the more-or-less permanent queue outside this payphone that the scam was rumbled, and some spoilsport from the Direction Generale des Telecommunications came along with a bag of tiny pliers to fix the thing. How much we'd cost the state by then, heaven knows.

Once the Rue de Castiglione payphone had been repaired, I had to take up my pen again and write letters. From my lonely attic I wrote hundreds, probably thousands of letters, not a few of them ruing the amount of telly I was missing. The cultural ramifications of this were significant, and remained so for years afterwards. For example, whenever people made jokes about *Tenko*, the every-expense-spared drama about an all-female prisoner-of-war camp in 1942 Singapore (and you'd be surprised how often they did), I didn't have a clue what they were on about. It had been transmitted while I was away, so that was that, and while I didn't ever resort to the subterfuge forlornly attempted by Martin Earnshaw, who pretended to have watched everything that Jez Sykes and I had watched, I found myself retrospectively sympathizing with him. It was no fun, then or even now, to be a gooseberry in a conversation about telly.

Eventually, after I had been in Paris for almost a year, I gave notice to the landlord of my attic room and returned to Southport to prepare for university, and, almost more excitingly, to reacquaint myself with the television set.

On the way home I stayed for a couple of nights at my grandmother's house in north London, and surprised myself by watching every minute of the *Nine O'Clock News*, which it turned out had made the news itself while I was away, Richard Baker, Kenneth Kendall and Peter Woods having been sacked to make way for the more youthful John Humphrys and John Simpson. While working on this book, incidentally, I decided to see if some of those old-timers were still around, and discovered that, at least at the time of writing, Kenneth Kendall was alive and well and living on the Isle of Wight running an art gallery with his male partner. In the 1970s, there was no question of the public at large learning that a BBC newsreader was gay. Indeed, it was always faintly surprising to discover that they had anything at all below waist level, hence the widespread delight when Angela Rippon came out from behind a desk to perform that high-kicking dance routine on the 1976 *Morecambe & Wise Christmas Special*. It would be stretching a point to call that a where-were-you-when-you-watched-it? moment, since virtually the entire nation was at home peeling a satsuma or twiddling a Quality Street wrapper, but it is undoubtedly a TV moment enshrined in the collective memory.

Returning to the news itself, I had gone through most of the 1970s considering it the very definition of tedium. For the first few years of the decade, every bulletin seemed to begin either with the latest strike of dockers or motor-industry workers, or with some new IRA outrage, or an atrocity in Vietnam. There were only a few headline stories that captured my young imagination, among them the disappearance of the Labour MP John Stonehouse, whose clothes were found on a Miami beach in November 1974 but was later found to have faked his own suicide, after being arrested in Australia (by semi-inept detectives who rather sweetly thought they'd caught the missing Lord Lucan) where he had hoped to set up a new life with his mistress, Sheila Buckley. This story later inspired clever David Nobbs to create *The Fall and Rise of Reginald Perrin*, so the news couldn't be too airily dismissed as tedious, not when it could generate such fine comedy.

And yet, from the time I started becoming aware of the news, in the late 1960s, it was something that grown-ups watched enthusiastically and children just as enthusiastically tried to avoid. It might have been more appealing had the distant war in Vietnam not seemed to lead the news headlines night after night in the late 1960s, although not, perversely, on the night *News at Ten* began, in July 1967. For their curtain-raising programme, the big nobs at ITN had dispatched reporters all over the world, and all of them were told to sign off individualistically – 'Sandy Gall, *News at Ten*, in Saigon' – which had never been done before, to show how excitingly international *News at Ten* was. The idea on that first night was that viewers would be struck not only by the unprecedented device of having two newscasters, but also by the thrilling global flavour of the news. Then, with reporting teams ready for action in Alabama, in Vietnam, all over the place, the Ford car workers inconsiderately went on strike, most inconveniently not only for the management at Ford, but also for the folk in charge at ITN. *News at Ten*'s first sign-off was 'Richard Dixon, News at Ten, Dagenham'.

Moving slickly from Richard Dixon to Richard Nixon, in 1973 Vietnam and even industrial disputes at Ford were suddenly eclipsed by the Watergate crisis. I didn't even begin to understand Watergate, and I don't recall my parents ever trying to explain it to me, but the names – Nixon, Haldeman, Ehrlichman, Dean – were somehow singed into my consciousness, which perhaps explains why I later became fascinated by that unusually shameful period in American history.

In 1992 Jane and I went to the States on holiday, visiting Virginia and Washington DC. The summer before, in New York, I had bought brunch for Quentin Crisp and got a nice article out of the encounter for the newspaper I then worked for, the *Hampstead & Highgate Express*. This time I wondered whether I could perchance write something about Watergate, which had strictly speaking unfolded outside the Ham & High's circulation area, but there had to be a connection with north London somewhere. After all, we were taught at the Ham & High that the rest of the world more or less rotated round north London. So before leaving England I had written to Ben Bradlee, the legendary newspaperman who had been editor of the *Washington Post* when his reporters Bob Woodward and Carl Bernstein so famously broke the Watergate story, telling him who I was (nobody) and asking (cheekily) for an interview.

I didn't expect to get a reply, yet when we arrived at our hotel in Washington there was, to my astonishment and delight, a message from Bradlee suggesting an appointment the following day. But before I went to see him I thought I'd better find out whether there was a handy anniversary to which I could peg the interview, so I phoned the *Washington Post* switchboard and asked to be put through to the newsroom.

I explained to a woman there that I was a reporter from a local newspaper in London, in Washington hoping to write something about the Watergate crisis, and could she possibly tell me whether there was a handy anniversary looming. She listened patiently, in truth more patiently than I deserved, and then she said, 'I'll just put you through to Bob Woodward.' It was like calling the Vatican with a minor question about doctrine and being put through to the Pope. Before she could redirect my trivial request towards Woodward – played by none other than Robert Redford in the film *All the President's Men* – I stammered something about not wanting to put him to the trouble and put the phone down. That's my own Watergate story, such as it is. I rather wish now that I'd held my nerve and stayed on the line to speak to Woodward. It would have made a satisfying connection with all those 1970s editions of the BBC's *Early Evening News* which I sat through wondering what impeachment meant.

The trouble with the *Early Evening News*, which came on at 5.50 p.m. every weekday, was that it marked the end of children's programming. No sooner had Zebedee said it was time for bed on *The Magic Roundabout* than Richard Whitmore or someone was telling us about boring adult stuff. Whitmore, I should add here because I can't imagine where else I'd slip it in, has spent his post-newsreading years writing some extremely useful books, among them the definitive history of outdoor toilets in Hertfordshire. For that I salute him. But because the solemn faces and grave voices of Whitmore and his colleagues were so representative of the end of children's television and the start of a long evening of viewing for grown-ups, which we knew would culminate in the order to go to bed, I think my generation developed an instinctive dislike of the news. Jane freely admits that to this day she feels a childlike desire to sulk when the news comes on, an impulse that did not serve her especially well when she was a BBC producer working on Radio 4's news programmes *The World at One* and *The World This Weekend*.

Sometimes, I confess, I do what my parents tried annoyingly to do with me, and encourage my own children to watch the news. The problem is that, like so much else, the news has changed dramatically since I was their age. It's much more gruesome than it used to be, as was neatly observed by the pop star Noel Gallagher when I interviewed him for a television documentary in 2006. The documentary was called *We Love the Royle Family* and was commissioned to coincide with the reunion of the Royles in a marvellous stand-alone episode titled 'The Queen of Sheba'. I talked to lots of famous people about their devotion to the show, among them Gallagher, whose song 'Half the World Away' was used as the theme music. He told me that the spectacle of the Royles slobbing in front of the telly in their front room reminded him powerfully of his own family, with one notable difference.

'I always remember being put to bed before *The Sweeney* because

Jack Regan might say the word "bastard",' he said. 'I mean, what is television like now? Fucking hell. *Look North* in the 1970s had stories about cats getting stuck up trees. Now it's like, four people get beheaded at a post office queuing for their giros and nobody bats a fucking eyelid.' Indeed.

17

Jack Regan and John Thaw: A Tale of Two Very Different Men

I have paid fleeting homage already to *The Sweeney* in this book, and recalled my sorrow at having to sell our brown Ford Granada to my cousin James following my father's death, but now is the time to evoke it more comprehensively. If you grew up in the 1970s, and were male and heterosexual, then the odds are that Detective Inspector Jack Regan and Detective Sergeant George Carter loomed large in your consciousness.

A conversation about formative television with anyone who was in their early-ish teens around the time that *The Sweeney* began in 1975 will sooner or later, and probably sooner, embrace Regan and Carter. I use the word 'embrace' with some reservation, incidentally. It is a faggoty, fruity, poofy word (as Regan and Carter might have said) to use in connection with two men of such formidable machismo.

While I was writing this book, I spent an entertaining evening reminiscing about 1970s telly with Craig Cash, who with Caroline Aherne wrote *The Royle Family*, in which he also featured as Denise's gormless husband Dave. Sure enough, it didn't take long for *The Sweeney* to pop up. Craig clearly remembered an episode of *The Sweeney* featuring two Australian villains, which he said had a huge impact on him because it ended with the baddies, shockingly, getting away! This was rare, perhaps unprecedented, in a primetime detective series. It might have happened all the time in real life, but it had certainly never happened to Dixon of Dock Green.

Incidentally, it's amazing how, more than three decades after the event, we can still dredge up memories like Craig's. I have a similarly vivid memory of watching an episode of *Z-Cars* while I was waiting one day at our next-door neighbour's, Mrs Watson's, for my mum and dad to get home from work. I can't have been more than eight, yet the cliffhanger of an ending has stayed with me all these years. Some scallies of about my age were on a motorway bridge about to let a paving-stone drop onto a passing car. I was riveted. But just as they let it drop, the celebrated theme music – Fritz Spiegl's famous arrangement of the old folk song 'Johnny Todd' – started up, and the credits rolled. It was the first time I had been left in suspense by a TV programme, and I practically counted the minutes until the next episode, although the strange thing is that I can't recall what happened. I still wonder, sometimes.

To stick with the *Z-Cars* theme for a moment, it stirs me now not only because it evokes my childhood, but also because it evokes the football club I support. Influenced by my friends from three doors along, Jez and Chris Sykes, I started supporting Everton FC at the beginning of 1970, the season in which they won the league championship. And as fellow Evertonians will know, the *Z-Cars* theme is played as the teams take the field before every match at Goodison Park. A few years ago, I listened with delight to an edition of *Desert*

Island Discs in which Sue Lawley interviewed the theatrical impresario and celebrated Everton enthusiast Bill Kenwright. Lawley wanted to talk about the theatre; Kenwright preferred to talk about Everton. And when he chose a history of Everton as the book he would take to his desert island with the collected works of Shakespeare and the Bible, and chose the *Z-Cars* theme as the record he would take ahead of all his other favourites, she could hardly disguise her bewilderment. For listening Evertonians, it was a hoot.

On a more sober note, after the 11-year-old Everton fan Rhys Jones was tragically shot dead in August 2007, the *Z-Cars* theme was played ahead of a Champions' League game at Anfield, the home of Everton's city rivals Liverpool FC, as a way of demonstrating the community's shared horror at what had happened. Was any TV theme tune ever played, anywhere, to such poignant effect? I doubt it.

As for the episode of *The Sweeney* that Craig remembered so vividly, thanks to the exhaustively researched *Shut It! A Fan's Guide to 70s Cops on the Box*, by Martin Day and Keith Topping, I can reveal that it was transmitted on ITV on Monday 13 October 1975, and was called 'Golden Fleece'. It was the first episode of *The Sweeney* to reach top spot in the viewing charts, with 8.8 million viewers, and also demonstrated the show's growing self-confidence, with a direct reference to its main competitor, *Kojak* on BBC1. 'Who loves ya, baby?' Regan growled, handing a lollipop to Carter.

By then, Carter was a widower. His 29-year-old wife Alison had been killed by a hit-and-run driver in the episode transmitted a fortnight earlier, which I had watched in a kind of stupefaction. Coppers' wives weren't supposed to die. TV coppers weren't even supposed to have wives. When did we ever see Mrs Steve Keller or Mrs Mike Stone crossing the road in *The Streets of San Francisco*?

Roger Marshall's script milked the poignancy remorselessly. 'Body on the slab, that's all,' muttered Carter. 'Nothing. You can't relate to them all, can you? Only this time it isn't just a body, it's my wife's body. Sudden death. My wife's sudden death. Form 44. How many of those have we had to fill in, eh, guv?' It was searing stuff, although I can remember feeling very uncomfortable with Carter's subsequent tendency, over the next few weeks, to pickle his sorrows in alcohol. When you are thirteen, a little poignancy goes a long way.

As was cleverly spotted by the makers of the 2007 BBC hit *Life on Mars*, in which a modern-day detective travelled back to 1973 and effectively joined forces with Jack Regan, in the form of Phillip Glenister's gloriously unreconstructed DCI Gene Hunt, *The Sweeney* provides as strong an evocation as any television programme of a world gone forever. One of the fascinations of watching old repeats is making the then-and-now comparisons. For example, in the pilot episode broadcast in June 1974, the hard-drinking Regan paid 76p for two large Scotches. In October 1975 a return train fare from London to Durham was £11.24. And a year later a bent businessman called Tony Grey (played by John Hurt in a decidedly non-Quentin Crisp kind of way, bent in this 1970s instance meaning corrupt) advertised for computer programmers, offering £5,000 a year. Needless to say, Jack Regan was not wholly acquainted with computer technology. 'What's a cursor?' he asked, gruffly. 'Someone we nick for obscene language,' Carter replied. How we tittered at their banter, the like of which had never been heard on a British cops-and-robbers show.

The other fascination in watching *The Sweeney* these days lies in the casually sexist and racist dialogue, as so effectively mined in *Life on Mars*. While both the audience and John Simm's character Sam Tyler, transported more than three decades back to the Manchester of 1973, winced at the political incorrectness of those times, it was worth remembering how insensitive we all were back then. Jack Regan habitually referred to black women as 'coloured birds', or addressed men of dubious sexuality as 'ducky', and not even Mary Whitehouse objected. It was the violence in *The Sweeney* that really bothered her, and she was supported by a report by an eminent psychologist, Dr William Belson, in 1977. Ominously titled 'Television Violence and the Adolescent Boy', it found that 'teenagers exposed to violent programming committed 49 per cent more violent and anti-social behaviour' than those who spent their time more wholesomely engaged.

I don't remember there being any more violence than usual at KGV on the mornings after *The Sweeney* had aired, even though it was invariably the main topic of conversation. But maybe there was. Physical intimidation, after all, was not an unknown phenomenon at my school. First-year pupils, who went by the disparaging collective name of 'newts', were often targeted by boys higher up the school, some of whom were known to take great pleasure in forcing the head of a particularly vulnerable newt into a toilet bowl and flushing the chain.

This was never done to me partly on account of the fact that my friend from Lynton Road, Jez Sykes, was in the year above me and was one of those boys with whom nobody messed. When early in my 'newthood' I happened to mention to Jez that an unsavoury second-year named Price was regularly picking on me, he memorably and heroically held Price against a wall by the tie-knot and tightened it, reducing the knot from the size of a large vegetable samosa (at boys' schools in the 1970s it was thought that one's toughness and the dimensions of one's tie-knot were in direct proportion) to the size of a plectrum. Moreover, by the time the first series of *The Sweeney* began I was starting the spring term of my second year, and was thus relatively safe. But there must have been some bullies who were inspired by the uncompromisingly tough Regan and Carter (whose names, by an odd coincidence, were but a letter away from anticipating the 39th and 40th Presidents of the United States, occupiers of the White House between 1976 and 1988) to make life a misery for younger boys. And I do remember that when a new boy to the school called Hawksworth joined my class, 4B, in 1975, he was swiftly given the nickname 'Haskins' in honour of Jack Regan's boss. I don't know why. It can't have been that Hawksworth resembled Detective Chief Inspector Haskins, who was played by the almost-bald Garfield Morgan. Prosaically, it must simply have been that both their names began with H.

Whatever, there has never been a decade in which television has had more influence on the nation's secondary schoolchildren than it did in the 1970s. To a very large extent this is because, in an era of only three channels, we were all watching the same stuff. I once interviewed the actress Meera Syal, who is only a few months older than me, and she recalled that on the mornings after *Till Death Us Do Part* had been aired, with Alf Garnett talking about coons and so on, the casual racism at her school in Wolverhampton always seemed to be ratcheted up a notch or two. All the innate racists in the school had watched it, and none of them were bright enough to realize that the joke was on rather than with Johnny Speight's monstrous creation.

Apart from there being only three channels, there was bugger-all else to do of an evening. Even the video recorder had yet to be invented, let alone PlayStations and MSN and the other technological toys that occupy my own children for hours on end, or would if we didn't flog them into playing the occasional wholesome game of Monopoly.

The other thing about the 1970s was that there was for the very first time a whole slew of programmes seemingly aimed directly at adolescent audiences, the likes of *Starsky and Hutch*, *Alias Smith and Jones*, and much of the drama output from Lew Grade's ATV, which sent a generation of schoolboys to bed at night dreaming of the exquisite Alexandra Bastedo of *The Champions*.

Whether *The Sweeney* was one of those programmes aimed primarily at impressionable youths is a moot point. Its producer, Ted Childs, was quick to point out in the face of the damning Belson

Report that around half the audience was over sixty, and that if the series really did incite violence among its viewers, then the nation's shopping precincts would be full of 'marauding OAPs beating the rest of us over the head with pension books'. Very few schoolboys dared to miss it, however, for all the reasons I have outlined earlier in these pages about peer pressure. To be forced onto the periphery of a conversation about *The Sweeney* was a terrible thing. It could certainly never be admitted that you hadn't been allowed to stay up for it in case Jack Regan said 'bastard'. At least Noel Gallagher had the excuse of only being seven years old in January 1975.

The Gallagher brothers, coincidentally, grew up in the same work-ing-class Manchester suburb, Burnage, as John Thaw had twenty-five years or so earlier. It was Thaw himself who told me that, with a quiet chuckle, when I interviewed him for the *Radio Times* in 2001, not too long before he was diagnosed with the cancer of the oesophagus that would eventually kill him.

I didn't tell him that I had myself grown up with Jack Regan as the definitive copper in my life. There was no need. He must have esti-mated my age and realized as much. He must also have realized that meeting him was a slightly unsettling experience for those of us who, despite all those years of him playing the gentle, cerebral Inspector Morse, still thought of him as Regan. In person he was much more like Morse, although he had been toughened immeasurably by a deeply traumatic episode when he was seven years old. That's when his mother walked out on the family to set up home with another man, and he never saw her again.

In preparing my feature I spoke to his younger brother Ray, who had emigrated to Australia, and was more revealing than Thaw him-self ever was about their mother's abrupt departure. 'It made him very tough on the outside,' Ray Thaw told me. 'He decided that nobody was going to harm us again, that we would survive no matter what.' I also spoke to the actress Sheila Hancock, Mrs Thaw, who reckoned that what he always described simply as 'the awfulness' had had a different significance. 'To trust women has been difficult for him,' she said.

After his mother scarpered, the most influential woman in his life was his grandmother, his father's mother Vera, who lived a short bus journey away in West Gorton, alongside Bellevue Zoo. 'She was very extrovert, to the extent of dressing up in silly clothes for a laugh,' he told me. 'So was my mother, from what I remember. And I was a show-off, too, as a child. I've had it knocked out of me since becoming an actor, because I have always thought of acting as a very serious business. If you ask anyone who has worked with me, they will tell you that I carry the script around with me like my last will and testament. So I've become more and more introverted, although, having said that, I'm getting slightly more outgoing now.' He paused. Conversations with him, and I had several, were peppered with long pauses. 'Slightly,' he emphasized.

I could scarcely imagine, I said, what a culture shock it must have been for a Burnage lad to arrive at RADA on a scholarship in the late 1950s; one of his classmates, just to rub it in, was the frightfully well-spoken Sarah Miles. He chuckled, and told me how his dad couldn't afford the train fare from Manchester, so they all piled into his Uncle Charlie's old Ford Thames van – him, his dad, Ray, Charlie, and Charlie's daughter Sandra. They dropped him off near RADA, at the corner of Gower Street. 'And the first person I saw was a student going up the two steps into RADA with an overcoat over his shoulders, a real cliché of an actor luvvie. I thought, "My God, it's true."'

Thaw himself was always the antithesis of that cliché, yet the embodiment of another one, the *Billy Elliot* cliché of the blunt working-class Northerner finding his vocation in London in, as Jack Regan would have put it, the poofy arts. Ray Thaw fuelled this *Billy Elliot* image by telling me how proud he and his father were when John won his scholarship. 'I remember us going to watch him on stage in

London for the first time. *Chips with Everything*, I think it was. When he came on I felt like standing up and screaming, "That's my brother!" But Dad calmed me down. He whispered to me, "If we keep quiet, we might hear what people say about him."'

Thaw's career took off quickly. In 1964, aged twenty-two, he landed his first lead role on television, playing a military policeman in a series called *Redcap*. A year earlier, in a play called *Semi-Detached*, he had understudied his hero, Laurence Olivier. 'I used to watch him like a hawk from the wings,' he said. 'And when he told me that he was taking a week off, I said, "I'm twenty-one, playing a man of sixty-five. I'll never get away with it." He said, "Do what I do, baby. Amaze yourself with your own daring."'

I suppose that's precisely what he did as Jack Regan, whose swaggering aggression made him famous, and yet was so unlike his real self. When I asked Thaw what made him emotional, he said classical music. 'Schubert, Bach, Mozart, Sibelius . . . the brilliance, the genius of it. Was it Lenin who said, "Who could create such beauty whilst living in this vile hell?" Music does that for me, too,' he said. He must have related to Morse's love of opera. Regan, by contrast, would almost certainly have assumed Nessun Dorma to be a Japanese camper van.

18

'Down with CI5': Bodie, Doyle, and the Predicament of the 1970s Actor

I confess that I hardly ever watched Thaw playing Morse, brilliant though I know he was in the part, and I suspect that I'm not alone among folk of my generation. Even all those years after *The Sweeney*, it felt disorientating to watch him playing a copper not in the habit of barking, 'Get yer trousers on, you're nicked!'

As a short aside, in the summer of 1986 I came back to England from Emory University in Atlanta, Georgia, where I had spent a year on a post-graduate scholarship. As part of my course I got myself an internship at the fledgling Cable News Network, part of Ted Turner's Atlanta-based media empire. It was Turner's belief that a twenty-four-hour rolling news station was the way of the future, but not many people shared his vision; indeed CNN was widely derided in media circles, and rudely dubbed Chicken Noodle News for the perceived triviality of its content.

On the morning of 28 January 1986 that all changed. At CNN's offices downtown I watched the launch of the space shuttle *Challenger*, an event overlooked by the major networks but covered live by CNN. Precisely seventy-three seconds into what should have been a standard flight, *Challenger* disintegrated, killing the seven crew members on board. One of them was Christa McAuliffe, a 37-year-old teacher from New Hampshire who had been selected from more than 11,000 applicants to be the first civilian in space. My job at CNN in the weeks leading up to the *Challenger* launch had been to liaise with schools across America, where the kids were all doing projects about McAuliffe's adventure. Thousands, maybe millions, of schoolchildren saw it come to a catastrophic end as *Challenger* exploded in mid-air. Overnight, albeit in the most terrible way imaginable, Turner's faith in round-the-clock news provision was vindicated. Never again was CNN called Chicken Noodle News.

Anyway, having had a tiny part in a pivotal TV moment, I returned to England convinced that it was my destiny to become a mover and shaker in the television industry. Persuading the BBC to share this sense of destiny, however, proved beyond me. So instead I relied on a helping hand from my then-girlfriend's aunt, who was an executive with Central Television.

She kindly arranged for me to have a trial as a script-reader, one of a posse of reasonably literate people whose job it was to scrutinize the thousands of scripts sent in, mostly speculatively, and to pass the best efforts on to the next tier of decision-makers. I was sent a handful of scripts to see whether I had a discerning eye, and decided that there was no point in sitting on the fence. I had to be decisive, unequivocal, with my judgement. One of the scripts was for an episode of a new detective series, adapted from a novel. I hated it. 'Stilted dialogue, implausible plot,' I wrote. 'My advice is that you shouldn't touch this with a bargepole.'

This dud I told them not to touch with a bargepole turned out to be the first episode of *Inspector Morse*, 'The Dead of Jericho', to which Central had already committed £500,000, with John Thaw firmly on board to play Morse. The script had been written by Anthony Minghella, later to become famous as the Oscar-winning director of *The English Patient*, and whose premature death in March 2008 was mourned by the entire film world, but at the time his name meant nothing to me. I didn't realize that 'The Dead of Jericho' was already commissioned; I thought, naïvely, that it was a script sent in on spec, and that they were waiting with interest for my valuable opinion. Anyway, the dud became the first of thirty-three two-hour films in a series which ran for thirteen years, one of the greatest success stories in the history of British television. My own career as a script-reader was, by contrast, one of the most dismal failures in the history of British television. It lasted three weeks. Clearly, and despite all those years I had spent riveted to the screen, I had no kind of eye for what might constitute a decent TV programme. It seems worth adding that a few years later I became a national-newspaper TV critic, first for the *Mail on Sunday*, then for the *Independent*.

I know I'm not the only person who hardly ever watched *Morse* because of the legacy of *The Sweeney*. My friend Craig's mum is another, although for diametrically opposite reasons. She couldn't watch Morse because she had always hated Jack Regan. 'She used to say that Regan had a chip on his shoulder,' Craig told me. I love that. It shows how sometimes actors completely inhabit the characters they play, not in their own minds but in the public's perception. Or maybe it's just the perception of my friends' mothers, my pal Pete's mum, you will recall, having been astounded to find Raymond Burr, released from Chief Ironside's wheelchair, walking freely down the stairs on *Parkinson*.

Sometimes this perception is the bane of an actor's life, never more so than in the case of Martin Shaw, who from 1977 to 1983 played Ray Doyle, increasingly grudgingly, in *The Professionals*.

The Professionals rode the *Starsky and Hutch* bandwagon, the one that screamed round corners on two wheels. As Day and Topping wrote, *Starsky and Hutch* was the embodiment of a new TV phenomenon, the 'buddy' series, which replaced the previous Hollywood-inspired penchant for maverick cops who bucked the system. When producer Brian Clemens approached London Weekend Television chief executive Brian Tesler (whatever stymied my own later ambitions in television, it was obviously nothing to do with being called Brian) with a couple of ideas, one of them, tentatively titled *The A-Squad*, about a pair of wisecracking anti-terrorist agents, got the nod. The title was later changed to *The Professionals*.

I was never as smitten by *The Professionals* as I was by *The Sweeney*. It seemed altogether less realistic, partly because unlike *The Sweeney*, which purported to lift the lid on the modus operandi of the Flying Squad, the law enforcement agency it portrayed was the fictitious CI5, a transparent effort to blend the CID and MI5, with the improbable consequence that Bodie and Doyle were charged with tackling everything from armed robberies to Cold War spy scandals. That said, in 1984 when angry Libyans besieged the British Embassy in Tripoli following the shooting of WPC Yvonne Fletcher outside the Libyan People's Bureau in London, feeling that their country was being unfairly victimized, they kept shouting 'Down with CI5!' It turned out that a dubbed version of *The Professionals* had recently been shown on Libyan TV.

The other problem I had with it was that Bodie (Lewis Collins) and Doyle appeared to have been cast for their looks as much as their acting abilities, which couldn't really be said of Regan and Carter. In fact the similarly attractive Anthony Andrews had been the first choice to play Bodie (which would surely have scuppered his chances of playing Sebastian Flyte in *Brideshead Revisited* four years later), but he was dropped when it was decided that he and Shaw had insufficient chemistry on screen.

It is easy these days to forget just how those very names, Bodie and Doyle, became entrenched in popular culture, although one still gets occasional happy reminders. My wife was sitting in the waiting-room at a veterinary surgery in our local town of Leominster a few years ago, and was amused to hear the receptionist call through to the vet: 'Mrs Harrison's just been on the phone. We had Bodie in last week and now Doyle's not very well.'

What kind of creatures Bodie and Doyle were, she never found out, but it was nice to know that the names lived on. In the late 1970s and early 1980s they were downright iconic, which of course also meant that they were ripe targets for comedy. *The Two Ronnies* performed a joint send-up of *The Professionals* and *Tinker, Tailor, Soldier, Spy* in a sketch called 'Tinker Tailor Smiley Doyle', with Ronnie Corbett playing a bumbling version of Doyle, while the Comic Strip team, even less subtly, produced a spoof called 'The Bullshitters', with Keith Allen as Bonehead, Peter Richardson as Foyle, and Robbie Coltrane as their grumpy boss Commander Jackson, not so coincidentally the namesake of Gordon Jackson, who enjoyed one of the more interesting careers in 1970s television, memorably playing phlegmatic Mr Hudson in *Upstairs, Downstairs* before taking the role of Bodie and Doyle's superior, George Cowley. I expect that too must have been exploited in the odd comedy sketch, Cowley ordering the seizure of a terrorist arms cache before sitting down for a cup of tea and a muffin with Mrs Bridges.

One can only imagine how all these parodies played with Shaw, who felt increasingly hostile towards the show even while it was being aired, considering, not entirely without justification, both the storylines and his own character to be gruesomely one-dimensional. Aptly enough, Paul Michael Glaser had harboured similar misgivings about *Starsky and Hutch*, feeling that it harmed his reputation as a serious, versatile actor. He duly quit as Starsky after four series, whereupon a plan was hatched to kill him off and introduce Starsky's younger brother Nick as Hutch's new partner. Happily, the idea was abandoned.

In recent years, Glaser has at least come to acknowledge his debt to Starsky. As far as I'm aware there has been no such gesture from Martin Shaw. Not only that, but being a serious (and arguably over-serious) actor, he reportedly exercised his right after *The Professionals* ended to veto repeat showings. On ITV at least, *The Professionals* went unrepeated, and when I was commissioned by the *Radio Times* to interview Shaw, around the time that he started starring in *Judge John Deed*, I heard that it was safer to tango through a minefield than to ask him about *The Professionals*. I never did do the interview. The stipulations about what I could and couldn't mention became so tiresome that eventually the project fell by the wayside.

In fairness to Shaw, there are quite a few other actors who get peculiarly huffy at being asked about the roles that made them famous. It was my misfortune in the mid-1990s, in a hotel just off the Strand in London, to interview Bernard Hill, whose most celebrated role then, and forever, was Yosser Hughes in Alan Bleasdale's immortal *Boys From the Blackstuff*. I knew that as in the case of Shaw and the taboo subject of Doyle, Hill was almost neurotically sensitive about Yosser, and so I had to tiptoe around the subject like a cat burglar, wondering when to time my lunge for the jewels. In the event I didn't have the bottle, and contented myself with talking to him about everything else he'd ever done but not *Blackstuff*, which seemed absurd, like interviewing Leonardo da Vinci and not mentioning *The Last Supper*. Anyway, we then left the hotel together, and a bloke on an adjacent building site, bless his hard hat, promptly bellowed out 'All right Yosser!'

The streets of London can be fertile ground for interviewers. You think the job's done, only to emerge from a hotel or restaurant with whoever you've just interviewed and there get handed your best paragraph. I once spent a most enjoyable hour in the lounge of the

Berkeley Hotel in Knightsbridge, chatting to Ronnie Corbett, who, I should add, is hugely convivial company and an altogether delightful fellow. We then exited onto the pavement, still chatting away, at which point he spotted a traffic warden sticking a ticket on his Bentley, which had overrun its allotted meter time by less than a minute. Corbett set off as fast as his little legs could carry him, shouting, 'You wicked bastard!' It was a priceless insight into the life of a comedian for whom the world, if only fleetingly, had stopped being funny.

Another man who effectively shuns the role that made him famous is James Bolam, who played the working-class, work-shy cynic Terry Collier in the hit 1960s comedy *The Likely Lads*, and its 1973 sequel *Whatever Happened to the Likely Lads?* In 2007 there were vague plans to reunite Terry and his old mucker, the upwardly mobile Bob Ferris, played by Rodney Bewes. The writers, Dick Clement and Ian La Frenais, were up for it, even revealing what might have become of the Likely Lads forty-five years on. 'Bob was always very ambitious,' said Clement. 'He would have gone into the building trade, founded his own small business but gone bust. Terry would have been hit by a bus while crossing the street in Newcastle and been awarded compensation. Of course, seeing his friend who never did a proper day's work now having all the money would be a bitter irony for Bob. We always felt the best comedy came when he was miserable.'

Bewes was up for a reunion too, as was Brigit Forsyth, who played Bob's domineering wife Thelma. But Bolam was no more willing to play Terry again than Martin Shaw might be to play Doyle or Bernard Hill Yosser. Which of course was not something any of these fine actors should be pilloried for, although it seems a shame that they have turned their backs so emphatically on the characters with which we still associate them. On the other hand, the fact that we still associate them with those characters was precisely why they turned their backs in the first place. Scarcely had *Whatever Happened to the Likely*

Lads? finished than Bolam was back playing roguish Jack Ford in the gritty drama about life in South Shields between the wars, *When the Boat Comes In*. Later still he went on to play Harold Shipman, for heaven's sake. One can see why he wanted to shrug off the ghost of Terry.

In the case of him and Bewes, moreover, there was an added twist. They were said to loathe each other, and to have stopped speaking more than thirty years earlier, after Bewes related in a newspaper interview the story that Bolam's wife, Sue, had told her husband while he was driving that she was pregnant, causing him almost to crash the car.

It doesn't seem like the most indiscreet tale ever told, although maybe Bolam has a different version. Either way, it seems as though he felt his co-star had collaborated in an invasion of his cherished privacy. He hasn't given many interviews down the years, but in one of them he said, tellingly, 'I'm having new track rods fitted on my car. I don't want to know anything about the man who's doing it. Why should he want to know about me?'

As Bewes recalled the episode, he realized that he had perhaps spoken out of turn and decided to ring Bolam to forewarn him. 'There was this dreadful silence. He put the phone down. I called him back. He didn't answer. He hasn't spoken to me since.'

Nor is he likely to again if Bewes was correctly quoted in the *Daily Mail*, confirming that, like Shaw with *The Professionals*, Bolam vetoed repeats of *The Likely Lads* for some years. 'He justified it by saying, "It's a retrospective step in my career." But eventually they did show the series again, and I'd love to have asked Jimmy, "Did you send the repeat cheque back because of your principles?" It's all terribly sad.'

Whether or not it's terribly sad, it's certainly worth reflecting that several of the seminal small-screen performances in that era were given by actors who either could not have been less like the characters they portrayed, or embarked on the rest of their television careers desperately trying to divorce themselves from that particular piece of their past, or both. For those like Craig's mum, and Pete's mum, which in truth is all of us to a greater or lesser extent, who think that actors must be at least a teeny bit like the characters they play, this is hugely disappointing. Which is why I am devoting much of the next chapter to *Dad's Army*, because I think you'll be reassured to learn – after the shock of discovering that the man inhabiting Jack Regan was a Schubert-loving, Keats-quoting aesthete – that Arthur Lowe was very much like Captain Mainwaring, and that in John Le Mesurier there was a great deal of Sergeant Wilson.

19

'Don't Tell Him, Pike!': Debunking the Curse of *Dad's Army*

Dad's Army started as long ago as 1968; so long ago, in fact, that the third episode was abruptly ripped off the air so that the BBC could give full coverage to the Soviet invasion of Czechoslovakia. This was a year after the dawn of the colour television era, although, as I have explained already, at 58 Lynton Road the sun carried on rising in monochrome.

I must say that I don't remember watching *Dad's Army* in black-and-white, but for six years I must have done. I certainly remember watching it with my dad, who would chortle happily in his Parker Knoll armchair, and whose favourite character was Captain Mainwaring. He'd met more than a few Captain Mainwarings in his time, he used to say.

In 1994 I met the man who had called Captain Mainwaring 'dad'.

I had read a short item in a newspaper about Arthur Lowe's beloved Victorian steam yacht, *Amazon*, on which he had lived for much of the time, and which more than a decade after his death had been put up for sale by his son Stephen. My interest piqued, I managed to contact Stephen, who lived in the far north of Scotland. He told me a little more about his father, and invited me up to see the yacht.

Stephen looked, I was delighted to find, just like his father would have looked behind an unkempt ginger beard. He sounded like Arthur, too: gruff, not given to displays of emotion. An engaging, mildly eccentric man of forty-one, he lived with his wife and baby daughter in a tumbledown cottage just outside Inverness, across the road from a dull stretch of the Caledonian Canal where *Amazon* was moored. Arthur Lowe had bought *Amazon* for £2,000 in 1968, the year he first squeezed into Captain Mainwaring's tunic. He, his wife Joan and Stephen lived on board for six months a year, Arthur generally wearing a padded Arctic suit Joan had given him. Though he never sailed *Amazon* himself, always hiring a professional skipper, he loved to think of himself as a hardy English seadog, sailing into the night in worsening weather. Arthur was a romantic. 'Like most romantics, he went through life in a state of slight disillusionment,' Stephen told me.

Amazon spent most of her time bobbing gently on the Thames outside the television studios at Teddington. 'But I do remember sailing up the Seine to Paris in a heatwave,' said Stephen. 'Arthur stood on the bridge purple-faced. He would not take off his padded Arctic suit.' Stephen admitted that in private Arthur could be disconcertingly like Mainwaring. Modest delusions of grandeur, honest, loyal, pompous, stubborn, a compulsive organizer, frequently curt. Later, I talked to Jimmy Perry and David Croft, the co-writers of *Dad's Army*, about him. Perry remembered sitting with Arthur in a restaurant in Great Yarmouth. A chap came round the tables, playing a guitar. 'Not here,' muttered Arthur, with a Mainwaring-like wave of his hand. 'Go away.'

Stephen Lowe suggested that despite his father's success, Arthur never really felt professionally fulfilled. 'I think he saw time running out. He was fifty-one before he had his first real success, as Leonard Swindley, the draper in *Coronation Street*. His career didn't move fast enough for him and he got depressed. Funny men do. My mum would buy my dad yellow waistcoats to cheer him up.'

The problem was that Arthur Lowe wanted to be a movie star. He'd made his film debut as a journalist in the Ealing comedy *Kind Hearts and Coronets* and it was a world that fascinated him. Of course, as Mainwaring, he made – and, thanks to the never-ending repeats, continues to make – far more people laugh than most film actors. But those priceless pauses were not always borne of immaculate comic timing. 'Very often he was wondering what the hell he was supposed to say next,' David Croft told me. 'He never used to take his script home. He'd say, "I'm not having that rubbish in my house." So he'd read it for the first time in the taxi and would finish learning it on the set. I used to field complaints from the rest of the cast.'

The affection in which the *Dad's Army* team held Lowe is pleasing but quite surprising, given how obstreperous he sometimes was. 'He could be bloody awkward,' said Perry. 'In the U-boat episode he was supposed to have a bomb down his trousers and Private Fraser was supposed to fish for it. Being Arthur, he didn't read the script until an hour before filming. "I'm not having this, James," he said. "Tell your partner I don't have bombs down my trousers, and I'm certainly not having John Laurie's arm down my trousers." There was no persuading him. We had to rewrite the scene and stick the bomb down Corporal Jones's trousers.' After that episode Arthur had a clause added to his contract. He would not remove his trousers, nor tolerate bombs down them.

He was born in Derbyshire in 1915 and brought up in Levenshulme, Manchester, the son of a market train manager. He married Joan in 1945. It was her second marriage, his first, and a great

155

boost to his confidence. Moreover, with Stephen's arrival in 1953 came another outlet for his organizational zeal. 'He'd always organize the cricket matches in the park, and our home movies were planned and directed to the nth degree,' said Stephen. 'But he'd organize others, never himself. He went through life half an hour late.'

Perry concurred. 'At The Bell Hotel in Thetford, where we stayed during the making of *Dad's Army*, Arthur would always come down late for breakfast, out of breath and red-faced. "James," he'd say, "these early mornings interfere with my lavatorial arrangements." I suggested All Bran. "All Bran?" he said. "Are you insane?" But after two mornings he declared that All Bran had changed his life.'

Everyone associated with *Dad's Army* was at some stage invited to spend time on the *Amazon*. It was Arthur's joy to entertain on board, exchanging the padded Arctic suit for a navy-blue blazer with brass buttons. To his eternal regret he'd been rejected by the merchant navy because of poor eyesight, so he was thrilled when Stephen went to sea in 1970. 'I think he'd far rather have gone to sea than been an actor,' says Stephen. 'At sea he would have been one of the lads. As an actor he never really was.'

Boozy late nights out with fellow thespians were not really Arthur's scene, still less boozy mornings. John Le Mesurier often used to start drinking at 10 a.m., having spent most of the night before at Ronnie Scott's jazz club in Soho. Arthur liked Le Mesurier, but heartily disapproved of his lifestyle. It was ironic, therefore, that towards the end of Arthur Lowe's life people used to think he was drunk, because of his habit of nodding off at all hours. In fact, for the last five years of his life, he suffered from narcolepsy, a chronic inability to stay awake. Stephen Lowe told me that he had a signature of his father's which simply trailed off; Arthur had conked out in the middle of an autograph.

As for his great joy in life, *Amazon*, Stephen showed me around with as much pride as Arthur would have done. There was a huge sign alongside her proclaiming 'Museum Ship', but she got few visitors, despite the distinction of being the oldest wooden steam yacht afloat – she was built in Southampton in 1885, and even I, a committed landlubber, could see that she was an immensely handsome vessel. Stephen showed me the wind-up gramophone, which would stand on deck in the evenings as Arthur and Joan danced. He also showed me the semicircle Joan had cut out of the bar on account of Arthur's tubbiness; without it she couldn't squeeze by when he was fixing drinks.

Since his father's death in 1982, Stephen had been chartering the boat and running her as a museum, but the charter market was in decline and casual visits didn't generate nearly enough money to maintain her. Besides, he wanted to buy some security for his daughter's future. So he put *Amazon* on sale, for £185,000. I never heard whether he sold her, although I'm sure he did, and I'm sure too that he was true to the promise he made me, that on the day his father's beloved boat was finally sold, he would 'take a bottle of whisky, climb to the top of a distant hill, and not come down for some considerable time'.

I can't remember asking Stephen Lowe whether his dad ever called him a 'stupid boy', as Mainwaring so often did Private Pike, played by Ian Lavender. Whatever, a couple of years later I further indulged my affection for *Dad's Army* by interviewing Ian Lavender for the *Mail on Sunday*, and was astounded to find that he was about to celebrate his fiftieth birthday. Private Pike, Britain's favourite 'stupid boy', about to turn fifty! It seemed like one of those birthdays liable to make an entire nation feel older. For most generations there is somebody famous whose age reminds you of your own advancing years. For my mother's generation, born in the mid-1920s, it's Marilyn Monroe. In the year that Lavender turned fifty, Monroe would have turned seventy. She could have made a sequel to *Bus Stop* called *Bus Pass*. For my generation, or at least for me in particular, it's

Bonnie Langford. I was horrified a few years ago to see her on a TV chat show with a bald, middle-aged husband in tow. I'd half-assumed she was still six. But the ageing of Private Pike, the juvenile weed from *Dad's Army*, makes more than one generation realize how old they must be getting.

I interviewed him in a hotel in Holland Park. That day, he told me, he had received two cheques in the post. One was for £2.33, covering video sales of *Rising Damp* (in which he'd had a bit part) to Canada. The other was for a far more substantial £11.16 – *Man About the House* overseas sales to Hong Kong. Unlike Martin Shaw, and James Bolam, and Bernard Hill, Lavender had nothing but affection for the role that had made him famous. Not for a second did he regret being cast as Frank Pike. But starring in *Dad's Army* for nine years at the start of an acting career, rather than towards the end of one like most of the cast, had squeezed him into a pigeonhole marked Situation Comedy. Despite a run in *EastEnders*, his main acting work since *Dad's Army* ended has been in TV sitcoms and as a sought-after pantomime dame. He was even offered the part of the clown in a West End production of *The Merchant of Venice* starring Dustin Hoffman, but declined, saying that he wanted a straight part. 'I ended up playing one of the brothers, Salerio or Salanio, I can't remember which,' he told me. 'They're always known to actors as the salads. I was one of the salads.'

At the time I met him, Lavender had no work in prospect, although this didn't worry him unduly because he'd just survived a brush with bowel cancer, casting perspective on his problems. But his cancer added some credibility to the conviction among some over-superstitious thespians that *Dad's Army* was somehow jinxed. They cited the deaths of so many of the original cast, conveniently overlooking the fact that many of them were, not to put too fine a point on it, of dying age. On the other hand, James Beck, who played the spiv, Private Walker, was only forty-two when he passed away in 1973.

Edward Sinclair, the verger, was sixty-three. Arthur Lowe wasn't particularly old at sixty-six. Even the founder of the *Dad's Army* Appreciation Society, a haulage contractor from Yorkshire who went by the excellent name of Tadge Muldoon, had expired in 1995, following a dreadful car crash.

Lavender told me how he had landed the role of Pike only a short time after leaving Bristol Old Vic Theatre School, and that the opportunity to work in such venerable company seemed heaven-sent. 'I was very much a sprog,' he said, 'but Clive Dunn [Corporal Jones] in particular used to look out for me, make sure I wasn't forgotten. And I like to think I'd been taught to learn, so I knew that actors who'd been around for thirty years or more might just have something I didn't. Younger actors don't seem to realize that now. In many ways it was like going to school every day. I learnt how to work a laugh. With Arthur, it was more a case of what he didn't say, what went through his eyes, whereas Clive worked a laugh quite differently.'

Hearteningly, Lavender reckoned that pretty much all the cast had simply played exaggerated versions of themselves. I would have been inconsolable if he'd told me that John Laurie, who played the tetchy, doom-mongering undertaker, Private Fraser, had been eternally sunny, or Clive Dunn a paragon of order. I already knew that Arthur Lowe had not been self-deprecating and winsome.

'Arthur was a pompous little man but I was very fond of him,' he said. 'Unlike Mainwaring he would burst his own bubble occasionally. John Laurie could be cantankerous, but he was a startling raconteur and had a wicked sense of humour. I got on with him from the start. Do you know, I remember him saying to a new make-up girl, "You're a bonny wee thing." And in all innocence he actually tweaked her tit. If me or Jimmy Beck had done that we'd have been kicked somewhere nasty, but she blushed beautifully.

'There was a lovely rivalry between John and Arnold Ridley (Private Godfrey), who were both about the same age. Arnold had been badly injured by a bayonet during the First World War, and he woke up in pain every day. John would wind him up terribly. As soon as Arnold let it be known that he wasn't sure whether he was up to a certain scene, John would immediately be so fit it wasn't true.

'In some ways, John Le Mesurier was very like Sergeant Wilson. Apparently, he had turned up for his basic training in the war, as Private Le Mesurier, at the wheel of an open-top Austin Tourer. He was wearing a dinner jacket and had his golf clubs and some jazz records in the back. John used to play vague, and the make-up girls would fall over each other to help him. There'd always be three or four girls running to get something for him.'

I had intended my interview with Lavender to be mainly about him, but he talked so captivatingly about his old co-stars that I decided to turn the piece into a more general feature on *Dad's Army*, to which end I drove up to East Anglia to talk to David Croft again. Over a memorably civilized alfresco lunch with the patrician Croft and his charming wife, in their idyllic home in the middle of the Norfolk countryside, Croft, who also produced and directed *Dad's Army*, confirmed that, as the series wore on, he and Perry had tailored the dialogue to suit the actors.

'Oh yes,' he said, 'Clive Dunn, for instance, was a terrific waffler. He was the only one who ad-libbed his own material, and very often he'd hit on something in rehearsal and we'd say, "That's marvellous, let's keep it in," but then he'd forget what it was he'd just done.

'And, as Ian says, John Le Mesurier would sit all alone and the girls would just queue up to do things for him. He'd murmur, "My dear, your hair is so charming that way", and of course they'd melt. I once heard him say to a particularly beautiful make-up girl, "I say, could you wind my watch?" Wilson, Croft added, settling the speculation once and for all, really was intended to be Pike's natural father. 'In my mind he was, although in those days one didn't go into all that.'

All the same, Perry and Croft never intended Pike to play much of a part in *Dad's Army*. But Lavender had other ideas. 'He realized quickly,' Croft told me, 'that unless he did something he was going to disappear. For instance, he found that long scarf himself, just turned up wearing it one day, and built up the character very cleverly, basically out of self-defence so we couldn't get rid of him. We ended up writing a very good episode around him, "The Making of Private Pike", in which he got a girlfriend.'

For Lavender and most *Dad's Army* fans, however, Pike's finest hour came when the platoon was captured by a U-boat crew in the first episode of the sixth series, the episode in which Arthur Lowe refused to allow a bomb to be placed down his trousers. It was transmitted on Wednesday 31 October 1973, and in my Letts Schoolboy Diary I wrote 'watched new *Dad's Army* – brill!!!!' (like all schoolboys, I suffered from exclamation-mark incontinence), little knowing that it was but the first of dozens of viewings of what is now the famous sequence when Philip Madoc, playing the U-boat captain, demanded to know the youngster's name, and Mainwaring barked 'Don't tell him, Pike!' Much as I love the intelligent sophistication of the comedy in *Frasier*, for example, or *Yes, Minister*, Mainwaring's exhortation represented comedy at its simplest and most sublime. 'I told David I'd never be able to keep my face straight,' Lavender told me. 'And I didn't. He cut away from me a split second too late and if you watch it now you can just see me starting to crack up.' I've checked, and he's right.

'It's incredible,' he added, 'that there were all those catchphrases every week like "Don't panic!" and "Stupid boy!" and that was only one line in one episode. Yet so many people remember it. Even when I get fan letters in pantomimes, at least a quarter of them have "don't tell him, Pike!" at the bottom.'

Around the time I interviewed Lavender, the then-controller of BBC1, Alan Yentob, had risked ridicule by scheduling repeats of *Dad's Army* early on Saturday evenings, directly against ITV's hugely popular *Baywatch*. Pamela Anderson making the most of her tits on ITV versus the Walmington-on-Sea Home Guard making tits of themselves on BBC1: most industry insiders predicted no contest. And they were right, but not in the way they anticipated. Yentob had the satisfaction of seeing *Dad's Army* garner almost 10 million viewers, against a shade over 7 million for *Baywatch*.

Yet nobody in the late 1960s and early 1970s would have identified *Dad's Army* as one of those shows likely to last for eternity in repeat heaven. Ian Lavender had a theory for this. 'I think it's partly because *Dad's Army* was dated even then,' he suggested. 'It's harder to repeat other good comedies – *The Good Life*, say – because it's important to know what contemporary attitudes were.' That's partly true, but it's also true that sometimes we don't appreciate until years later just how good particular programmes were. Popular as *Dad's Army* was at the time, it was no more popular than the classroom comedy *Please Sir!*, for example. Yet nobody would want old episodes of *Please Sir!* to be popping up all the time now, except those entitled to repeat fees, that is, and possibly not even them.

20

'I 'Ate You, Butler!': Forgettable Sitcoms, and the Age of Innuendo

Paradoxically *Dad's Army* does not stir the nostalgic juices like other more dated sitcoms, the reason being that all those repeats mean that it hasn't faded in the collective memory. Were it not for my ever-reliable Letts diary, I wouldn't know whether I first watched the U-boat episode on the day it first went out or ten years later. So let me devote this chapter to those 1970s sitcoms that few of us have watched since, unless we're really sad and asked for the boxed set as a fortieth birthday present. *Mind Your Language, Citizen Smith* and *Get Some In* all spring effortlessly to mind. I watched each of them religiously, and was accordingly very sorry indeed to read in 1997 about the sad death, aged only fifty-two, of Barry Evans, who played Jeremy Brown, the chirpy Englishman teaching a variety of all-too-archetypal foreigners (a sexy Frenchwoman, a randy Italian, a humourless German, an Indian with a wobbly head) in *Mind Your Language*.

Evans wound up working as a mini-cab driver in the Leicestershire village of Claybrooke Magna, and was found dead in a rundown house alongside an empty whisky bottle and a spilled container of aspirin. A friend of his, 18-year-old James Leadbitter, was later accused of attempted murder, although the charge was subsequently dropped. Leadbitter told police that he had visited Evans on the day he died to say that he wouldn't be calling again, whereupon Evans had 'become upset'. The coroner recorded an open verdict, which is more than can be said of the popular verdict on *Mind Your Language*. It has become one of the favourite whipping-boys for those who castigate 1970s television for its political incorrectness, on account of its undoubtedly rigid racial stereotyping, but I don't mind admitting that I was quite fond of it at the time. It certainly didn't offend those contemporary attitudes of which Ian Lavender spoke, but perhaps that is more an indictment of contemporary attitudes than of *Mind Your Language*.

Less offensive to posterity, but still well and truly mired in the early 1970s, was *Man About the House*, which started in 1973 and became a huge favourite of almost everyone I knew, except poor old Jonny Cook whose dad wouldn't let him watch ITV on account of it being 'a bit council estate'. The credits, had they ever rolled in the Cook household, would have been grist to Mr Cook's mill. To symbolize the subject matter of a man sharing a flat with two women, they featured not only two sets of ladies' underwear and a set of Y-fronts, but also, as my friend Chris recalls it, two cats and a chicken. I must say that I can't remember the cats and the chicken, but if it were the case, then for the time it was an enormously subtle stroke of innuendo (two pussies and a cock, if I have to spell out the reference), and one, I dare say, that even the eagle-eyed Mrs Whitehouse missed.

It was, of course, the heyday of innuendo. I subscribed to two magazines, the educational *Look & Learn*, and the 'junior *TV Times*', *Look-In*. *Look & Learn* was above any form of innuendo but *Look-In* wasn't. On 25 October 1975, which as it happened was my fourteenth birthday, the Pop Quest quiz in *Look-In* invited readers to reassemble an anagram to reveal the name of a top singer. The singer was Alvin Stardust. The anagram, dreamt up either by someone in editorial with a sense of humour, or by someone almost completely guileless, was Daril Vastnuts.

Man About the House, as everyone of my generation recalls, starred Richard O'Sullivan, Paula Wilcox and Sally Thomsett as Robin, Chrissy and Jo, the ménage-à-trois renting a flat – for the record, or perhaps the anorak pocket, it was 6 Myddleton Terrace, Earls Court – from the feckless Mr Roper (Brian Murphy) and the libidinous Mrs Roper (Yootha Joyce). As in the case of the blonde one and the dark one from Abba, it was almost mandatory among boys of my age to favour either Chrissy or Jo over the other. Despite my usual preference for blondes, I fancied Wilcox's Chrissy more. Apart from anything else, it was only three years since I had been to the pictures to see *The Railway Children*, in which Sally Thomsett had played the decidedly unfanciable middle child, Phyllis.

Not, I should add, that her *Railway Children* co-star Jenny Agutter suffered from the same association. *Walkabout*, the 1970 Nic Roeg film in which she obligingly took all her clothes off in the Australian outback, sent my testosterone haywire, and after catching it by accident late one night on television I scrutinized the TV listings on a daily basis for about three years, determined not to miss it if by some joyous chance it was shown again, which sporadically it was. Some years later I interviewed the lovely Miss Agutter for one of my Telly People features in the *Mail on Sunday*, and it was all I could do not to fall at her feet and thank her for having shown me what the naked female form looked like without the pubic hair airbrushed out, as it frustratingly was in *Health and Efficiency*, the naturist magazine that was common currency at KGV, officially equal in value to a set of poker dice or 50 Bazooka Joes.

H&E, now that I think about it, was a pretty poor source of sex education, scarcely any better than the underwear section of the Littlewoods' or Grattan's catalogue from which I had previously derived my adolescent thrills. When I was fifteen, however, I made a significant step forward by acquiring a small stash of *Penthouses* from reliable contacts in the shoplifting business. Not very imaginatively I kept them under my bed, and was horrified to get home from school one day to find them gone. 'By the way,' my mother casually said over supper that evening, 'if you're looking for your girlie magazines, I've put them in the spare bedroom with your old *Look & Learns*. I thought that was the category they belonged under.' I remember opening my mouth, trying to think of a suitable riposte, then closing it again. It's been more than thirty years now, and I still haven't thought of one.

Given what sexual innocents I and most of my friends were for at least the first half of the 1970s, and in my case for most of the second half as well, it is amusing to reflect on how knowing we pretended to be while enjoying the nudge-nudge, wink-wink, double entendre comedy of that era, as personified by Benny Hill singing 'Ernie'. There was even an advert for milk, that most wholesome of drinks, straplined 'Are You Getting Enough?'

On the Buses was another example: to the despair of Luxton and District depot's long-suffering inspector Blake (Stephen Lewis, whose catchphrase 'I 'ate you, Butler' was another important tool in the repertoire of those of us who fancied our talents as impressionists), drivers Stan and Jack (Reg Varney and Bob Grant) were forever chasing 'birds', while Stan's sister Olive (Anna Karen) would periodically suggest connubial relations with her supremely uninterested husband Arthur (Michael Robbins). With Mildred Roper facing precisely the same predicament with her husband George in *Man About the House*, it's a wonder that an entire generation didn't grow up thinking that the marital condition in middle age is all about nymphomaniac wives and husbands with any sex drive they might once have had shrivelled to nothingness.

Moreover, it was Anna Karen's unfortunate fate as Olive to remain synonymous with ugliness for more than three decades after the Luxton and District depot closed its doors for the last time: up and down the country even now there are men who will still venture the observation of a plain, rather fat, owlish-looking woman that 'she's a ringer for Olive from *On the Buses*'. And this despite the rumour at KGV circa 1974 that Anna Karen was in real life a highly attractive former model (although unlike the rumours that John Inman was married with three kids and Clint Eastwood, in the argot of the time, a raving woofter, this one had some roots in reality: Karen, who rather exotically hailed from South Africa rather than south London, had indeed been a burlesque dancer in her youth).

Unlike its treatment of *Dad's Army*, the passage of time has not been kind to *On the Buses*. It's still possible to catch old episodes if you scroll for long enough through the satellite channels, but it's a bit of a trial to sit through one from beginning to end. That's unless you're a certain Paul Harrison, who has posted on the internet his enduring devotion to *On the Buses* not on account of the comedy, but on account of the buses:

> It is a well-known fact that *On the Buses* was filmed at London Wood Green, depot of the Eastern National Omnibus Company. From this depot, every day, the 251 service to Southend would operate via the town of Rayleigh and right past my door. These buses were Bristol FLF-type Lodekkas fitted with 70-seat bodies built by Eastern Coachworks of Lowestoft. Those used in *On the Buses* were delivered to ENOC in 1967/68 and fitted with semi-automatic

transmission and Gardener 6LX 10,225cc diesel engines. I remember travelling on vehicles used in the series during the run. For example, AEV 811F (fleet number 2917) was a real favourite, and a frequent runner on the 251. One week AEV was missing for two days; it was being used for filming!

There's really nothing I can add to that.

On the Buses, even though it got decent viewing figures, ran for seventy-four episodes and contributed a lasting synonym to the vernacular, is one of those sitcoms regularly cited by those who would counter the idea that the 1970s was some sort of golden age for television comedy. *Mind Your Language* is another, as is *Love Thy Neighbour* and all sorts of little-remembered series, including one so bad that even I at the age of fourteen realized it was rubbish, the execrable *Yus, My Dear*, a vehicle for the fomer boxer Arthur Mullard (a vehicle which some people wished, as Hilary Kingsley and Geoff Tibballs sweetly put it in their excellent book *Box of Delights: The Golden Years of Television*, had been an oncoming train). Mullard was a fixture on the Bob Monkhouse-hosted game show *Celebrity Squares*, and for a while was accorded the status of a national treasure, a status which just about survived even his notorious double-act with the veteran comic actress Hylda Baker on *Top of the Pops* in 1978, when they made a shambles of a spoof, not an easy task, of the *Grease* duet 'You're the One that I Want'. Yet after his death in 1995, Mullard's daughter Barbara claimed that he had sexually abused her for years and had driven her mother to commit suicide. His friends, she added, had not been conspicuously surprised by this revelation. So I don't feel too bad about panning *Yus, My Dear*.

On the positive side, it was also the decade which yielded *Fawlty Towers*, *Porridge*, *Rising Damp* and *The Good Life*, while *Dad's Army* and *Steptoe and Son* continued their form from the 1960s, and *The Likely Lads* spawned a sequel that was just as good as the original.

Whether or not this made the 1970s a golden age for sitcom will be debated forever, but it was by any standards a golden age for commitment to primetime comedy. Hardly any night of the week was without a primetime sitcom, and *Man About the House* bore not one but two spin-offs, *George and Mildred* and *Robin's Nest*. Even the Americans got in on the act, buying the format and turning it into *Three's Company*, a big hit on ABC in the late 1970s, which in turn gave birth to *The Ropers*, the US version of *George and Mildred*.

By now, knowing how very undiscerning I was during my teens, comedy-wise, you won't be surprised to learn that I greatly enjoyed *Robin's Nest*, in which Richard O'Sullivan's character, Robin Tripp, opened the eponymous restaurant with his live-in girlfriend Vicky, played by Tessa Wyatt.

Just cast another eye over that last sentence, by the way. Does it shock or horrify you? Do you feel moved to write to *The Times*? Or to petition your MP? In 1977 you might have done, because never before had two members of the opposite sex been shown living in sin, as it was then charmingly known. Not in anything so frivolous as a situation comedy, anyway. To portray Robin and Vicky not only sharing a roof but also sharing a bed, the writers Johnnie Mortimer and Brian Cooke had to get the prior approval of the Independent Broadcasting Authority – that same admirable organization, you'll recall, that a couple of years earlier had erased 'sexual intercourse is a poor substitute for masturbation' from the script of *The Naked Civil Servant*, replacing it with 'Wasn't it fun in the bath tonight?'

Had Mortimer and Cooke been denied permission, they would have had to engineer a quick wedding for Robin and Vicky, though in fact the sinners did get married in the second series, and by the end of series six they were the proud, if predictably harassed, parents of twins. The envelope might have been pushed, but it wasn't pushed that far: in 1977 an unmarried couple living together were still expected to tie the knot eventually, on television as in life.

21

Making Doughnuts Like Fanny's and Johnnie's: Food and Drink in the 1970s

Apart from the hot potato of cohabitation, the other theme in *Robin's Nest* was the hot potato itself or, at any rate, food. *Look-In* magazine, guilelessly assuming that somebody playing a chef must perforce be interested in cooking, ran an interview with Richard O'Sullivan in its issue of 18 June 1977. Asked whether he could cook in real life as he could in the series, he replied: 'Well, I can do roasts. I don't make sauces and stuff like that. I like simple, tasty foods best. Good fish and chips, curries, a good takeaway Chinese.' No, in other words, although *Look-In* did persuade him to part with his favourite recipe for Spaghetti Bolognaise, which went as follows: 1 medium onion, 1 oz dripping, 1 lb minced beef, 15 oz can of tomatoes, good pinch of dried basil, 8 oz spaghetti. Gordon Ramsay eat your heart out. Actually, he'd probably prefer to.

Anyway, food is worthy of a chapter of its own in any book about television in the 1970s, and particularly one written by me, because from the age of about twelve to the age of eighteen, when I was forced to negotiate the seven flights of stairs to my Parisian attic several times a day, I was what might uncharitably be called a tub of lard.

This I ascribe largely to hitting adolescence when I did, roughly coinciding with the introduction into the nation's shops – and more specifically into Holders' newsagents at the end of Lynton Road – of Curly-Wurlies and cans of strawberry Cresta. It was also something to do with being an only child. There being no other children with whom to sit down eating child-sized portions, I sat down with adults and ate adult-sized portions. Heinz spaghetti hoops on toast at half-past five, which constituted an evening meal for most of my friends, was not my idea of a proper feed. More often than not, I enjoyed a three-course meal with my parents at eight o'clock. And after my dad died, my mum, nobly intent on not letting standards slip, continued the ritual for just the two of us.

Compounding this, I was plain greedy. On weekdays my mother valiantly restrained herself in the production of my packed lunches – a cheese sandwich, a Thermos flask of tomato soup and an apple was standard fare – but this was no more successful than Mr Williams's later confiscation of the television, because once I got to school I would go to the shops to supplement my lunch with a cheese and onion pie, and then pester Neil Hunt into letting me have a chunk, if not all, of his mum's chocolate refrigerator cake. My mum didn't make chocolate refrigerator cake, although it wasn't because she was a poor cook. On the contrary, she was a terrific, imaginative cook, and our tiny pantry always contained things that nobody else's pantries or larders did: when we were about seventeen, my friend Pete Venables and I often used to wind up at my house after evenings at the pub, either discussing football or our mutual lack of success with the girls that we fancied. At some point during these sessions we would always get peckish, and I would make a quick snack for us both. Pete still remembers the night I offered him a stuffed vine leaf with his cheese sandwich. 'What the fuck is that?' I think he said. For Southport in 1979, it was a wholly reasonable response.

I can't imagine where my mum found stuffed vine leaves in 1979. Maybe there was a specialist Greek shop near the warehouse in Liverpool. I do remember that one corner of our lounge was a shrine to her weekly *Cordon Bleu* magazines which, thirty-plus years on, she still has, even though the fashion for hollowing out tomatoes and stuffing them with cream cheese has diminished somewhat, thank God.

When I was writing this book she sent me the first issue, just to prick my memory. It is undated but priced 4s/6d, so it must date from the late 1960s or early 1970s, before decimalisation. The front cover features a young woman in a vibrantly patterned orange, yellow and pink dress, looking not unlike Alison Steadman in *Abigail's Party*, and gazing at a plate of Chicken Veronique seemingly unsure whether to eat it or make love to it. On the back there are suggested menus for each day of the week. Saturday's suggested starter, before the Chicken Veronique, is Tomato Gervais, which should perhaps enjoy a twenty-first century revival, in honour of the man who gave us David Brent.

To make Tomato Gervais – more prosaically known as tomatoes stuffed with cream cheese – the *Cordon Bleu* tip was to sprinkle fresh chives on top, unless 'neither fresh chives nor the AFD (accelerated freeze-dried) ones are available'. Imagine that, a world in which chives might not be available. It was also advised that the cheese mixture should be softened with two or three tablespoons of double cream 'or the top of the milk'. Along with white dog turds, the 'top of the milk' is a phenomenon that enjoyed its heyday in the 1970s, and has vanished from our lives, which seems to me a crying shame, not that there's any point crying over the top of the milk, of course.

I can still recall the Tomato Gervais being placed with a flourish in front of my dad and me, almost certainly on a Saturday evening – precisely as recommended by *Cordon Bleu*, although more because a weekday evening after a hard day's graft packing bras was no time for my mum to be stuffing a tomato.

About once every couple of months, she would get home from a day in the warehouse so exhausted that she couldn't face cooking, and so my dad would take us out for dinner at The Boulevard at the northern end of Lord Street. She was probably no less exhausted on all the other nights, but The Boulevard was a strictly limited treat. As a consequence, what a treat it was! In my Letts diary there is the following entry for Thursday 6 February 1975: 'Woke up. Had breakfast. [It never occurred to me that these two activities, waking up and having breakfast, could be safely assumed and did not have to be faithfully recorded.] Went to school on train. Got to school. Not friends with Andy. Had lessons. Made up with Andy. Packed lunch was squashed. Lessons. Platford was off. Lost keys somewhere between English and chemistry. Went home on bus. Went to Heppy's. Mum and dad came home at 6.30. Mum tired, so went to Boulevard. Missed *Persuaders* but didn't mind that much. Brill meal!!!! Went to bed at 9.45.'

That I was reasonably happy to forsake *The Persuaders* – one of my favourite shows, starring Roger Moore and Tony Curtis as amateur sleuths Lord Brett Sinclair and Danny Wilde, shows how inexpressibly devoted I was to The Boulevard. I'm not the only one with 1970s memories entwining *The Persuaders* with eating, by the way. In his book *Eating for England*, the food writer Nigel Slater recalls chocolate bars from that era that are now extinct, such as the Golden Cup, the Texan bar, the Aztec bar, and the Summit bar. 'I have yet to meet anyone else who can remember this little bar of cherry nougat coated in milk chocolate,' he writes of the Summit bar. 'I am unsure whether it was Cadbury's, Fry's or Mackintosh's (no-one will actually admit to it), but it really did exist, if only for a moment. Its short life was around the time we were glued to our screens watching Danny Wilde and Brett Sinclair driving around Monaco as *The Persuaders*.'

On that particular Thursday night, though, I managed to unglue myself. With a visit to The Boulevard as the alternative, I didn't mind going into school the next morning and not being able to discuss how Wilde and Sinclair had outwitted the international jewel thieves. Last time I looked, incidentally, The Boulevard was a bingo hall. Most of the places that I revered as a child have gone, including all three cinemas on Lord Street: the ABC, Palace and Odeon. But of them all, The Boulevard was the most magical.

That was where I first encountered the avocado pear, possibly on that very evening in February 1975, although had it been so, I'm sure I would have diarized the encounter. It was always an avocado pear, incidentally, never just an avocado. We said things in full in the 1970s. Continental quilts, balaclava helmets, avocado pears, all loomed large in the vocabulary of the lower middle classes.

The avocado pear at The Boulevard was halved and came, as a starter, in a bespoke white avocado pear dish, which seemed to me to be the epitome of sophistication. In the shallow cavity where the pip had been was a small pool of French dressing, and when I mashed this up with the flesh of the avocado pear I thought it the most delicious thing I had ever eaten.

Sometimes, just to ring the changes every six months or so, we went to the Fox and Goose instead. This was a Berni Inn, replete with red velour seats and Irish coffees that appeared to be served in the same large glasses in which the prawn cocktails had earlier appeared. I always had haddock and chips at the Fox and Goose. It cost £1.25 and came on a kind of oblong plate that was big, but not big enough to accommodate the heavily battered haddock. Maybe the intervening years have distorted the facts but, as I recall it, I have seen smaller whales than those haddocks, although I wonder now how much of them was fish, and how much was batter?

Nigel Slater, who is three or four years older than me, writes evocatively about the 1970s Berni experience in *Eating for England*. 'There was something distinctly glamorous about the Berni Inn, with its mock Tudor beams, smell of grilled steak and plaice, and whiff of lager-and-lime.' For a starter he always chose melon, cut into a boat with an orange sail and a maraschino cherry, followed by steak garni, medium rare. 'Steak garni always sounded so much more exotic than plain steak,' Slater recalls, 'despite the fact that the "garni" was actually only half a tomato and a bit of cress.'

An episode in the first series of *Life on Mars* tapped into the memories we all have, those of us of the right vintage, of Berni Inns in the 1970s. The time-travelling Sam Tyler took his boss, the Jack Regan doppelgänger DCI Gene Hunt, out for a curry, a relative novelty in Manchester in 1973. 'When I said different,' muttered Hunt, 'I meant maybe a Berni Inn.'

We never went out for curries, either. I don't remember there being a single Indian restaurant in 1970s Southport, and there were only a couple of Chinese restaurants. According to Christina Hardyment's book *Slice of Life: The British Way of Eating Since 1945*, the real proliferation in Indian and Chinese restaurants came in the 1980s; in 1950 there were only six Indian restaurants in Britain, and still only 2,000 by 1970.

As for the town's Chinese restaurants, maybe we avoided them because of the rise of what my father called yobbery. In his novel *Sour Sweet*, Timothy Mo recalls the 'strange and widespread habit' among English customers in Chinese restaurants in those years 'of not paying bills, a practice so prevalent as to arouse suspicion that it was a national sport. Loud and rowdy behaviour was more comprehensible, including fencing with chopsticks and wearing inverted rice bowls on the head like brittle skullcaps, writing odd things on the lavatory walls, and mixing the food on their plates in a disgusting way before putting soy on everything.' My parents wouldn't have liked that sort of behaviour at all.

In 1982, this 'new' ethnic cuisine was given TV exposure for the first time, in *Madhur Jaffrey's Indian Cookery*, an eight-part series which, to the ill-concealed surprise of more than one BBC executive, got excellent ratings. But by then it was Delia Smith who had inherited from Fanny Cradock the mantle of Britain's favourite TV cook, which Cradock had handed to her, quite unwittingly, with her reprehensible behaviour on Esther Rantzen's show *The Big Time* in 1976, when she was witheringly patronizing to a farmer's wife given the chance to cook for an ex-Prime Minister. In its way this was just as bad, and at least as career-damaging, as Ron Atkinson's ill-timed and ill-chosen comments years later about Marcel Desailly.

Before then, Cradock and her husband Johnnie were favourites of mine, if only because their existence as the nation's best-known cookery-show hosts – at a time, don't forget, when there were hardly any cookery shows to host – enabled me (and thousands of other schoolboys) to crack the gag about making our doughnuts turn out like Fanny's and Johnnie's.

Nor was it every TV cook who could inspire an entire TV drama. In October 2006 her story was dramatized on BBC4 and called *Fear of Fanny*, starring Julia Davis in the title role, with Mark Gatiss of *The League of Gentlemen* as poor, henpecked Johnnie. *Fear of Fanny*, which included the episode from *The Big Time* that cooked Cradock's goose, was reviewed in the *Guardian* by the doyenne of TV critics, the venerable Nancy Banks-Smith.

'In 1976 the long-threatened disaster arrived,' Banks-Smith wrote.

The Big Time was a programme in which amateurs tried to be professional. Gwen Troake, a rosy, roly farmer's wife from Devon, had won the chance to cook for the prime minister, Edward Heath. It was not a prize to set the blood pounding but, in a praiseworthy attempt to appeal to his nautical bent, she planned to serve a seafood platter, roast duck and coffee cream ('I thought with the

rum it would be very nautical'). Fanny's comments, though liber-
ally peppered with darlings, were devastating: 'You could kill pigs
with that menu. Do you have any friends in Devon, dear? Living?'
And that was the end of her TV career but, curiously, she was well
ahead of her time. Nowadays TV judges reduce defenceless members of the public to tears on a regular basis.

Nancy Banks-Smith was right. Cradock's withering, snobbery-
fuelled assault on poor Gwen Troake was pretty tame by the
standards of modern-day humiliation on TV, yet at the time she was
deemed to have behaved with monstrous condescension, and indignant viewers jammed the BBC's phone lines, calling for her head on
a platter, perhaps with an apple in her mouth.

It was duly served up. She was never asked to appear on television
again and died, alone and unmourned, in a Sussex nursing home
shortly after Christmas Day 1994, aged eighty-five. Her subsequent
obituaries told quite a story. She had been married four times, twice
bigamously, and had abandoned the sons of her first two marriages.
Moreover, although she hooked up with Johnnie Cradock in 1939,
they did not actually marry until 7 May 1977 – another, rather unexpected, connection with *Robin's Nest*. It was one thing for Vicky and
Robin to be cohabiting out of wedlock, but honestly, who'd have
thought it of Fanny and Johnnie?

I always watched Fanny Cradock with a kind of appalled fascination. She was like no woman I had ever come into contact with, and
for that I gave thanks. Nor, in truth, was she such a good cook, which
I think I sensed even at the time. I had far more admiration for the
ever-cheerful Graham Kerr, who concluded his show, *The Galloping
Gourmet*, by diving into the front row of the audience and dragging
someone on to the stage to taste what he had just created. God, how
I wanted to be that person.

The other noteworthy thing about Kerr was his gender. Outside restaurant kitchens, men didn't cook in the 1970s, at least not the men I knew. I can't remember ever seeing my dad in our kitchen at 58 Lynton Road, although that was partly because it was only about three feet square, and there was scarcely room for anyone except my mum, who was in there every evening except on the rare occasions we went to The Boulevard or the Fox and Goose (to which, rather racily, and with a familiarity belying our infrequency as customers, we all referred as 'the Fox').

It was Graham Kerr, not my dad, who showed me that it was acceptable, indeed admirable, for men to cook. Not that I cooked what he did, which was probably just as well given my already expanding waistline, because practically everything he made called for a truckload of clarified butter. But by the age of ten I could at least make a decent omelette. Some degree of proficiency in the kitchen was useful because in the terminology of the time I was a latchkey kid, letting myself in (except when I lost my keys between English and chemistry) when I got home from school because both parents were working.

My own kids have never had that experience and, partly as a consequence, have never shown all that much interest in the rudiments of cooking: after all, there is always a parent on hand to whizz up something nice. In some ways I think that's a shame, just as I regret the fact that a family meal out is not the treat for them that it was for me and indeed, across the Pennines, for Jane, for whom a Saturday-afternoon tea at Cole Brothers department store in Sheffield was the highlight of the week, if not the month.

Maybe, paradoxically given the food revolution that has convulsed Britain since the Black Forest gâteau years, there simply aren't as many treats to be had these days. The Cole Brothers cafe, just like the Marshall & Snelgrove cafe in Southport to which I was sometimes taken, had silver teapots, silver milk jugs and silver sugar bowls wielded by waitresses in black frilly aprons, and Jane tells me that as a little girl she used to walk backwards out of the room because she was desperate to see the waitress's response on discovering her tip. For our children, the whole business of going out to eat en famille is taken utterly for granted.

Jane's equivalent of The Boulevard was a place called The Swiss Cottage just off the A1 near Pontefract, a venue so revered by her and her older sister Jackie that neither dreamt of crossing the threshold unless they were wearing their best maxi-skirts. Jane's mum also reminded her recently that a visit to the restaurant at the new Trust House Forte service station on the M1 was considered a rather special family outing. Once or twice, when they went for a Sunday-afternoon drive to Clumber Park in Nottinghamshire, both girls had to take a change of clothing in case they stopped to eat at Woodall services on the way home.

Jane remembers *The Galloping Gourmet* too, and she too yearned to be the person called up by Kerr to share his culinary creation. Clearly, our partnership was meant to be. She also remembers, a year or two before she met me, inviting some friends to her flat in north London for dinner one evening, and one of them, Ian, seeing all her vegetables and herbs already chopped and assembled in little dishes waiting to be cooked. 'Very *Galloping Gourmet*,' he said.

Like making a crack about the Milk Tray Man, or the Slimcea Girl, or Bernie the Bolt, or saying 'give us a twirl', a reference to *The Galloping Gourmet* is a bonding exercise between two people of roughly similar age, and it is my possibly biased belief that the 1970s delivered more of these terms of reference than any other decade. At any rate, what will my children's bonding exercises be in 2038? I suppose one of them might be 'Keeeeep dancing!' as uttered thirty years earlier by Bruce Forsyth on *Strictly Come Dancing*, which rather impressively will mean Forsyth's catchphrases spanning almost a century if you think that while my generation thinks back to 1975 and remembers 'Give us a twirl' and 'Nice to see you, to see you nice', and 'Good game, good game', and 'All right, my love', my parents' generation in 1975 had warm memories of him saying 'I'm in charge!' while operating the Beat the Clock on *Sunday Night at the London Palladium* in 1958. Dear old Brucie. Didn't he do well?

As for *The Galloping Gourmet*, Ian got it right with his reference in Jane's flat, because Kerr too used to have all his ingredients already prepared and in little dishes, very unlike Jamie Oliver with his bish-bosh chopping and slicing and trimming and flattening. On the other hand, if Jamie has a televisual antecedent it is surely Kerr rather than Cradock, much as I'd like to give the old moo a spin in her grave by suggesting that she paved the way for such an ineffably common young man.

Kerr, by the way, is often wrongly described as a Kiwi, or Canadian, or Australian. He had connections with all those countries but he was born and grew up in England, moving to New Zealand in 1958. There he somehow got himself appointed chief cooking adviser to the Royal New Zealand Air Force, but was then given a posting in Australia, where someone spotted his telegenic qualities and gave him a TV programme called – I love this – *Eggs with Flight Lieutenant Kerr*. In 1969 the nomadic Kerr moved with his wife Treena to Canada and that's where *The Galloping Gourmet*, produced by Treena, was conceived. It didn't last long, alas, because the Kerrs were involved in a nasty car crash which left him temporarily paralysed. But he recovered, and I'm pleased to report that, at the time of writing, he is alive and well and still cooking professionally, although the clarified butter has taken a back seat since 1986, when Treena suffered a heart attack. Graham Kerr, the man who on an edition of *The Galloping Gourmet* once gave us poached eggs in Chartreuse sauce, became a standard-bearer for a healthy diet. He is an eggs-in-Chartreuse-sauce poacher turned gamekeeper.

At the end of the day – or at the end of this chapter, anyway – the striking thing about food programmes in the 1970s was how thin they were on the ground. I have before me a battered edition of *TV Times* covering the ITV schedules from 10–16 November 1974 (bizarrely, *TV Times* could not carry the BBC schedules, nor could *Radio Times* cover ITV, which suited my friend Jonny's parents and all those who refused to let the fiendish commercial channel into their homes, but was a hellish nuisance for the rest of us) and on ITV that week there was not a single programme that had anything to do with food.

It wasn't as though we weren't interested. The magazine has plenty of adverts for food (Green Giant Sweetcorn Niblets – 'that sun-ripened splash of gold adds a touch of excitement to any family meal') and kitchen equipment (the Moulinex Mixer 'makes light work of tangy lemon meringue pie ... only £5.60'). Moreover, on the 'Dear Katie ...' page at the back of that edition of *TV Times*, at the top of which there is a photograph of agony aunt and dedicated problem-solver Katie Boyle striking a strangely sensual pose with a pen resting decorously between her lips, a Mrs Alderson from Appleby in Westmorland (a county that has now gone the way of poached eggs in Chartreuse sauce, consigned to the dustbin of history) writes plaintively: 'There is such a multitude of additives in our food, I am interested to know what hydrolized protein, monosodium glutamate and emulsifier are – especially emulsifier, as it appears in almost everything.'

To which Katie replies:

I, too, have often wondered what these additives are, so I think lots of people will be interested to know that hydrolized protein is a processed natural protein used to give flavour – Marmite or Yeastrel, for instance. Monosodium glutamate is made from soya beans, and the Chinese have used it for 300 years or so. Emulsifier is any substance that can be beaten up with oil and change the taste from oily to creamy – in a mayonnaise made with oil and egg yolk, the egg yolk is the emulsifier. Now here's another additive – £5 to add to your purse for the most interesting Letter of the Week.

Bravo, Mrs Alderson! Although, had the choice been mine, the *TV Times* Letter of the Week for 10–16 November 1974 would have gone to Mrs D.P. Wilson from Cardiff, who appealed to Katie Boyle for help with the following heart-rending problem: 'Since I became a widow, one of my difficulties is that I simply cannot do up or undo my zip. I have a Victorian button hook and a back-scratcher, but, alas, my only remedy to date is to go out into the street and wait for a lady to come along and unzip me.'

I do hope she's not still waiting.

22

'Greetings, Grapple Fans': Wrestling From Bletchley, and Brent Town Hall

There is no obvious segue from a chapter about food to a chapter on sport, except that the 1.30 race at Doncaster on Saturday 10 November 1974, advertised in that same copy of *TV Times*, was the two-mile, four-furlong Berni Inns Chase. It was the first race of that afternoon's ITV Seven, which my father watched, as usual, while I played football on the rec with my Lynton Road friends Jez and Chris Sykes, and John Hepworth. That evening I was permitted, according to my 1974 Letts Schoolboy Diary, to stay up to watch *Kung Fu*. I never quite knew what was going on in *Kung Fu*, but I loved it all the same. It starred David Carradine as a Chinese-American Buddhist monk called Caine, a drifter and martial arts specialist who abhorred the use of violence unless it was absolutely necessary, which of course it was every week, albeit in slow-motion.

That same month, coincidentally, a wrestler called Kung Fu had appeared for the first time on *World of Sport*, in the usual 4 p.m. wrestling slot which continued until Dickie Davies started bringing us the football results at ten to five. Behind his mask and exotic name, Kung Fu was plain Eddie Hamill from Belfast, who had adopted the pseudonym in homage not to Carradine, I later discovered, but to a Korean martial arts expert he'd met a few years earlier in Turkey. Whatever, a man who worked by day as a lifeguard in Rhyl, as Hamill did, needed a bit of mystery, and the oriental name provided it. Kung Fu was one of my favourite wrestlers, just behind the flamboyant ponytailed baddie Jackie Pallo, and the wrestling was my favourite part of *World of Sport*, with the exception of *On the Ball*, the football preview presented by the ever-genial Brian Moore and often featuring the never-genial Brian Clough. In the 1970s, football, like television, was full of Brians.

That Saturday I got in from the rec as usual in time to watch the wrestling. My diary doesn't record whether my dad was in a good mood or a bad mood. It depended on how many winners he'd picked in the ITV Seven and it was usually the latter. That day's wrestling, the *TV Times* tells me, came from Bletchley and featured Ricki Starr, Zoltan Bocsik and Leon Fortuna. It was a pretty unremarkable bill, featuring none of the characters I wanted to see after commentator Kent Walton had delivered his familiar salutation: 'Greetings, grapple fans!' and before he delivered his standard farewell, 'Have a good week, till next week.' There was no Kung Fu, no Mick McManus, no Les Kellett, no Big Daddy, no Adrian Street, no Kendo Nagasaki, no Jackie Pallo. Those of us who come from the 1970s mutter these names with nearly as much reverence as schoolboys of the 1950s talk about Denis Compton and Len Hutton, or Tom Finney and Stanley Matthews.

Pallo, who sometimes pretended to bite his opponent if he was otherwise pinned to the canvas, was the one I loved to hate no less than did the brolly-wielding grannies at ringside. I was gratified to discover years later that he had been less of a faker than many of his contemporaries, and that when blood was called for to make a headbutt look real, he at least had the decency to bite his own lip; many of the others like to produce 'the claret' by nicking themselves with a concealed razor blade.

In February 2006, alas, Pallo found himself in a half-nelson from which there was no escape, not even by pretending to bite. It was the Big C that got him, an opponent even more formidable than Big Daddy. And with time-travelling to the 1970s conveniently in vogue at that time thanks to *Life on Mars*, many of us read his obituaries and were propelled directly back to Saturday tea-times in front of a gas fire three decades earlier. For some of us, Jackie Pallo was a name as powerfully evocative of the kipper-tie decade as Lord Lucan, Red Rum and Gilbert O'Sullivan.

In truth, Pallo, born in 1926, was strutting round the wrestling rings of England long before the 1970s, and long before *World of Sport*. But it was *World of Sport*, the programme that began in 1965 as ITV's rival to *Grandstand*, which made him a star. For television snobs like Jonny Cook's dad, the fact that the commercial channel showcased such downmarket fare as wrestling merely emphasized the intrinsic superiority of the BBC. In the *Observer*, Clive James asked:

What is it about Dickie Davies that makes you feel less wretched about [the *Grandstand* presenter] Frank Bough? By any rational standards, Frank ought to be definitively awful: the whole time that his stupefying ebullience is sending you to sleep, his RANDOM use of emphasis is JERKing you awake. Dickie doesn't do any of that. On the contrary, he speaks with exactly the same degree of measured excitement about every sporting event that turns up on a Saturday afternoon anywhere in the world. Perhaps that's the trouble. Understandably keen about the World Cup, Dickie Davies folds his hands, leans forward and smiles at you from under his moustache. Equally keen about the World Target Clown Diving Championships, he folds his hands, leans forward, and smiles at you from under his moustache.

Almost every week from 1968, when he took over from Eamonn Andrews as *World of Sport*'s main presenter, Davies folded his hands, leant forward, smiled at us from under his moustache, and introduced the wrestling from Brent Town Hall, Wolverhampton Civic Hall or some other salubrious venue. It later transpired that his measured excitement on the screen was as much an act as Pallo's villainy in the ring, and that he didn't rate wrestling one bit. When Davies heard that Pallo had passed on, he rather wittily opined that it was an unprecedented example of Pallo not faking it.

Yet Davies and his paymasters recognized the value of wrestling to ITV. Slowly but surely, it began to exert a vicelike grip on the nation that was worthy of Pallo himself. Everyone knew that it bore almost no kinship to the noble art of wrestling as depicted on ancient Greek urns, but by the 1970s we were hooked, even though it was strongly rumoured even then that Pallo's bouts with his arch-enemy Mick McManus were no less choreographed than Pan's People's moves on *Top of the Pops*. When Pallo wrote his autobiography, in 1985, we knew it for sure. The book was called *You Grunt, I'll Groan*. But even then there were impressionable schoolboys and gullible grannies who refused to believe that a Boston Crab was anything other than the most painful physical predicament known to man. And among the gullible grannies was the Queen Mother, no less, said to be a particularly avid fan. So too was Margaret Thatcher.

Much of the credit for wrestling's popularity in the 1970s belonged to an Englishman, born Kenneth Beckett, who served with a Canadian squadron during the Second World War, cultivated a Canadian accent, and changed his name to the racier Kent Walton.

Cleverly recognizing that he needed a niche if he was to succeed in sports broadcasting, Walton became the Voice of Wrestling in the same way that Dan Maskell was the Voice of Tennis and Eddie Waring the Voice of Rugby League. And don't forget how nice it was to have cast-iron certainties in the worst decade of industrial strife since the 1920s. That ritual sign-off 'Have a good week . . . till next week' was a sign of stability even if the week ahead was a three-day one. As for the belief that he was Canadian, it followed him to his grave: when Walton died in 2003, aged eighty-six, one obituary bracketed him with his 'compatriots' Bernard Braden and Hughie Green as having made an impact on British television.

It was ironic that Walton should have encouraged such artifice, because even though he knew better than almost anyone that the Terrible Turk and the Masked Madagascan both came from Rochdale, he always insisted that wrestling was a proper sport and not a circus act. 'Let's see if we can get a close-up of those red eyes, if you're lucky enough to be watching on a colour set,' he used to say of the masked Nagasaki, sounding very much as though the prospect excited him enormously.

In all this he was helped by the wrestlers themselves, Pallo notable as one of the most convincing among them. The snarling might have been fake, but the pain looked real. Pallo, in fact, once ended up in Walton's lap at ringside, having been 'hurled' over the ropes in front of the usual crowd of histrionic pensioners baying for blood. Many of the stars invented little idiosyncrasies and nurtured them devotedly. McManus used to pretend that his Achilles heel was his ears, not such an improbable image when you consider the extraordinary contortions into which these beefy men got themselves, and each other. 'Not the ears, not the ears,' he would cry. For his part, Pallo used to hate it when anyone grabbed his ponytail, which in those days was a rather more outré hairstyle than it might be considered now.

Some of them had stranger ring personas than others. Another favourite of mine, for reasons that I'd rather not try to analyse here, was the peroxided and mincingly camp Welshman Adrian Street. In reality, almost inevitably, he was emphatically heterosexual, and when I last heard of him he was running the splendidly named Bonecrusher Academy, a wrestling school near Pensacola in Florida. Speaking of wrestling in America, incidentally, their Worldwide Wrestling Federation achieves the impossible by making our own version, as championed for over twenty years by *World of Sport*, look understated and very nearly refined. Yet it died a sudden death in December 1988 when Greg Dyke, the controller of ITV Sport, decided that it presented the wrong image of the channel to advertisers. Like Benny Hill a year later, it no longer suited the times. All the same, what times they were.

In all honesty, they were not unequivocally good times, not with almost continual industrial unrest, relentlessly rising unemployment figures, and *Yus, My Dear* on television. Maybe it was better to be a child in the 1970s than a grown-up, with only a slow puncture in the Spacehopper to worry about, not a burdensome mortgage or a precarious job. There was certainly something childlike about the pantomime-style wrestling on *World of Sport*, yet some really serious grown-ups liked it, among them the Home Secretary Roy Jenkins, who was once spotted in the audience at a Royal Albert Hall wrestling night, applauding Giant Haystacks.

Among the royal family it wasn't only the Queen Mother who loved it, but also the Queen herself. Simon Garfield, in his book *The Wrestling: The Hilarious True Story of Britain's Last Great Superheroes*, includes the following segment from the diaries of one of Roy Jenkins's colleagues, Labour Cabinet Minister Richard Crossman:

At midday I had to shoot off to Buckingham Palace for the first of our new-style Privy Councils. The Queen had agreed that after the formalities we should withdraw to the Caernarvon Room next door and have drinks with her. The Queen was in tremendous form. After the Council, when the drinks were circulating, she began to describe to me a television programme she had seen yesterday of a wrestling match . . . An all-in wrestler had been thrown out over the ropes, landed on his feet, and after writhing in agony had suddenly shot back into the ring, seized his opponent and forced him to resign. She said what tremendous fun that kind of all-in wrestling was. 'Do you want a Royal Charter for them?' I asked. And she said, 'No, not yet.' It was interesting to hear what a vivid description she gave of the whole scene, writhing herself, twisting and turning, completely relaxed. It was quite an eye-opener to see how she enjoyed it.

Given her passion for horse-racing as well, the Queen must have loved *World of Sport*, although she probably took the corgis for a walk during the scrambling from Lydden in Kent, or the badminton from Coventry, or whatever filled the hour or so between the ITV Seven and the wrestling. Unless of course she switched over to watch Eddie Waring raising his trilby before Castleford played St Helens on *Grandstand*. 'Philiiiip, the rugby league's on!' 'Oh, spiffing!' I think that's a perfectly plausible exchange.

23

Harvey Smith on Sanyo Music Centre, *Match of the Day* and Barry Stoller, and Other Great Sporting Combinations

It is odd, in a way, that my generation thinks back to televised sport in the 1970s with such unbridled affection, for really there was very little of it, certainly when compared with today. It seems perverse to suggest that Rupert Murdoch has devalued sport, with three Sky channels offering non-stop coverage, not to mention Eurosport, Setanta etc., but as any economic historian would tell you of the global fiscal chaos in the 1970s, an excess of something leads inexorably to its devaluation. When I was the age my children are now, the only regular television programmes devoted to sport were *World of Sport* and *Grandstand* – one of which you had to choose over the other because they were on at the same time – plus *Match of the Day* on a Saturday night, ITV's *The Big Match* on a Sunday afternoon, and

Sportsnight on a Wednesday evening. Actually, in the north-west of England we also had *Kick-Off* early on a Friday evening, a preview of the weekend football presented by Elton Welsby, a suave fellow with dark ringlets who would have looked like a matinee idol had he not been only 3ft 8ins tall, or so it seemed when my friends and I spotted him in the flesh outside Goodison Park one Saturday afternoon.

ITV's other early evening programme in the north-west, I should add, was *Granada Reports*, presented by Bob Greaves and Tony Wilson. To me Wilson was just a TV presenter. I didn't know until years later that he was also the founder of Manchester's legendary Hacienda nightclub and a founder of Factory Records, and consequently one of the most influential movers and shakers in the British record industry. It still seems bizarre to me that while all this moving and shaking was going on he was also presenting *Granada Reports*, and even more bizarre that he was permitted to do so while advertising his hatred of the Bay City Rollers with an 'I Hate the Rollers' badge on his lapel. We never saw Angela Rippon wearing an 'I Hate Boney M' badge.

Wilson's opposite number on the BBC was the perma-tanned Stuart Hall, who presented the regional news programme *Look North* and, from the early 1970s, *It's a Knockout*. I loved *It's a Knockout*, and felt a kind of proprietorial pride in the fact that the north-west's own Stuart Hall, with none other than Eddie Waring, was the front man. On the couple of occasions it was transmitted from Southport's open-air bathing lake (which I never visited without getting a verruca, but that's by the by), I sat down in front of the telly breathless with excitement, in the hope that I might recognize members of my home-town team. I never did, of course. I wouldn't have been able to identify my own mother behind a 12ft inflatable pirate suit.

Efforts have been made down the years to resurrect *It's a Knockout*, not least, and to the embarrassment of the entire nation, by Prince Edward in 1987. With the stark exception of that spectacularly misconceived *It's a Royal Knockout*, I'm not sure why it's not still going. I'm sure my kids would enjoy it. But maybe they wouldn't. Maybe the daft challenges would look downright anaemic compared with soap actors and footballers' wives being made to crawl through snake pits on *I'm a Celebrity, Get Me Out of Here!*, which is really just *It's a Knockout* for a fame-obsessed age.

Of all the outlandish games on *It's a Knockout*, and its international stablemate *Jeux Sans Frontières*, I can remember only the one in which ungainly 12ft pirates had to walk the plank while dodging jets of water fired by the opposition, their task being to throw vast pieces-of-eight into a treasure chest suspended from a palm tree. I'm not ashamed – well, maybe just a little ashamed – to say that I thought this was hilarious. So did my dad, until he expired. And so did Stuart Hall, who looked every week as though he too might expire, following a seizure brought on by too much mirth. He sometimes had to put his arm round the referee, Arthur Ellis, seemingly as a means of standing up.

Ellis was a former international football referee, but it was still stretching a point to call *It's a Knockout* sport. In retrospect, just as bizarre as Tony Wilson presenting a news programme wearing an 'I Hate the Rollers' badge was that *Sportsnight*, presented by either David Coleman or Harry Carpenter, offered the nation its only midweek opportunity to watch proper sport. I exclude *The Superstars*, in which different sportsmen competed in disciplines other than their own, because, riveted though I was by it, and hugely as I enjoyed the spectacle of Kevin Keegan falling off his bike and sliding on his back across a cinder track, I realized that it was essentially a contrivance.

Besides, *The Superstars* went out on Friday evenings, and was effectively part of the weekend. All there was through the week for sports nuts was *Sportsnight*, and as a result I watched whatever was on, thus forming an attachment even to sports that did not really interest me, such as show-jumping, which featured on *Sportsnight* with a persistence that eventually wore me down. I started to enjoy it, and the names of the show-jumpers of that era, the likes of the Schockemöhle brothers Paul and Alwin, loom as large in my memory as the quintessential 1970s footballers Frank Worthington, Alan Hudson and Stan Bowles. So do even the names of their horses, such as Penwood Forge Mill, ridden by Paddy McMahon, and Harvey Smith's mount Sanyo Music Centre, whose curious name bemused Clive James in the *Observer* as much as the rest of us. 'You might have imagined that Harvey was mounted on a piece of stereo equipment,' he wrote, 'but Sanyo Music Centre, though it has a leg in each corner like certain types of radiogram, is in fact a living creature with no provision for the electronic reproduction of sound.'

In the 1970s I didn't know much about Clive James apart from his brilliant television column every Sunday, but that was enough. To earn a living from watching the telly seemed to me an extraordinarily neat trick, and by the end of the decade it was one I vaguely hoped to emulate at some point in my own life. It was ironic, given that my mother had earlier identified television as the one factor likely to scupper my exam results, that reading James's sparkling prose on television every week had kindled the desire to make some sort of a career out of writing. But it had, making me focus a little harder on my English literature A-level course.

One of my set texts on that course was *The Go-Between* by L.P. Hartley, which I studied under the patient tutelage of my form tutor T.B. Johnson – an English teacher whose study looked onto the area where my friends and I played football every lunchtime, and who invariably took afternoon registration with at least one muddy imprint of a football on the window behind him.

I haven't read *The Go-Between* since I was eighteen, but I have often quoted its famous opening line – 'The past is a foreign country; they do things differently there' – and I do so again here.

T.B. Johnson is no longer around to disapprove of my applying this splendid line to football, a game he heartily disliked largely on account of it posing a daily threat to his study window, and it fits perfectly in the case of *The Big Match*, which exemplifies how truly foreign the past can sometimes be. *The Big Match* was the 1970s equivalent of Sky's big Sunday match now, except that it featured merely the highlights of an encounter that had taken place the previous afternoon. How mad is that? Or at least, how mad was I – and every other football enthusiast in the country – for waiting, sometimes with feverish anticipation if our own team was involved, to watch a match twenty-four hours after it had taken place?

I suppose I could have employed the tactic of trying not to find out the result, which in a world without text messages might have been achievable. That's what Terry and Bob did in a celebrated episode of *Whatever Happened to the Likely Lads?*, 'No Hiding Place', transmitted on Tuesday 20 February 1973. Accepting a £10 bet that they could not go a whole day without discovering the result of an England match, they eventually sat down to watch it, only to find that it had been postponed because of a waterlogged pitch. My schoolfriend Mozzer and I once had the same experience, staying up to watch the highlights of a Scotland international against Bulgaria, in which our hero, the Everton goalkeeper George Wood, was due to play. Mozzer came round to my house and we sat up until 11.35 p.m. to watch the highlights, then learnt that the match had been postponed because of fog.

Anyway, *Whatever Happened to the Likely Lads?* brings me inexorably to the subject of theme tunes, not yet explored at length in this book, but a far more evocative reminder of 1970s television than the printed word. Never mind scratch-and-sniff, if there were such a thing as scratch-and-listen technology, this book would be the complete package. None of us actually needs to watch old episodes of *Whatever Happened to the Likely Lads?* and *Bless This House* and *The*

Liver Birds; all we need is the theme music to propel us backwards through time. The theme music for *It's a Knockout*, I should add, was 'Bean Bag' by Herb Alpert and the Tijuana Brass. No wonder my dad enjoyed it. As discussed earlier in these pages, every dad in the 1970s had to have at least one Herb Alpert LP. It was decreed by an Act of Parliament.

I should also give a nod here to the late Ronnie Hazlehurst, who passed away in October 2007, aged seventy-nine, and whose obituaries recorded his genius for writing, arranging and conducting the music for dozens of TV comedies. He had a particular talent for fitting the musical theme to the comedic theme, for example by using a cash register in the music for *Are You Being Served?*, and Big Ben's chimes in the music for *Yes Minister*. He also rose splendidly to the occasion when told that a production had gone so over budget that there was hardly any money left for the music, as in the case of *Some Mothers Do 'Ave 'Em*, for which he used piccolos to sound out the programme title in Morse code. It takes a certain kind of genius to decide that piccolos playing a tune in Morse code might be just the ticket.

Hazlehurst it was, too, who came up with the theme to *The Likely Lads* in 1964, although the *Whatever Happened to the Likely Lads?* theme is arguably more memorable, the plaintive 'What Happened to You?', written by Ian La Frenais and Mike Hugg, formerly of Manfred Mann. I loved all these theme tunes, but it was sporting theme music that made my pulse race like nothing else, not least the opening credits of *World of Sport*, with the light aircraft trailing the programme title like those warnings over Cornish beaches to swim only between the flags. We tended to be a *World of Sport* rather than a *Grandstand* household only because of the ITV Seven, which didn't always please me, but yielded dividends on the marvellous day that the normally word-perfect Dickie Davies unaccountably did a Trevor McDonald and, trying to refer to cup soccer, by accident referred to 'cop succer'. And it wasn't the image of Theo Kojak with a lollipop in his mouth that made me laugh.

As for the music, I would have watched *World of Sport* and every other sporting programme on TV even if they had been introduced by Chopin's Funeral March, but of course they weren't: then, as now, producers of sports programmes were unerring in their selection of the most uplifting tunes available, exemplified best of all by Barry Stoller's *Match of the Day* theme (which dates from 1968, the year it replaced the original choice, Arnold Stock's 'Drum Majorette'), although the one that really got me going was the music at the start of the BBC's Test Match coverage, 'Soul Limbo' by Booker T. and the MGs (or Book a Table and the Maitre D's as one of their biggest fans, John Lennon, liked to refer to them).

I'm not sure that there is any piece of music that evokes my 1970s youth quite as powerfully as 'Soul Limbo', nor was there anything other than cricket that could reduce me to a prostrate position on the couch for five whole days, short of the BBC showing an entire series of *Alias Smith and Jones* back to back. It's odd in a way, because I consider myself just as much of a cricket enthusiast now as I was then, yet even if I didn't have all the duties of the bread-winning paterfamilias I have become I don't think I could now sit enraptured in front of the telly watching every ball of a five-day Test match. Yet in the summers of 1975 and 1976 in particular, when Ian Chappell's Australia and Clive Lloyd's West Indies toured England, it seemed as natural as breathing. Five whole summer days could pass with nothing – apart from seeing to the odd zit – to deflect me from the cricket.

Perhaps when I am a portly old grandad that time might come again, but I doubt it, and at the end of the day's play I certainly won't be tirelessly bowling a tennis ball at the garage door in the attempted manner of Mike Hendrick trying to dislodge Rick McCosker. It had to be at the end of play because nothing could get me vertical while the Test match was on, not even during the tea-break, when the

BBC's main cricket presenter Peter West, his pipe smoke practically curling out of the televison set into the room, would chat to some old-timer about his role in the infamous Australia v England Bodyline series of 1932/33.

All the Bodyline players have departed for the celestial pavilion now, of course, as has West himself, after a decent-enough knock of eighty-three. I remember him with particular affection because in 1987, after my brief and inglorious script-reading career, when I was trying to get a career in print journalism off the ground, I wrote to him requesting an interview.

I had trawled through a copy of *Who's Who*, and written to fifty famous people whose home addresses were listed. My brilliant scheme was to write up the interviews, then sell them to some publication, thereby creating a portfolio with which I could dazzle the editors of national newspapers who would fall over each other in the unseemly rush to hire me. Needless to say, it didn't quite work out like that, partly because hardly anyone replied. Nine out of fifty celebrities answered and of those nine, just four agreed to meet me. Jonathan Miller and Melvyn Bragg (may the gods bless and protect them and keep their hair luxuriant) were two; Brian Johnston and West were the others.

West had been the Barry Davies of his day, commentating on myriad sports for the BBC. Not a lot of people know, incidentally, that West, Davies and *The Big Match*'s Brian Moore all went to the same school, Cranbrook in Kent. Obviously the timetable there comprised double maths, history, RE, double commentary, physics. But he also presented *Come Dancing*, chaired numerous panel shows and, according to the obituaries in September 2003, finished second in a *News Chronicle* poll to find the television personality of 1953 (he was pipped by Benny Hill).

For me, he was above all the face of the BBC's cricket coverage, in which role he was roundly abused by the England fast bowler Bob

Willis in an interview after the famous Headingley Test of 1981. For some reason Willis remained furious with the media even after England had so memorably beaten the Australians, and West very publicly copped his anger. 'Come on, Bob, you've won a Test match, taken 8 for 43, can't we find a happier theme?' West eventually implored. It must have tickled him towards the end of his days to see Willis himself wielding a Sky Sports microphone, part of the media establishment he once held in such disdain.

By then I was no longer in touch with him, but we corresponded for a few years after our interview, which was published – oh, rhapsody! – in *Gloucestershire Life* magazine. I have a copy of his 1986 autobiography, *Flannelled Fool and Muddied Oaf*, in which he wrote, 'to Brian, may your ambitions be realised.' That they largely have been is down in some measure to him and his kindness. I hope he's happy up there in that celestial pavilion, still puffing on his pipe, and enjoying the company of so many other sports broadcasters who made their mark, on me at least, in the 1970s.

Another was Dan Maskell, the so-called Voice of Wimbledon, whose pared-down style of commentary, I was rather offended to find, once featured on an American TV show designed to take the piss out of funny foreigners. It's one thing taking the piss ourselves, out of the Japanese or indeed the Americans, but it came as a shock to find British TV on the receiving end. The object of the American audience's hilarity was a snatch of Maskell's commentary, or rather non-commentary, from the BBC's coverage of Wimbledon one year. As I recall it, an entire game passed without Maskell uttering a word, not even one of his 'Ooh I say!' or 'Peach of a volley!' exclamations. Then, after the last point, the umpire said, 'Game to Borg.' There was a pause, then Maskell grunted: 'So, game to Borg.' The audience cracked up.

Maskell, of course, belonged to that golden generation of sports commentators who understood that if nothing could be added to the picture, it was best to stay quiet. On the other hand, sometimes a commentator's excitement lifted a spectacle even if you could see precisely what was happening, and even if it was conveyed by vocal cords so pickled in claret and port and good Madeira that any semblance of animation had long since been drowned, as was the case in 1970 when the veteran golf commentator Henry Longhurst watched the American Doug Sanders, clad all in purple, stand over the short putt he required to win the Open Championship. 'This is what people dream about,' murmured Longhurst, 'that you've got this one with a left-hand borrow, downhill, on the last green at St Andrews, to win the Open.' Sanders missed it. 'Missed it,' said Longhurst. 'And there but for the grace of God . . .'

Old Henry Longhurst's commentary that day was pitched perfectly for the sporting occasion, and the 1970s was full of other examples, including the following two transcendent moments from arguably the greatest decade there ever was for sporting excitement on television.

'This is great stuff, Phil Bennett covering, brilliant, that's brilliant, John Williams, Brian Williams, Pullen, John Dawes, great dummy, David, Tom David, the halfway line, brilliant by Quinnell, this is Gareth Edwards . . . a dramatic start . . . WHAT A SCORE!' bellowed Cliff Morgan on 27 January 1973, as the Barbarians made the perfect start against the All Blacks at Cardiff Arms Park, in what is still widely considered to have been the greatest game of rugby union of all time.

About eighteen months later, the eyes of the world turned to another sporting encounter that would become the most exalted, most written-about sporting event in the history of sport. 'Suddenly Ali looks very tired indeed,' said Harry Carpenter, ringside in Kinshasa, Zaire, at the world title fight between heavyweight champion George Foreman and the challenger, Muhammad Ali, the so-called 'Rumble in the Jungle'. 'In fact Ali, at times now, looks as though he can barely lift his arms up . . . Oh, he's got him with a right hand! He's got him! Oh, you can't believe it. And I don't think Foreman's going to get up. He's trying to beat the count. And he's out! Oh my God, he's won the title back at thirty-two!'

When Sanders missed his putt, when Edwards scored his try, when Ali decked Foreman and won back the world title, I was watching. Longhurst, Morgan and Carpenter would doubtless have protested otherwise, but I knew that I was in the right place at the right time. Never mind St Andrews, Cardiff and Kinshasa, 58 Lynton Road in front of the telly was unequivocally the place to be.

24

Some More of the Women in My Life: Val Singleton, Jenny Hanley and Miss Penelope

Like all those who spent the 1970s in front of the telly, the love affair had been kindled in the 1960s, among others by Windy Miller on *Camberwick Green*, Florence and Dougal on *The Magic Roundabout*, Bernard Cribbins on *Jackanory*, Peter Glaze and Leslie Crowther on *Crackerjack*, Skippy the Bush Kangaroo and Dr Marsh Tracy on *Daktari*, Johnny Morris on *Animal Magic*, Basil Brush, Pinky and Perky, and of course Peter Purves, John Noakes and Val Singleton on *Blue Peter*.

Blue Peter is one of those enduring, age-defining programmes – *Doctor Who* is another – of which different generations have different memories. For me, and everyone born within a few years of me, Peter, John and Val will always be the definitive presenters, and Biddy Baxter the definitive editor. We never saw Baxter, never knew how old she was or what colour hair she had, yet her name became a reassuring landmark of my childhood, no less than the Belisha beacon at the end of Lynton Road. I found similar reassurance in the name of Flick Colby, the Pan's People choreographer, which appeared at the end of *Top of the Pops*.

So it was disconcerting when these pillars of certainty were removed from my childhood, for instance in 1972, when Val Singleton left *Blue Peter* to 'pursue other projects'. I admit to keeping an eye on Val's successor Lesley Judd once my KGV schoolmate Jeff Brignall had pointed out to me that you could occasionally see a pair of nipples poking through her cheesecloth blouse, but I knew even then that that was no reason to watch *Blue Peter*. There was no proper adolescent arousal to be found in *Blue Peter*. That's what *Magpie* was for.

I'll come back to *Magpie*, but sticking with nipples and *Blue Peter*, which is not an association that pops into a chap's mind every day, my wife Jane later ended up working with Val Singleton on the Radio 4 current affairs programme *PM*, and Val gave her a tip that has stood her in excellent stead down the years – that when you're not wearing a bra it's a good idea to wear sticking plasters (as opposed to sticky-backed plastic) over the nipples. Apparently, Val had once delivered a report to camera from the deck of a ship on a cold day, and had been miserably aware of her nipples standing to attention like a pair of subalterns on parade, being inspected by a rear-admiral. She resolved to do something about it on similar occasions in future, and Jane has benefited directly from her resourcefulness, which may in turn, I suppose, have been a legacy of working on *Blue Peter* and doing clever things with squeezy bottles for so many years.

News and current affairs were not, in truth, great strengths of Val's. She once asked a court reporter at a big trial whether he thought the defendant *looked* guilty. But she was unflappable and had a terrific radio voice, and most of all a supreme confidence in her own ability, which was conveyed at the microphone as it had been in front of the camera. Maybe she drew confidence from knowing that her audience was largely made up of those who had been children between 1962 and 1972, hanging on her every word. In April 2007, by the way, she turned seventy, which is another of those shocking milestones – rather like Private Pike turning fifty – to make us all feel older. On the other hand, dear old Val was always a little on the motherly side; I don't know any men of my generation who lusted after her (or women, despite the endlessly recycled rumour about her and the singer Joan Armatrading being lovers, which even today you can find being earnestly discussed in internet chatrooms, and is 100 per cent urban myth and which Val herself tried to nail in the summer of 2008 by boasting that she had once had sexual relations with Peter Purves, as disturbing an image for my generation as Sooty shagging Sue).

The same was emphatically not true of *Magpie*'s Jenny Hanley, who was an object of adolescent lust at least as potent as Suzi Quatro, Debbie Harry and the blonde one from Abba, and for some of us, the revelation that she celebrated her sixtieth birthday in 2007 is even more shocking than Val Singleton turning seventy. I find it almost impossible to think of Jenny Hanley being older than twenty-eight.

Magpie started in 1968, directly inspired by the success of *Blue Peter*, although ITV executives hoped to make it a little trendier. This was not a difficult task, since anything less trendy than *Blue Peter* would have worn an Ena Sharples-style hair-net and organized whist drives. That said, as Hilary Kingsley and Geoff Tibballs noted in *Box of Delights*, *Magpie* never had anyone to compare with the fearless John Noakes. 'If Noakes was haring round the Isle of Man TT course, the *Magpie* team would be in the studio playing with their Scalextric, and if he was scaling the north face of the Eiger you had a feeling they'd answer it by purchasing a return ticket on the Snowdon mountain railway.'

Actually, that's a bit harsh. The *Magpie* team did their best, stunt-wise, and, to its eternal credit, the show made newspaper headlines in 1971 when a teenager resuscitated a boy by giving him the kiss of life as he'd seen it demonstrated on *Magpie*, which was a boast *Blue Peter* couldn't make. Nor could either Noakes or Purves claim to look anything like the super-cool Marc Bolan, unlike *Magpie*'s Mick Robertson. And then there was the gorgeous Hanley, who lacked Val Singleton's assurance with sticky-backed plastic (not to mention sticking plasters) but had been a model, which was pretty cool, and indeed had featured in the 1968 Bond film *On Her Majesty's Secret Service*, which, though it is dreadfully unfashionable to admit now, remains one of my favourite Bond films. My dad took me to see it at the Palace in Southport, and along with Katharine Ross undressing in *Butch Cassidy and the Sundance Kid* and Robert Wagner very alarmingly catching fire in *The Towering Inferno*, Diana Rigg's sudden death in *On Her Majesty's Secret Service* was among the most striking cinematic images of my adolescence.

But much as I loved 'going to the pictures', as we charmingly called it in 1960s and 1970s Southport (less charmingly, my own kids call it 'going to Vue', our nearest multiplex), it was the small screen that dominated my life and provided most of the images that defined my childhood. Among them, of course, were the *Doctor Who*-hunting Daleks. In one of the amusement arcades on Nevill Street in Southport, there was a life-size Dalek in which, for 5p, you could swing round exterminating people, aiming in particular at the miserable old crone who handed out change from a small booth. This, my friends and I speculated, appeared to be her actual home. Between about 1972 and 1975 we spent a lot of time in that arcade, but we never saw her set foot out of the booth. Maybe she took the same view of me and the Dalek. I loved that Dalek.

As I ventured earlier, *Doctor Who* occupies a similar place to *Blue Peter* in popular culture, insofar as different generations accord different actors the honour of being 'definitive'. For me it was Jon Pertwee, who played the third incarnation of the Doctor after William Hartnell and Patrick Troughton, from 1970 to 1974, and it pleases me that my children too will grow up thinking of a definitive Doctor Who; in their case David Tennant. I can see that Tennant is excellent in the part, but after Pertwee I never really had any truck with later incarnations, such as Tom Baker and Peter Davison.

Mind you, I had even less truck with Worzel bloody Gummidge, whom Pertwee played after giving up his role as Doctor Who. That always seemed like a betrayal to me, a Time Lord metamorphosing into a scarecrow. Although Pete Duel's suicide had impressed upon me that my dramatic heroes were just actors doing a job, and sometimes bore no resemblance in real life to the characters they played, it was particularly hard to reconcile time-travelling and inter-galactic heroes with the banalities of everyday existence. Pertwee later explained that one of his reasons for quitting as Doctor Who was the sudden death of his great friend Roger Delgado, who played the renegade Time Lord, the Master. The news that Doctor Who and the Master had been the best of friends was unsettling enough, though not as unsettling as the circumstances of Delago's death. He was killed, in June 1973, when his car plunged into a ravine, in Turkey. He was there on location, making a comedy film called *Bell in Tibet*, and I can remember clearly how discombobulated I was to learn that the Master had been killed in a car crash in Turkey. While making a comedy film! It wasn't at all the sort of thing that ought to have happened to a renegade Time Lord.

By comparison with some of my friends, however, I was not a huge fan of *Doctor Who*. Science fiction generally did not really light my fire, which is why I had to break some disappointing news to my friend Avril, when I told her that I was writing a book about television in the 1970s, and she asked how many chapters I was devoting to *The Tomorrow People*. 'Never watched it,' I said, to her disbelief. Avril grew up on a farm on a hillside near Welshpool, and the family television set could only receive ITV, which made *The Tomorrow People* – a sci-fi adventure for children, which ran from 1973 to 1979 – even more precious. Apparently, teleportation – or 'jaunting' as the show's precocious youngsters preferred to call it – was achieved by fiddling with something called a 'jaunting belt'. And from time to time Avril is still wont to say, much to the amusement of her loved ones, that she wishes she was wearing her jaunting belt.

Why I never wholly embraced science fiction I'm not really sure. I faithfully watched everything produced by the so-called father of Supermarionation, Gerry Anderson, from *Thunderbirds, Captain Scarlet, Joe 90, Fireball XL5* and *Stingray* to his live-action shows *UFO* and *Space 1999*, but I could never quite make the leap of imagination required to transport myself across, as it were, the final frontier. If I was going to watch a battle between good and evil, I preferred it to happen on horseback.

Oddly, Anderson himself was similarly ambivalent about the puppets that made him famous. I interviewed him once, and found him a rather odd cove, who felt that his fate had been sealed as early as 1957, when he was asked to direct a children's series for ATV. The film production company he ran was in trouble, and so he took the job, only to find that the star of *The Adventures of Twizzle* was not an actor, but a small puppet with red hair and extendable legs. 'My dream of becoming Stanley Kubrick', he said, 'fell to pieces in an instant.'

Accordingly, he never had much time for the heroes of International Rescue, or even for the totty in *Thunderbirds*, Lady Penelope Creighton-Ward. I quite fancied Miss Penelope, as her loyal chauffeur Aloysius Parker called her. It wasn't so much her pink amphibious Rolls-Royce that I found alluring, as the graceful way she smoked cigarettes. Not many puppets have ever mastered the art of smoking, but Miss Penelope did it with the élan of Grace Kelly.

The series was named after an American airstrip, Thunderbird Field, where Anderson's older brother Lionel, an RAF pilot in the Second World War, completed his basic training. Lionel later flew thirty-eight missions and eventually went missing over enemy territory, so one would think that, if only for that reason, Anderson might feel some kind of sentimental attachment towards *Thunderbirds*. But no. 'I always used to think that they were terrible,' he said. 'I didn't see much on screen but the faults. I couldn't get a puppet to pick something up, or to walk. Their mouths were like letterboxes flapping open and shut. But I got to the point where I thought I'd better stop running down these pictures, because everybody in the world except me seems to like them.'

In August 2001, at an auction of television memorabilia, somebody in the world liked *Thunderbirds* so much that he (it can only have been a he) paid £38,000 for the original Parker, while a telephone bidder in America snapped up a mere cast of Lady Penelope, albeit from the original mould, for £16,000. For once, far from International Rescue saving the world from madness, it was itself the source of the madness.

Anderson was duly incredulous. It was only because he was a frustrated feature-film director that *Thunderbirds* and his other creations looked the way they did. He tried to make the puppets look and behave like actors, and to enhance that illusion he introduced special effects. The head of ATV, Lew Grade, thought he was a genius. Anderson once told the *Independent*'s Matthew Sweet that he could still vividly remember the 7.30 a.m. meeting at which he pitched *Thunderbirds*. In Grade's office, they drank coffee from little silver cups and smoked huge Havana cigars. Grade then leant back in his chair and asked Anderson to sock him with his new idea. Anderson warned that it was going to be costly, and that he wasn't sure whether Grade would want to risk backing it. 'You have to believe me,' Anderson said, 'but he got up from his desk, came round the table and grabbed me by the scruff of the neck. I thought he was going to hit me. I was really quite scared. He pulled me out of the chair into the centre of the office, and he said, "You see that light bulb? If you want to make a television series about that light bulb, I'll back it." So we sat down and I told him about International Rescue, and at the end of twenty minutes he told me to go off and start work.'

I can believe that anecdote, because when I met Grade, towards the end of his long life, he told me that he had recently thought of a way in which *Joe 90* could be revived. 'Everything is about genes these days,' he said, waving his Monte Cristo around. 'So we could inject that young boy with the genes of the strongest man in the world, the greatest surgeon in the world, and do it that way.'

I found it hugely uplifting, I later wrote, to find a nonagenarian – Lew 90 – enthusing about the way in which a puppet series about a nine-year-old boy might be remade for a modern audience. I found it less uplifting when his successors in the executive corridors of the nation's television companies did the same thing, eschewing original ideas in favour of updating old Lew Grade productions. According to the old one-liner, nostalgia ain't what it used to be. That's nonsense, of course. Nostalgia is more, and much bigger, than it ever was. And television is the trough at which the nostalgia frenzy feeds. Yet the twenty-first-century makeovers of old ATV dramas were almost anti-nostalgic. For some of us, decades-old episodes of *Randall and Hopkirk (Deceased)* exert a strong Proustian influence. In our mind's eye we want to see Mike Pratt, Kenneth Cope, iffy plots and wobbly sets, and not have them obscured by Vic Reeves and Bob Mortimer. When we think of *The Prisoner*, we want to remember the young Patrick McGoohan being enigmatic in Portmeirion, not the octogenarian version doing a cameo in a remake.

Still, I console myself with one thought. It is too late to update one other collaboration between Lew Grade and Gerry Anderson, *Space 1999*. So we are left with unsullied memories, such as my horrifying realization, sometime in 1975, that 1999 was likely to fall well within my lifetime and how the hell would the universe and I cope with that cosmic gas cloud?

25

The Final Frontier: From Captain Kirk to Captain Pugwash

That thought struck me one Sunday afternoon when I was sitting in the lounge in Lynton Road watching the latest interstellar activity on Moonbase Alpha. Despite my vague suspicion of science fiction, rare was the episode of *Space 1999* that I missed. But on this particular Sunday I was hit as if by a meteorite with the realization that in 1999, this distant year being presented as an informed vision of the future, with folk wearing funny white suits and driving gull-wing jet-propelled cars, and with a nuclear-waste dump on the far side of the moon unfortunately blowing up and inconveniently knocking the moon out of orbit, I would only be thirty-seven years old, considerably younger than both my parents were on that very afternoon. I found this immensely unsettling, and from then on watched *Space 1999* with diminished enjoyment.

I recalled all this many years later when I bumped into Martin Landau – who had played John Koenig, the commander of Moonbase Alpha – at the Playboy Mansion in Los Angeles. Hugh Hefner was holding a St Valentine's Day party, to which I had been sent by the good old *Radio Times* to shadow Ruby Wax shadowing Hefner for a BBC documentary. One of the lesser celebrities there was Landau, who spent much of the evening clutching the pert rear of a woman young enough to be his granddaughter, if not his granddaughter's granddaughter. I was tempted to tap him on the shoulder and ask if he thought this was decorous behaviour for the commander of Moonbase Alpha, but, regrettably, I didn't.

I suppose, thinking about it now, that *Space 1999* was conceived at a time when the triumphant *Apollo 11* mission was fresh in the memory, when it looked as though by the end of the century more giant leaps would have been taken – not by Neil Armstrong or even our old friend Manny Klein, but by mankind in its relationship with space. The idea that by 1999 human beings might be living on the moon probably didn't seem remotely absurd in 1973. Even the Cadbury's Smash aliens looked plausible.

The more prosaic impulse behind *Space 1999* was the opportunity to fill the considerable gap left by *Star Trek*, which had finished in 1969 after only three years, having been nothing like as successful during its original transmission as it would later become. A little later, *Blake's 7* tried to get in on the act as well. But neither *Blake's 7* nor *Space 1999* were hits remotely on the scale of *Star Trek*, which took the planet by storm when its seventy-nine episodes were repeated in the early 1970s. It took a little while for the actors to cotton on to the magnitude of the hit they were associated with: when Leonard Nimoy, the entirely human alter ego of Mr Spock, was shown round the Johnson Space Center in Houston, Texas, he was astounded to find astronauts asking for his autograph before he could ask for theirs. Later, when an episode of *Star Trek* on an American network was interrupted with a news flash because a genuine space mission had run into trouble, viewers protested in their thousands that their favourite programme had been needlessly vandalized.

This was the phenomenon that Anderson, Grade and others hoped to replicate with *Space 1999*, not that they ever did. For whatever reason, the *Star Trek* formula was unique in capturing the imagination even of those of us who weren't particularly interested in what might or might not transpire in the outer reaches of the galaxy in the twenty-third century, perhaps because we could recognize something of what the show's creator Gene Roddenberry had intended when he first pitched the idea to NBC: that its space-age setting should in a sense be incidental, and that the stories should borrow heavily from C.S. Forester's novels about Horatio Hornblower, the Napoleonic-era naval captain engaged on noble missions far from home, as well as from popular TV westerns. He envisaged *Star Trek*, he said, as a '*Wagon Train* to the stars'.

He also saw it as a way of addressing a number of issues of burning importance in 1960s America, not least that of racial prejudice. Roddenberry wanted his Starship Enterprise to be a multi-racial vessel, in which neither colour nor creed would stand in the way of promotion. It was partly with this in mind that he cast the lovely Nichelle Nichols as Lieutenant Uhura. It was also because he was shagging her at the time, but never mind. Whatever the reason, Nichols became one of the first black women to feature in a major TV series on American television, and although she felt tempted to leave in the first season, feeling that her role 'lacked significance', she was reportedly persuaded to stay by none other than Dr Martin Luther King Jnr, a big *Star Trek* fan.

I love the idea that Martin Luther King was a Trekkie. Or, perhaps, a Trekker. Most *Star Trek* fans prefer the latter term, feeling that 'Trekkie' has trainspotterish connotations. I discovered this distinction in the year 2000 – a suitably space-age kind of year – in a bar on Page Street near the Houses of Parliament. Someone had tipped me off that *Star Trek* fans assembled there on Saturday nights, so I went to see for myself, and asked a man dressed as a Klingon to explain the difference between a Trekkie and a Trekker. 'A Trekker dreams what it's like to have sex in zero grav,' he said, 'whereas a Trekkie dreams what it's like to have sex.' He narrowed his eyes and looked around. There were no rogue Trekkies in tonight, he added. But we were surrounded by lots of Trekkers, all gazing at an episode of *Star Trek: Deep Space Nine* on an array of large screens.

Suspended from the ceiling was a vast model of the Starship Enterprise. The Klingon told me proudly that it was unveiled one Christmas by Dave Prowse, the actor who played the physical form of Darth Vader in *Star Wars*. I found that, within the confines of science fiction, most Trekkers are liberal with their affections. Some even went to Page's Bar on Sunday nights, otherwise known as *Xena: Warrior Princess* nights, swapping their Star Fleet tunics for Xena-style boob tubes. The women, too.

I talked to a young woman called Brooke, who liked the Xena get-togethers but preferred the Trekker evenings. She was dressed as an alien from the planet Romulus, wearing a black bob wig, pointy ears, and, since Romulan blood is copper rather than iron-based, subtle green face paint. She told me that she had once been in full garb, making her way home from Page's, when an aggressive drunk lurched over to her. 'Which frigging planet are you from?' he snarled. 'Romulus,' she said coolly, successfully removing the wind from his sails.

I also talked to a guy called Bob Benton, the manager of Page's Bar, who tried to explain *Star Trek*'s unique appeal. 'I was going to make Page's a *Coronation Street* theme bar,' he said, 'but I had always been a big fan of *Star Trek* and decided that would work better. The thing about *Star Trek* is that it deals with every problem the world has ever had, like one-parent families and drug abuse.' I looked at him closely. He wasn't kidding. I decided not to share with him my twenty-year-old *Star Trek* joke. 'Uhura, Uhura.' 'Yes, captain?' 'Nothing, I was just clearing my throat.'

Such irreverence, I decided, would probably not be well received at Page's Bar. Not even Mr Sulu, confronted by an Archon, would be as fiercely defensive as those punters were about their habit. As Brooke from the planet Romulus said: 'People think we're sad gits sitting round a table sharing half a shandy. In fact, we start drinking before noon and carry on till four in the morning. It's great fun, and it's a way of making friends with a real cross-section of society, from airline pilots to roadsweepers.'

I could see Brooke's point. If people are dressed up to the Deep Space Nines, they stand a better-than-usual chance of overcoming their social inhibitions. But Christian, a gay teacher from Suffolk, offered a slightly different perspective. 'I came out last March,' he told me, 'and it was coming to Page's every weekend that gave me the confidence.' I could see the sense in that. Mr Spock, master of logic, would have understood too.

A few days later I wrote a newspaper article about my evening at Page's Bar, and was rather gratified to find that it caused quite a bal-lyhoo in Trekker circles, with various keepers of the faith hotly debating on websites whether my tone was affectionate or sardonic. Either way, they recognized that I was not a fellow traveller. I had watched the show faithfully enough in the 1970s but it had never been one of my favourites, not even when, in 1973, it was revived in cartoon form with the original actors supplying the voices.

The cartoon has yet to feature in this book, partly because I'm writing principally about the 1970s, and all the cartoons I loved as a kid – *Tom and Jerry*, *Wacky Races*, *Top Cat*, *The Flintstones*, *Wait Till Your Father Gets Home* and *Scooby-Doo*, each of them produced by the extraordinarily prolific Hanna-Barbera company – originated in the 1960s or earlier. I should just add, though, that in January 2007 I was fascinated to read the obituary of one Iwao Takamoto, the creator of *Scooby-Doo*! In my paper his obituary was alongside that of a great nuclear physicist, who was the first man to split a proton or eat an electron or something, and I just loved the contrast: the world-renowned scientist, side by side with the man who invented *Scooby-Doo*.

I didn't read the scientist's lavish obituary, but I can tell you all about Takamoto's. When he was sixteen, he and his family, who were Japanese immigrants, were interned in the Californian desert following the Japanese raid on Pearl Harbor. But it was during this period that Takamoto was given lessons in drawing by two fellow internees, which means that in a roundabout way it is possible to say that Pearl Harbor gave birth to *Scooby-Doo*. This pleases me greatly. I can also tell you that Scooby-Doo was modelled by Takamoto on the Great Danes bred by a woman at the studio, and that the name Scooby-Doo was taken from Frank Sinatra's little riff at the end of his song 'Strangers in the Night' (I always thought, when listening to my parents' records while I was growing up, that it must be the other way round, and that after Sinatra had reflected so melodically on love being just a glance away, a warm, embracing dance away, he was for some reason eager to record his admiration for a cartoon dog).

But the best thing I can tell you about *Scooby-Doo* is that my friend Chris Taylor admits to having had 'early erotic thoughts' about Scooby's friend Daphne – 'the fit one', as Chris still describes her. This admission, I feel, puts into context my own mild feelings for Lady Penelope in *Thunderbirds*, and indeed my reliance on the underwear sections of Littlewoods and Grattan catalogues. It really was an age where you had to find your adolescent thrills in whatever way you could, whether in a mail-order catalogue or a children's cartoon series.

Both Chris and Jonny Cook, I was delighted to find on my beer-and-nostalgia-fuelled evening out with them, which doubtless would have been fuelled by beer and nostalgia whether or not I'd had the excuse of researching this book, shared my affection for another Hanna-Barbera production, *The Banana Splits Show*, which in the early 1970s ran every morning of the school holidays and to which I was hopelessly devoted.

The Splits were an animal version of the Monkees, consisting of a dog called Fleegle, a gorilla called Bingo, a lion called Drooper and an elephant called Snorky. I was particularly fond of the hippyish Drooper, whose job in every show was to take out the 'trash', and read out letters from viewers in a segment called 'Dear Drooper'. Inside the fleecy animal costumes, I have subsequently learnt, were four actors: Jeffrey Winkless, Terrence Winkless, Dan Winkless and James Dove. The Winklesses were brothers, the sons of a certain Nelson B. Winkless Jnr, who was a jingle writer for the show's sponsor, Kellogg's. James Dove, who occupied the Snorky costume, was later fired, apparently, he said, because he made it plain that he thought the Winkless boys had been hired through nepotism. I was horrified even thirty-five years after last watching *The Banana Splits Show* to discover this. Snorky always seemed so emollient; who could have suspected that behind the floppy trunk he was a seething mass of resentment?

The best bits of *The Banana Splits Show* were the animated segments – The Arabian Knights and The Three Musketeers – and the live-action Danger Island, in which a white boy in permanent peril on a rainforest-covered island would call for his native helper by shouting 'Uh-oh, Chango!' At my primary school in Southport, Farnborough Road, 'Uh-oh, Chango!' was a frequent refrain in the playground. I craved a native helper of my own.

Jonny, Chris and I – three grown men in a Mayfair pub in the autumn of 2006 – had a short argument as to which was the pick of the *Banana Splits* segments. I liked Danger Island and Chris was a sucker for The Three Musketeers, but Jonny's preference was always for The Arabian Knights, in which valiant Prince Turhan and his cousin, the beautiful Princess Nidor (voiced by none other than Shari Lewis, better known as the voice of a singularly annoying ventriloquist's doll that was little more than a sock, called Lamb Chop) fought the evil Sultan Bakaar. They were assisted in this noble cause by Bez, a man who could turn into any animal (and if you're my age, you will now be silently mouthing the words of Bez's simple spell, 'siiiiize of an elephant / or a giraffe / or a flea') and their donkey, Zazoum. It was pure folly to pull Zazoum's tail, by the way – 'Just the last thing you should do,' said Chris, shaking his head disbelievingly, before heading to the bar to buy our umpteenth round of drinks – because he turned into a kind of whirling tornado, destroying everything in his path. In every episode, needless to say, someone did.

It is disheartening, looking back, to reflect that nearly all the programmes with which I was really smitten as a child came from America. I liked *The Clangers* and *The Wombles*, but not as much as I liked *The Addams Family* and *The Beverly Hillbillies*. Moreover, there were hardly any British cartoons on television apart from *The Adventures of Sir Prancelot* and *Captain Pugwash* (Seaman Staines, Master Bates, Ben Dover and Roger the Cabin Boy are further products of the urban myth department, by the way, and regrettably there is absolutely no evidence, as is still sometimes claimed by children of the 1970s seeking double entendres that never existed, that 'pugwash' is an Australian term for oral sex).

Sexual references or not, I had no time for either *Captain Pugwash* or even the superior *Sir Prancelot*, and the only other British-made cartoons that registered on my consciousness were the animated public information films advising us on the importance of being able to swim, or of observing the country code. No, the only cartoons I ever loved, in those pre-*Simpsons* days, were those that emerged from the Hanna-Barbera stable. If I did ever sit through a cartoon on the telly that had originated somewhere other than California, it was invariably squeezed between the Sunday Matinee (which almost always starred Terry-Thomas) and the arts programme *Aquarius*, and was something weird from Hungary or Czechoslovakia or East Germany, countries that also seemed to specialize in badly dubbed tea-time drama serials, such as *The Singing Ringing Tree*.

Even the British-made dramas for children seemed to lack something of the pizazz of their American counterparts. *The Adventures of Black Beauty* and *Follyfoot* were no match for *The Life and Times of Grizzly Adams* and *The Man From Atlantis*, at least not for a boy. Every fortysomething woman I spoke to while I was writing this book, on the other hand, waxed lyrical about *Follyfoot*. It was set on a farm, run by a kindly old colonel (Desmond Llewelyn, who was even more famous as the gadgets expert Q in the Bond films) as a home for old or unwanted horses, the kind of creatures on which my father habitually used to bet in the ITV Seven.

Maybe if I'd grown up with sisters, *Follyfoot* would have had more of an impact on me. It certainly made an impact in television circles, selling to twenty countries and even inspiring talk of a film adaptation. There were *Follyfoot* annuals, a *Follyfoot* comic strip in *Look-In*, and special editions of *Look-In* devoted entirely to *Follyfoot*, one of which is advertised in my November 1974 issue of *TV Times* – '64 colourful pages of stories, pin-ups, puzzles, picture strips, fascinating features and biographies of the stars, articles on showjumping and pony care. Plus a special competition with an Arthur English – alias *Follyfoot*'s Slugger – original painting to be won. Get your copy of *Look-In Follyfoot Special*, just 15p.' Every teenage girl of my acquaintance, which admittedly was a restricted field, bought the *Look-In Follyfoot Special*.

Even the theme tune, 'The Lightning Tree', performed by The Settlers, reached number thirty-six in the charts on 16 October 1971. On Craig Cash's estate in Stockport, meanwhile, a lad by the name of Brian Sweeney enjoyed a brief but dazzling celebrity on account of the fact that his drama teacher at St Anne's High School knew someone at Yorkshire Television and got Brian a part in *Follyfoot*.

There was nobody like that at my school, although my classmate David Lonsdale, one of the boys who sat round in T.B. Johnson's study discussing *The Go-Between* and trying to ignore the muddy imprints of footballs on the window, would later achieve dazzling celebrity of his own as David Stockwell, the village idiot in *Heartbeat*. He also played Ken Barlow's son Peter in *Coronation Street* for a couple of years in the mid-1980s, but in the 1970s, while we were at KGV, the highlight of his dramatic career was a turn as a cheerleader in the Granada pop show *Get it Together*. I am indebted, as Cyril Fletcher used to say from his capacious leather wing chair on *That's Life!*, to my friend Mike King for this recollection. He also remembers David striding out to bat in a house cricket match and a bunch of us on the boundary shouting 'C'mon, Lonsdale, get it together!' In reply, David threw his bat to the ground and stalked off in high dudgeon, shouting – and I do hope he won't mind me revealing this, now that he's a family man and an accomplished, highly respected actor – 'Fuck off!'

For cruel insensitivity and a sheer delight in winding up others, fifteen-year-old schoolboys are unmatched. Which might, come to think of it, be why I remember my schooldays with such unbridled affection.

26

Saturday Mornings, and Milkmen Called Ernie

At fifteen I still stayed in on Saturday nights. If I did go out it was only to babysit for Candice, the 13-year-old down the road, to our intense mutual embarrassment. When I was sixteen, however, I started going to pubs, and also landed that Saturday-evening job as a waiter. For me, the Saturday-night telly phenomenon was over, but it was great while it lasted.

Saturday night was the ultimate TV night in the 1970s, the sine qua non, as my Latin teacher Jack Clough might have said, and from time to time even now newspaper columnists of my generation (not least me) will write nostalgic laments on the subject of whatever happened to Saturday-night telly.

The build-up to it actually began in the morning, especially from 1976 with the introduction of the BBC's excitingly unscripted

Multi-Coloured Swap Shop. ITV's more anarchic counterpart, the ATV production *Tiswas* – an acronym which we were assured stood for 'Today is Saturday, Watch and Smile', although I've always suspected something ruder – had begun in 1974 but, maddeningly, our ITV region, Granada, chose not to transmit it until 1979.

There was much more autonomy in the ITV regions then, and far more regional advertising, for example, than there is now. Some of the jingles which practically provided a soundtrack to my life were only heard in the north-west of England. There was one, for a used-car dealership in Bolton, that will ring a loud clanging bell for all those who grew up in Granada-land. 'BOC, better people to buy from / Come and see, the Earls Court of the North!' I'm not sure why anyone might have thought that the Earls Court of the North would be a place worth visiting. Maybe it sounded better than Bolton. Whatever, the jingle can't have hurt business. BOC is still thriving.

But it was no good having the BOC jingle on ITV and not *Tiswas*. It seems ridiculous now to think that I went through most of my teens unaware of the marvellous cleavage of Chris Tarrant's sidekick Sally James, a cleavage of which my contemporaries who grew up elsewhere in the country still talk.

When *Tiswas* did arrive on Granada it presented a dilemma. Until the evening schedules started in earnest, when in most households BBC1 won hands down, Saturday viewing in the late 1970s was a battle between *Swap Shop* and *Tiswas*, *Football Focus* and *On the Ball*, and indeed *Grandstand* and *World of Sport*. In the early years of the decade, however, Saturday-morning telly was not as child-friendly as it would later become. On Saturday 10 November 1974, just to pluck a date at random, a child expectantly switching on the television set at 9.30 on a Saturday morning, and turning to ITV, would have been confronted with Shaw Taylor presenting *Improve Your Bridge*. I couldn't imagine anyone of my age, with the notable exception of Roderick Butterfield, who had my school's most gigantic brain, sitting down to watch *Improve Your Bridge* on a Saturday morning.

Still, for me and my friends in those years there was at least the exciting alternative of the Saturday-morning Cinema Club at the Odeon on Lord Street. Alas, Saturday-morning cinema clubs have gone the way of the Odeon on Lord Street. I can remember one in London too, round the corner from my grandma's house in Queen Elizabeth Drive, Southgate, to which I would sometimes be packed off when we were staying there for the weekend. But that cinema closed years ago and the Odeon on Lord Street is now a Sainsbury's. Lord Street, I should add for those unacquainted with it, is a handsome Victorian boulevard (hence The Boulevard, the restaurant where I first came face to face with the avocado pear), and is by common consent one of the most splendid thoroughfares in the north of England. But on its eastern side it used to have not one, not two, but three large cinemas – the ABC, the Palace and the Odeon – and now it doesn't even have one. I think that's sad. I'd also like to know what happened to the middle-aged usherette with the blonde hairpiece who worked at the Odeon, or it may have been the Palace, or even the ABC, from whom I used to buy my Kia-Ora and Choc-ices. I've been feeling guilty since 1972 for surreptitiously slipping a well-chewed piece of Bazooka Joe bubblegum into her pocket.

The irony of me writing plaintively in early 2008 about the cinema-going experience thirty-four years ago in 1974, incidentally, will not be lost on my parents' generation, who in 1974 were similarly nostalgic about the cinema-going experience thirty-four years earlier in 1940. My mother recently sent me an old programme from the Gaumont, Watford, dated August 1940, in which the new general manager, a lanky young man named Denis Norden, introduced himself to the Gaumont's customers.

As an insight into a world that was bygone even in the 1970s, it is worth reproducing here:

This is my first chance to introduce myself formally to the good people of Watford. Mr Byford, who has occupied this chair ever since the Gaumont opened, has left to give his services in Home Defence, and I am here to take over the duties he has so ably initiated.

The standard of entertainment which he achieved will be hard to surpass. But I promise you that every effort will be made to do so. His familiar policy – Only The Best Is Good Enough For The Gaumont – will be enthusiastically maintained, and the splendid reputation this theatre enjoys will be kept up and, I hope, embellished. A glance through these pages will show you that I start with no handicap in the way of programmes.

This is not perhaps the happiest month in which to take over the running of a strange cinema. Nevertheless, amid the 'whims and glories of August sun,' you will find no variation in the comfort and restful coolness which we shall assure for you inside the theatre. When you come to the end of a perfect day . . . remember that the Gaumont and myself are at your service, prepared to make your evening equally satisfying.

DM Norden

But back to the telly, in which arena the endearingly eager-to-please young Mr Norden would later distinguish himself. The BBC1 schedule for Saturday 23 October 1976, which of course featured *Doctor Who*, is itself like a TARDIS (which stood for Time and Relative Dimension in Space, and is not to be confused with *Tiswas*), in the sense that reading it will propel anyone over forty years of age backwards in time. Here are the day's listings for both BBC1 and BBC2, as they appeared in that week's *Radio Times*.

NICE TO SEE IT, TO SEE IT, NICE

BBC1

8.50am Ragtime

9.05 Indoors Outdoors Practical hints and tips

9.30 Multi-Coloured Swap Shop including *Hong Kong Phooey*, *News Swap* with John Craven, *Valley of the Dinosaurs*, weatherman Jack Scott answering your calls, *Swaporama* with Keith Chegwin and *Star Swap* with Roy Castle

12.27pm Weather with Bill Giles

12.30 Grandstand introduced by Frank Bough

5.05 The Tom and Jerry Show

5.15 News

5.30 The Basil Brush Show introduced by Roy North, with special guests David Essex and Guys 'n' Dolls

6.00 Doctor Who starring Tom Baker in *The Hand of Fear*

6.25 Bruce Forsyth and the Generation Game featuring Anthea Redfern

7.25 The Duchess of Duke Street with Gemma Jones

8.15 The Two Ronnies Special guest Barbara Dickson

9.00 Starsky and Hutch

10.10 News

10.20 Match of the Day introduced by Jimmy Hill

11.20 Parkinson

12.20am–12.22 Weather

BBC SCOTLAND as above except: **10.20** Sportscene **10.50**–11.20 Top Score

BBC2

3.05pm FILM: Anna Neagle in Derby Day *(B/W)*

4.30 Vision On

4.55 Dastardly and Muttley

5.05 The Money Programme

5.55 Open Door

6.25 Network *The Lady of the Ring* from BBC West

6.55 M*A*S*H

7.20 'Painting – was Damned Hard Work' L.S. Lowry (1887–1976)

8.05 News and Sport

8.15 FILM: Die Marquise von O . . .

9.55 The Lively Arts – in Performance

11.25 News on 2

11.30–12.55am **FILM: Storm Fear** *(B/W)*

For me, as for all my friends, the BBC2 listings were redundant. I liked *Dastardly and Muttley* – the *Wacky Races* spin-off – but not enough to miss Len Martin reading the classified football results on *Grandstand*. It's worth adding that Martin announced the results in every edition of *Grandstand* from the first programme in 1958 until 1995, the year he died, aged seventy-six. What else he did in his week, I don't know. Maybe he didn't do anything else. James Alexander Gordon, who has been reading the classified results on the radio since the reign of the late King Alfred, is a similar enigma. But in any definitive history of television Len Martin would still be entitled to a generous footnote, not only for his longevity but also for his marvellous intonation. You could almost always tell from the way he read the first half of the result what the second half was going to be, and although he liked to say that his nightmare result would be East Fife 4, Forfar 5, had it ever been the case he would still have dealt with it in his own masterly style.

Maybe, on reflection, it was that line of Martin's that inspired the wonderfully silly *Two Ronnies* spoof of the football results, which as I recall went something like 'Dumbarton 2, Dick Barton 1 . . . Motherwell 1, Dad sick as a parrot 0 . . . and now a half-time score just in, East Fife 5, Forfar so far 4'. The football results were certainly always fair game for comedy. I can also recall Benny Hill's myopic continuity announcer squinting at the autocue and saying, 'Leyton Orient beat Hawaii five-nil,' before correcting himself: 'No, sorry, later on it's *Hawaii Five-O*.'

Benny Hill is worth a little detour in any book about television in the 1970s, for perhaps more than anyone he embodies that decade's enjoyment of the saucy double entendre. The lyrics of his song 'Ernie, (The Fastest Milkman in the West)', which sold 600,000 copies and shot to the top of the charts just before Christmas 1971, offered a classic example.

> She said she'd like to bathe in milk; he said, 'All right, sweetheart,'
> And when he'd finished work one night he loaded up his cart.
> He said, 'D'you want it pasturise? 'Cause pasturise is best,'
> She says, 'Ernie, I'll be happy if it comes up to my chest.'

I was ten years old when Ernie soared to number one, not yet old enough to fully understand its cheeky content, and yet I loved it anyway. I also loved *The Benny Hill Show*, as anyone with a pulse should, it seemed to me in the 1970s. Yet by the mid-1980s the alternative comedy movement had decreed that Benny Hill's style of comedy belonged with the dinosaurs. The most blistering attack, as recorded by Mark Lewisohn in his magisterial biography of Hill, *Funny Peculiar*, was delivered by the stand-up comedian Ben Elton in an interview published in 1987 in the rock magazine *Q*.

'I believe,' said Elton, 'that the non-use of stereotypes – Irish people are stupid, women's tits are funny – is noticeable in my act. I mean, you have Benny Hill in the late '80s chasing half-naked women around a park when we know in Britain women can't even walk safe in a park any more. That for me is worrying. And while Benny Hill is chasing naked women about the park I could say "fuck" a thousand times on telly and I wouldn't be nearly as offensive as that.'

When Hill's show was subsequently axed, Elton got the blame. In the *Sun*, a disgruntled Richard Littlejohn came up with a cross but undoubtedly clever Ernie-inspired ode:

You can hear the Lefties howl,
And the right-on comics scowl,
And the chatter of the feminists
As the thought policemen prowl.

It continued:

Now Benny had a rival, a sneering little prig,
In shiny suit from public school, who liked to have a dig
At all the jokes which made us laugh
About knickers, bums and tits,
Couldn't understand why Benny Hill had millions in fits.
His name was Elton,
And he had the biggest ego on the Left.

Elton has been copping it ever since for his perceived priggishness in relation to Benny Hill, although the truth of the matter was that he had a point: *The Benny Hill Show* could be decidedly sexist. On the other hand, he got it dead wrong when he alluded to Benny chasing half-naked women round a park. In fact, it was the other way round: the half-naked women were always chasing Benny, as fans of the show, outraged by the first stirrings of what would later be called political correctness, were quick to point out.

That said, the off-screen Benny Hill did take a slightly unseemly interest in sex. The producer of 'Ernie', the veteran EMI man Wally Ridley, was driven mad in Abbey Road Studios on the day they recorded the song. 'He approached it in 50,000 different ways but the core of his whole being seemed to be sex,' Ridley told Mark Lewisohn:

Every song he wrote was about it and he wouldn't stop talking about it. He told me about some lady whose husband was in the navy, and if I took her out to a function she'd be happy to do whatever I wanted. He also boasted that he sometimes let a room in his second apartment to one of his producers, to screw some lady, and seemed to suggest that he could fit me up, too. It was endless. I had to say for him, 'Oh, for Christ's sake, Benny, we're here to record, stop all that bloody sex business and let's get on with the work.' The man was a professional, so he handled the recording session well, but if he'd only stopped talking about sex for five minutes it could have been a lovely afternoon.

As Lewisohn records, the content of *The Benny Hill Show* became lewder as the 1960s gave way to the 1970s. Significantly, Benny had moved from the BBC, where 'a core of suggestiveness' had run through his programmes, to Thames Television, where the sexual content became much more overt; where, in short, the core of suggestiveness became more of a corrrrr! As Lewisohn writes:

To a certain extent this reflected changes in society. A scan through any popular British magazine of the early 1970s – *TV Times*, for example – reveals an abundance of editorial and advertising material featuring scarcely dressed women, or women in tight T-shirts with no bra underneath, the kind of material that, within a few years, would be outlawed as 'sexist'. This was the allegedly 'permissive' era, when 'blokes' ogling at 'birds' who wore mini-skirts or hot-pants or bikinis was deemed fair game . . . especially in British TV comedy, a genre that had lost its 1960s radicalism and with certain honourable exceptions, was going right down the pan.

I'm happy to defer to Lewisohn in such matters, for he is also the author of the monumental *Radio Times Guide to TV Comedy*, and I can see that many of the sitcoms that delighted me and millions of others so much in the 1970s – *Are You Being Served?*, *Man About the House*, *Some Mothers Do 'Ave 'Em*, *On the Buses*, *Bless This House* – were not exactly leading the genre to new heights. Maybe it *was* going down the pan, although for those of us with a keen sense of the lavatorial, that wasn't necessarily a bad thing.

Incidentally, I would have enjoyed *Bless This House* even more than I did had I known then what I discovered from the 2007 obituary of Diana Coupland, the husky-voiced actress who played Jean Abbott to Sid James's Sid Abbott, that it was she and not Ursula Andress who sang the playful calypso 'Underneath the Mango Tree' in the iconic scene from *Dr No*, the first Bond film, when Andress, as Honey Ryder, emerged from the sea and into the fantasies of a million men. At the time Coupland was married to Monty Norman, the composer of the Bond theme, and was duly handed the gig. So there you are. The woman who sang so sensually about mango, banana and tangerine, sugar and ackee and cocoa bean, was not Honey Ryder from *Dr No*, but Jean Abbott from *Bless This House*.

27

'Nice To See You, To See You Nice': The Saturday-Night Phenomenon

The increasingly ribald tone of *The Benny Hill Show* that followed its move to ITV was quickly spotted, and excoriated, by Mary Whitehouse, who was by now running an energetic 'Clean up TV' campaign. She complained loudly and publicly about the 'degrading moral overtones' in Hill's work. Not even the indefatigable Mrs Whitehouse, though, could find any degrading moral overtones in *The Generation Game*, presented by a former song, dance and gags man who, coincidentally, Benny Hill himself had spotted and generously recommended to his director at the BBC, Ken Carter, way back in 1953. Carter did not act on this recommendation (the letter is still on file at the BBC, apparently), but of course Bruce Forsyth became a star anyway, and by the mid-1970s was, along with Benny Hill, Eric Morecambe and Ernie Wise, one of a gang of old troupers dominating light entertainment on television.

During Forsyth's tenure *The Generation Game* was obligatory Saturday tea-time viewing for just about everyone I knew. Until 1977, when I started going to watch Everton every Saturday through the football season, I doubt whether I missed more than half a dozen editions of *The Generation Game*, which began in 1971. In any case, by 1977 the golden age was over. Forsyth stopped hosting it that year and the following year his role was taken by Larry Grayson, who didn't do a bad job and somehow managed to make a catchphrase out of 'Shut that door!', but the show wasn't ever the same again.

The appeal of *The Generation Game*, of course, was not least rooted in the magical yet simple format – based on the Dutch TV show *Een Van De Acht* ('One out of Eight'), which had been devised by a Dutch housewife. But only Forsyth, in tandem with Anthea Redfern, the woman he'd met – it being the 1970s, almost inevitably – at a Miss Lovely Legs contest, could have made it the institution it became. And, pleasingly, he was kind of involved in its genesis, because the Dutch housewife (whose name has eluded all my research attempts, although I'm sure I wouldn't be able to pronounce it even if I could find it) had come up with the idea for *Een Van De Acht* after watching Brucie presenting Beat the Clock on an old edition of *Sunday Night at the London Palladium* she'd once seen on television while on holiday in West Germany.

In 2000, the bosses at London Weekend Television decided to bring back *Sunday Night at the London Palladium*, renamed *Tonight at the London Palladium* on account of it somewhat sacrilegiously being transmitted on Fridays. Brucie was asked to be the compère, as he had been decades earlier before handing over to his mate Jimmy Tarbuck (who had proved his mettle by introducing Petula Clark, having clean forgotten her name as she waited in the wings to come on, as 'someone who needs no introduction').

By then I already knew Brucie slightly, and managed to invite myself down to his handsome home on the Wentworth estate, so that we could talk about the golden age of variety before, perhaps, playing a few holes of golf. A housekeeper in designer leather trousers met me at the door – the Wentworth estate has very well-dressed housekeepers – and I was installed in Brucie's den, where I was able to have a good look at all the photographs of him as a benevolent paterfamilias, seated next to the fragrant Wilnelia, who, it seemed hard to believe, I had watched winning the Miss World contest with my mum and dad in Lynton Road, all those years before. I also knew that at forty, thirty-two years Brucie's junior, Wilnelia had only recently miscarried their second child. I've said it before in this book, but it bears echoing: didn't he do well?

After a while he trotted in, with those familiar, hurried, slightly camp little steps, looking dapper in a grey sleeveless cardie designed to facilitate the golf swing. 'Nice to see you, Brian,' he said, but I resisted the obvious riposte. We started talking about his beloved variety, and he told me, fully recognizing the irony, that he thought *The Generation Game* had played a significant part in its decline. 'Variety suffered as people shows took over, and *The Generation Game* was the first people show,' he said. 'Everything that's happened since has been a spin-off from *The Generation Game*.'

He was content, he added, with the generation he had been born into, in 1928. 'I was born at just the right time,' he said. 'A little earlier and I could have been killed in the war, as my brother was. Much later and I would have missed those golden years, when television was young and exciting.' He started out in show business at fourteen – as Boy Bruce, the Mighty Atom – so by the time he got his big break at the Palladium, aged thirty, he was already an old trouper. 'For years I went up and down the country doing variety,' he recalled. 'I was the second-spot comic, which is the hardest job in the world, the lowest form of animal life in show business.' Sometimes, he died. 'I had a terrible time at the Empress, Brixton. I don't know what it is now. I hope it's a bingo hall. I hated the place.'

In 1958 Val Parnell, who ran the Palladium, was looking for someone new to take over the *Sunday Night* show. 'I was doing summer season at Babbacombe,' Brucie recalled, 'and some friends of mine, François and Zandra, who did a novelty dancing act, persuaded Billy Marsh, an agent who worked for Bernard Delfont, to come and see me.'

It is often said that the age of variety is dead, and I have to be brutally honest here and say that the thought of a novelty dancing act called François and Zandra doesn't make me feel particularly inclined to mourn. But for their part in boosting the career of Bruce Forsyth, François and Zandra should be congratulated. Marsh recommended Brucie to Parnell, who offered him a six-week contract, and four years later, by then a household name, he was still at it, hobnobbing with the likes of Bob Hope, Bing Crosby, Sammy Davis Jr and Nat King Cole. But never, to his regret, Frank Sinatra. 'Sinatra never worked the Palladium,' he said, 'and I only met him once, very briefly, when he was appearing at the Festival Hall and my daughter Julie was in a group called Guys and Dolls, who were on the bill with him. Julie introduced us in the corridor before the show. I'm sure he had his eye on her, actually. She's a very attractive girl, my daughter.'

I'm sure she is, and to me that still seems like an opportunity missed. If Ol' Blue Eyes had fallen for Julie, and impetuously married her as he had been known to do on encountering a pretty girl decades younger than himself, then Bruce Forsyth would have wound up as Frank Sinatra's father-in-law. They could have recorded a duet called 'Come Fly With Me . . . With Me Come Fly'.

Brucie would have liked to be co-opted into the Rat Pack. It sometimes rankled with him that he came to be regarded as Mr Game Show when he could sing and dance and tinkle with the best of 'em, as indeed he did with Bob and Bing and Sammy and Nat. But the popularity in recent years of *Strictly Come Dancing* means that my children's generation knows him as a hoofer again, albeit a rather superannuated one, which is nice. The last time I spoke to him he had stopped fretting about the game-show tag, and told me that his only regret, apart from his ever-ascending golf handicap, was that he hadn't acted in more films.

'I'd more or less got the part in a film called *Candleshoe*,' he said, 'because David Niven had turned it down. But Niven changed his mind when he found out that Jodie Foster, who was a huge star even as a child, was going to be in it. And Lionel Bart wanted me as Fagin in *Oliver!* when Ron Moody wasn't sure whether to do it, which would have been wonderful for me.' Alas, Moody reviewed the situation, and that was that. It's interesting how even big stars, household names, look back on lifetimes of missed opportunities.

After an hour or so of chatting in his den that morning, Brucie informed me that he had to go upstairs for a lie-down. Recording six shows in twelve days had exhausted him. But he invited me to wait for him, which gave me a further opportunity to pry. Journalists love opportunities to pry. After forty-five minutes he came downstairs again, refreshed. 'Have you brought your golf clubs with you, Brian?' he asked. Naturally, I had. We went outside, where he zapped open an electronic garage door, revealing no car, just an electric golf cart. 'Put them on the back of my cart,' he said, which I did. We then climbed aboard and he reversed the thing out of the garage, then pointed it down the drive, where he zapped open a pair of elegant wrought-iron gates and we trundled out onto the highways and byways of the Wentworth estate, along with all the regular traffic. It was bizarre but wonderful, and I remember looking sidelong at his distinctive chin-dominated profile and wondering whether my dad, who loved *The Generation Game* unless he'd had a particularly bad afternoon on the ITV Seven, were perchance looking down.

*

If Noel Edmonds and Chris Tarrant vied for the title of Mr Saturday Morning in the 1970s, and Dickie Davies, the presenter of *World of Sport*, and his *Grandstand* counterpart Frank Bough – who years later was revealed to spend his leisure time at orgies sniffing cocaine, which merely intensified the respect my generation already felt for him – vied for the title of Mr Saturday Afternoon, then the title of Mr Saturday Night was a toss-up between Bruce Forsyth and Michael Parkinson.

An evening's viewing that began with *The Generation Game* ended up with *Parkinson*; it was practically the law, along with the requirement that all dads had to have at least one Herb Alpert LP. David Morrissey, the Liverpudlian actor and director whose father hated 'Denis' until he saw Debbie Harry singing it, told me that he loved *Parkinson* because his dad loved *Parkinson*, and that's how it was; if you were allowed to stay up beyond *Match of the Day*, it was one of life's pleasures to watch your parents watching *Parkinson*. The admiration I formed for old Hollywood stars like James Cagney, Fred Astaire and Henry Fonda derived at least as much from watching them talking to Parky, and watching my mum and dad watching them talking to Parky, as from seeing their old films.

Parky's ITV counterpart for most of the 1970s was Russell Harty, who, as a fellow Lancastrian, I should perhaps have favoured. But I could never quite warm to Harty, who seemed, perhaps anticipating the Jonathan Ross years, to project a little too much of his own personality onto proceedings. I wasn't the only one who couldn't quite warm to him. When he died in 1988, the *Daily Telegraph*'s tremendously posh obituaries editor Hugh Massingberd (known to *Private Eye* readers as Massivesnob), memorably dismissed him as 'an adenoidal northerner', whose contribution to British televison included 'sweaty gaucheries', a 'uniquely affected accent' and 'brazen sycophancy'. Even to me, that seemed a bit harsh.

Inevitably, there was a rivalry between Parkinson and Harty – they interviewed many of the same stars, and Harty did manage to get more out of some of them, such as the mildly batty Sir Ralph Richardson, who seemed to recognize some of the same mild battiness in Harty – but it was more perceived than actual. Once, when they were slightly mischievously seated next to one another at some function or other, and became aware of hundreds of pairs of eyes on them, hoping for them at worst to studiously ignore each other, and at best to have a punch-up, Harty quietly asked Parky whether he could dance. 'Only the foxtrot,' he replied, whereupon they took to the floor and danced an enthusiastic foxtrot. I imagine Parky led.

When LWT gave Harty a Saturday-night slot in 1978, to me it merely served to emphasize that Saturday night was synonymous with BBC1, even though Harty's co-host, in a show called *Saturday Night People*, was the man whose TV columns in the *Observer* had inspired me to want to write, Clive James. By 1978 I still yearned to write for a living, but what I really, really wanted to be was the next Michael Parkinson. At a time when most of my friends wanted to be the next Kenny Dalglish or Elvis Costello, I tended to keep this quiet. But even when I started going out with my mates on a Saturday night, even when Saturday nights meant five pints of bitter at the Snooty Fox, a bag of chips, and sometimes a chunder on the top deck of the number 17 bus, I still hurried home in the hope of catching Parky's last guest, followed by his cheery goodnight, and Laurie Holloway's jaunty 'derduddlurdurdlurdur . . .'

Now, while I wouldn't want to be accused of Russell Harty-like brazen sycophancy, here comes the most brazenly sycophantic sentence in this book. One of the joys of my career as a journalist has been a series of encounters with the men who bookended my Saturday nights in the 1970s, and my objective now is a game of golf with both Brucie and Parky, perhaps with Tarby along to make up the four. There, I've said it.

Actually, though, Parky is a relatively recent convert to golf. For years he remained deeply suspicious of the Royal & Ancient game, to the extent that in the 1970s he founded what he called the Anti-Golf Society. 'All my friends had started playing, like Jimmy Tarbuck,' he told me in 1999, in an interview for the *Independent*, 'and I was maybe a bit working-class chippy about it. Also, I didn't like clubs very much and still don't, because they exclude people. I have played most of my golf with a woman [his wife, Mary], and that's how you find out what it's like to be a second-class citizen.'

This denunciation of sexual inequality, I later wrote, was somewhat at odds with Parkinson's image as an unreconstructed son of South Yorkshire (the late Peter Cook used to bet his friends that there would never be an edition of *Parkinson* in which the host did not mention his Barnsley roots). He has himself encouraged that image down the years by confessing that he became stroppy and resentful when Mary briefly enjoyed a successful telly career of her own. Their marriage went through some turbulence, and in the end Mary's career gave way. So it could be argued that Parky the enemy of exclusivity was only ever a fair-weather friend of equal opportunities. Or that in later life he mellowed. Either way, there was no doubting the sincerity of his tirade against snotty golf clubs and, an object of particular loathing, the Marylebone Cricket Club.

'I wouldn't touch the MCC with a bargepole,' he huffed, and warmed to his theme. 'I don't believe in the honours system either.' Not even for showbiz types who do tremendous charity work? I asked. 'Not really, I've seen too many people getting involved in charity as a plan of campaign, in the hope of getting a gong. Let's give medals to the poor buggers who picked up the pieces after the Paddington crash, but to someone like me? For what? For being highly paid and having the time of our lives? I've never, ever woken up and said, "Sod it, I've got to go to work." Unlike my dad, who had to go down the pit every day.' I could hear Peter Cook stirring approvingly in his grave.

I was interviewing him that day because his talk show was up and running again after sixteen years off the air. Our paths had also crossed about five years earlier, and when I asked then whether there was any chance of *Parkinson* the chat show being revived, he pulled a face and asked why anyone who had interviewed Dame Edith Evans would possibly want to interview Madonna. He also pointed out that the vogue for straightforward chat shows seemed to have passed, that it was all about the host and no longer about the guest. In 1999 I brought all that up, and reminded him of what he'd said about Dame Edith Evans and Madonna. 'What changed?' I asked. 'I got a good offer,' he said, and roared with laughter. It wasn't to be the last time that he would end up contradicting seemingly heartfelt remarks. Only a year or so after Parky had so eloquently denounced the honouring of TV celebrities, I was interested – and I confess slightly disappointed, after being so impressed with his stirring 'man of the people' soliloquy – to read that Prince Charles had invested him with a CBE for services to broadcasting. And in the 2008 New Year's Honours List (shortly after his final show, which included clips of many of his favourite interviews, including one with Madonna) he became Sir Parky. But I can't really quibble with that. He had certainly served me well.

It turned out that Britain at large was more than ready, in 1998, for a return to the Parkinson-style chat show. The difference between then and the 1970s was that his guests were now people of my generation, who had grown up watching him on Saturday nights, or whose mums, like Robbie Williams's, had always fancied him. This was all a bit arse about face, as they say in Barnsley. If anyone has to be starstruck on a chat show, it should generally be the guy asking the questions. And yet the veneration worked to Parkinson's advantage. George Michael, born in 1963, was another with fond memories of BBC1's Saturday nights in the 1970s. So when he decided to share his recollection of events in a public lavatory in Beverly Hills, following his arrest for lewd behaviour by a cop posing as a gay pick-up, he got his people to contact Parkinson's people.

However, Parkinson had a problem. How was he going to open the show? He couldn't go in like Flynn, as it were, by quizzing George immediately about the arrest. 'But I knew that everyone would be waiting for me to ask the question,' Parky told me, 'and I couldn't bear the bloody tension. Then he rang me and said he wanted to get together. We sat down at The Ivy, and his first words to me were, "I've always wanted to get on your show . . . to think I had to show my dick to an LA cop to do it!"' Parky roared again. 'And I said, "I'm not writing you a script, but if you say that as soon as you walk on, I'll be home and dry and you will be too."'

Parkinson's George Michael interview in December 1998 enhanced the reputations of both men, and did no harm, either, to the sales of George's latest single. Their encounter was never intended simply as a soul-baring exercise. 'Of course not,' Parky said. 'He had a new record coming out. Do you think Bing Crosby came on my show because he was a personal friend? Bollocks! But if we had to have him singing his latest song, was that such a bad thing?' Nay, nay and thrice nay, as Frankie Howerd (the only *Parkinson* guest who ever begged to be scripted) might have said.

Yet even now there persists the notion that in the 1970s, Parkinson's interviews were somehow purer than they were decades later: that Danny Kaye or Lauren Bacall dropped in to the studio in White City just because they happened to be on their way to Heathrow Airport. As the man himself says, it's bollocks. On the other hand, I'm sure he'd be the first to admit that his guests in the 1970s had a star quality that his post-1998 guests, on the whole, lacked. Maybe that's because so many of them were stars from Hollywood's golden age, whereas the likes of Jeremy Clarkson and Trinny and Susannah can't even claim to be products of television's golden age. But even more of a factor than that is that the appeal of

Parky's show in the 1970s was inextricably linked with the Saturday-night vibe: *The Generation Game, The Duchess of Duke Street, The Two Ronnies, Starsky and Hutch,* the *News, Match of the Day, Parkinson.* The memory is almost enough to make a grown man cry.

28

A Dramatic Decade: Upstairs and Downstairs in Duke Street, with Benny from *Crossroads*

The Duchess of Duke Street lasted for thirty-one episodes and ran on BBC1 between September 1976 and December 1977, which in the scheme of things wasn't very long, but coincided perfectly with what for me was the halcyon period of Saturday-night telly. Yet it is little-remembered now, at least by comparison with dramas such as *Upstairs, Downstairs*, which was a similar confection about Edwardian domestic life, and was indeed produced by the same man, a former army officer called John Hawkesworth, who had himself grown up – above stairs – in Belgravia.

That all these years later *Upstairs, Downstairs* has a much greater claim on our affections than *The Duchess of Duke Street* is all the more noteworthy considering that it was an ITV production. In fact it was one of the first serials to show that independent television could, in the classy drama department, give the BBC a run for its money. When it almost inevitably became a hit in America, where even now it is widely assumed that we Brits acquire our stiff upper lips either in the drawing-room or in the pantry, everyone assumed that it had been made by the BBC, considered in the States, then as now, to be an impregnable bastion of quality.

The character from the fictional house at 165 Eaton Place who was clutched most emphatically to America's bosom was a woman with a formidable bosom of her own, the cook Mrs Bridges. The actress who played her, Angela Baddeley, suddenly found in the twilight of an unremarkable acting career that she was a star on both sides of the Atlantic, celebrated as the bossy but kind-hearted human face of domestic service. This was ironic, since in 1904 she had been born into a life of Edwardian wealth and privilege as Madeline Angela Clinton-Baddeley, and had based Mrs Bridges on one of the several cooks her family had employed when she was a child. Even as a married woman, she and her husband, the theatre director Glen Byam Shaw (who had been a lover of the poet Siegfried Sassoon, just to make things even less Mrs Bridges-like), had four servants.

Still, there was nothing lacking in the proletarian credentials of the two actress friends who conceived *Upstairs, Downstairs*: Jean Marsh's mother had been a housemaid in Hackney; Eileen Atkins was born in a Salvation Army women's hostel and her father, before becoming a gas-meter reader, had been an under-butler.

Marsh and Atkins originally had a comedy in mind, tentatively called *Behind the Green Baize Door*. Then they took out the comedy element and decided to call it *Below Stairs*, before rejecting that and flirting with *Two Little Maids in Town*, *The Servants' Hall* and *That House in Eaton Square*, before alighting on the more succinct and evocative *Upstairs, Downstairs*. Marsh took the part of the shrewish head parlourmaid Rose, with Atkins earmarked for the role of Sarah,

the troublesome under-parlourmaid, except that at the time she was –
irony piled upon irony – playing Queen Elizabeth 1 in Robert Bolt's
play *Vivat Vivat Regina!*

So the role of Sarah went to Pauline Collins, who in real life was
married to John Alderton, famous as the hapless teacher Mr Hedges
in *Please Sir!* This was a source of some confusion to those of us who
sort of thought that the characters in *Upstairs, Downstairs* were real –
not that I was quite as deluded as a family in Worcestershire, who
draped their front door with black crêpe paper when, in the fourth
series, which began in October 1973, the *Titanic* went down, taking
lovely Lady Marjorie Bellamy (Rachel Gurney) down with it.

It was further disorientating when Alderton himself joined the
staff at Eaton Square as the chauffeur, Thomas, especially as Lady
Marjorie's successor as Lord Bellamy's love interest was the fragrant
Hannah Gordon, who'd played opposite Alderton, as the ex-wife with
whom he was still in love, in the 1972 sitcom *My Wife Next Door*. I
don't know whether there was a smaller pool of actors available in the
1970s than there is now, but that sort of thing happened rather a lot.
Maybe it was simply the case, even more than today, that a good performance in one comedy or drama was liable to beget a part in
another, which was why Gordon Jackson, having scarcely performed
his last piece of butling at Eaton Place as that pillar of rectitude Mr
Hudson, seemed to pitch up so swiftly as Cowley, the head of CI5, in
The Professionals.

The part of Mr Hudson, the *Upstairs, Downstairs* butler, was first
of all offered to George Cole, who would have been fine except that
he was still so widely identified as Flash Harry, the spiv in the St
Trinian's films, an association that was perhaps a boon rather than a
hindrance once he started playing Arthur Daley in *Minder*. Jackson,
by contrast, was perfectly cast, even though he irreverently pointed
out that Hudson stood for everything he disliked most about British
society. A review in the *Daily Mirror* summed up his performance

nicely, suggesting that Jackson played Hudson 'with the air of a man who'd been a preacher in some joyless kirk'.

Like few other drama serials before or since, *Upstairs, Downstairs* quickly found a place in the nation's heart, and also in its terms of reference. Ruby, the put-upon parlourmaid with the face like a slapped arse, as schoolboys of the time unkindly put it, practically became a 1970s synonym for a hapless drudge. Television back then was a rich source of synonyms. Benny from *Crossroads*, for example, was a phenomenon similar to Ruby, but writ even larger. Britain's favourite village idiot, Benny was played by Paul Henry, whom it was almost impossible to think of as a bright, quick-witted actor, given that he was saddled with Benny's face. It was rumoured of Henry that when he took sabbaticals from *Crossroads* – one of which lasted for six months after he went to look for a spanner, which even by Benny's standards seemed a bit of a misfortune – he worked in grand Shakespearean productions. But most of us preferred to imagine that he was on a course somewhere learning to read, or to tell the time.

Like few other soap stars, Benny became an institution even bigger than the serial in which he featured. During the Falklands War in 1982, British troops none too affectionately nicknamed the Falkland Islanders 'Bennies'. And when their superiors told them that it had to stop, they renamed the islanders 'Stills', on the basis that they were 'still Bennies'.

The Duchess of Duke Street had nobody as iconic as Ruby or Benny, or even Mr Hudson, but it enjoyed tremendous popularity all the same. It starred Gemma Jones as Louisa Trotter, a former servant who'd worked her way up the social scale to become proprietress of the swish Bentinck Hotel. Such a rise might seem improbable in Edwardian London yet the drama was based on the real rags-to-riches story of one Rosa Lewis, a humble watchmaker's daughter from Essex who ended up running the Cavendish Hotel in Jermyn Street, and was already the model for Evelyn Waugh's fictional hotel-keeper in his novel *Vile Bodies*. Rosa was nicknamed 'the Duchess' by her regular clients. These included King Edward VII – with whom, towards the end of her long life, she liked to imply that she had enjoyed connubial relations – as well as Kaiser Wilhelm, Charlie Chaplin and none other than John Hawkesworth, the patrician *Upstairs, Downstairs* producer whose idea the series was.

The Duchess of Duke Street was one of those dramas I could watch with my mum, which was more – quite a lot more – than could be said of another big production of 1976, *A Bouquet of Barbed Wire*, with its implications of incest. I'll return to *A Bouquet of Barbed Wire* later, on the basis that no book written by a man who in 1976 was an adolescent walking round in a cloud of testosterone can possibly exclude it. Sticking for now with *The Duchess of Duke Street*, however, it sowed the seed of an ambition which I thought I might pursue if the Clive James-fuelled desire to become a writer came to naught. Hotel-keeping looked like fun, especially in a place like the Bentinck, with all those princes and showgirls coming and going. For about a year, when any solicitous relative or friend of the family asked me what I wanted to do when I left full-time education, I told them that I plannned to be either a writer or a hotelier, the latter notion shaped entirely by *The Duchess of Duke Street*.

Television in the 1970s was more influential than any careers adviser. I know two highly successful performers now, contemporaries of mine give or take a couple of years, who cheerfully admit that their careers were propelled by dramas they watched on telly when they were kids. One is David Morrissey, for whom it was an episode of *Colditz*, circa 1973, that made him want to act. As soon as he told me that, I knew which episode it was: the one in which Michael Bryant played a British PoW who faked madness so convincingly that he was eventually released on compassionate grounds from Colditz Castle, only for us to discover that in pretending to lose his mind, he'd actually lost it. I can even remember where I watched that episode – at my grandma's house in London – and it had a chilling effect on me. On David the effect was even more profound.

'I remember when Michael Bryant was scraping at the cobbles and he looks up and gives this wink, and you think he's fooled everyone,' he could still recall almost thirty-five years later. 'At the end, when he'd got away, I was euphoric. Then the other prisoners got a letter from his wife and it turned out he'd really gone mad. I was devastated, in bits. But that's when acting moved me in a way it never had before. And I thought "I want to do that . . ."'

Caroline Aherne, the comic genius behind *The Mrs Merton Show* and *The Royle Family*, once told me much the same thing about *Abigail's Party*, a BBC *Play for Today* which she watched, enraptured, in 1977. She was already a funny and gifted child, but watching Alison Steadman as the monstrous Beverley in Mike Leigh's largely improvised comedy of lower middle-class manners is what made her ache to be a performer herself.

My own more modest and relatively fleeting ambition to go into the hotel business did not quite come to pass as spectacularly as theirs, although I did land a job as a hotel porter during the year I spent in Paris, and was gratified to be reminded on a daily basis how strikingly similar the old-fashioned and somewhat eccentric Hotel Castille, on Rue Cambon, was to the Bentinck on Duke Street, of blessed memory. Moreover the manageress, a formidable little Frenchwoman called Mademoiselle Casado (I never knew what her first name was, or even whether she had one; she was Mademoiselle Casado even to people who had worked with her for thirty years), was the very incarnation of Louise Trotter. It never occurred to me to nickname her 'La Duchesse' but I wish it had. It would have fitted perfectly.

The clientele was quite like the Bentinck's, too. Many of our guests were aristocratic types, and the register was full of names such as Roosevelt and Eisenhower, elderly well-heeled Americans related to former Presidents who chose the faded elegance of the Castille over the opulent grandeur of places like the Ritz and the Meurice because it was more discreet.

Contrary to the popular image of Americans abroad, these people always tried to talk French, or at least the men did, having invariably completed a short correspondence course before setting off for Europe. Nor, with me in my bellhop's uniform, was there any reason why they should think me anything but a native, so they often talked to me in pidgin French and, on the orders of the stern Mademoiselle Casado, I always had to reply in kind.

On one memorable occasion, a nice old American man said to me, in truly execrable French: 'Bonjewer, Monsewer. Oo-ay la bureau de poste?'

As slowly and clearly as I could, I told him in French that the post office was just round the corner in the Rue des Capucines. He looked blankly at me, as did his wife. 'What did he say, Harry?' she asked. Harry plainly didn't have a clue. So, trying to save him from the humiliation of admitting that he wasn't at all sure, I translated for her. 'I explained to your husband,' I said in English, 'that to get to the nearest post office you must turn left out of the hotel, then turn into the first street on the right, the Rue des Capucines. The post office is along there on the left.' She continued to look blankly at me, doubtless unable to believe that a young Frenchman in Paris could be talking fluent English to her. A triumphant-looking Harry then turned to her. 'He explained,' he said slowly, as if talking to a half-wit, 'that we must turn left out of the hotel, then take the first street on the right, and the post office is along there on the left.' 'Ohh,' she said, happily, and they both walked away, almost certainly congratulating themselves on the excellence of his Berlitz language course.

I had some fun at the Hotel Castille, and some formative experiences both nice and not so nice. A veteran French film director who must remain *sans nom* even after all these years once asked me to take a bottle of Champagne to his room, and when I pushed the door open I was more than a little alarmed – as you might expect – to find him naked on the bed, vigorously masturbating. If that sort of thing ever happened at the Bentinck, and I imagine it probably did, we certainly never saw it on a Saturday evening on BBC1.

29

A Dramatic Decade, Part Two: Claudius and a Bouquet of Barbed Champions

Rather less was left to the imagination in *A Bouquet of Barbed Wire*, yet it wasn't nearly as raunchy as is often remembered by folk of my age, and the incest was only ever implied. Nonetheless, sex loomed larger than it ever had before in a major drama serial and the American actor James Aubrey, who played Gavin Sorensen, later summed up what a tempest of passion it was, especially given the way shooting schedules operate. 'I was introduced to the actress who plays my wife,' he said. 'About thirty seconds later I was in bed with her. Then I was beating her senseless and within a flash I was at her funeral.'

That actress was Susan Penhaligon, who played Prue Sorensen and whose marriage to Gavin left her father Peter consumed with highly inappropriate jealousy. Peter was played by the ever-excellent

Frank Finlay, an actor destined, however long and distinguished his CV, to be remembered for playing a man who wanted to shag his daughter.

For a few weeks in 1976, with these unseemly comings and goings being discussed in every launderette and at every whist drive, Penhaligon was briefly as famous as any soap actress is today. She was understandably tipped for TV stardom after playing pouting, tragic Prue – who popped her clogs in episode seven – yet it never quite happened. Years later I interviewed her in the Langham Hotel in London. She was about to go on tour in a play called *Deathtrap*, coincidentally with an even bigger star of the 1970s who also never quite achieved what was expected of him, David Soul. Anyway, in the interview we talked about *A Bouquet of Barbed Wire*, what she had done before it, and what had gone wrong for her afterwards. It was also an interview which gave me, in the ensuing newspaper article, a memorable opening paragraph: 'There are only so many times in the life of an actress when she is required to sit naked among a herd of goats circling her nipples with lipstick. For Susan Penhaligon, opportunity knocked just once, in the 1971 film version of Dylan Thomas's *Under Milk Wood.*'

She did not flaunt her body quite as excitingly in *A Bouquet of Barbed Wire* as she had in *Under Milk Wood*, yet she copped the worst of the maelstrom of publicity. 'Actually, I was one of the most moral characters,' she told me. 'My mother got into bed with my husband, my father with his secretary, but I only slept with my husband. And yet a lot of the more salacious reaction seemed to land on my shoulders. I was completely at sea with it. I just didn't understand how to deal with the intrusion into my private life. These days there would be more support.'

Oddly, my 1976 Letts Schoolboy Diary has nothing to say about *A Bouquet of Barbed Wire*. That's partly because its early episodes were rudely punctuated by my father's sudden death, which gave me other things to think about. But I can recall watching it avidly even that very week, in which Clive James gave it a modest thumbs-up in his *Observer* column. 'There are worse serials to get hooked on,' he wrote. 'It won't rot your brain like *The Brothers*. Nor will you see – as in so many other series currently on the screen – the roof of a coal mine fall on the hero's father. Instead there is plenty of solid middle-class adultery and incest. Sheila Allen is having a whale of a time as the Older Woman, who has welcomed her daughter's husband into her bed, which is roughly what her husband (Frank Finlay) would like to do with the daughter, and perhaps will, or even perhaps once did, or perhaps both.'

I meant to watch it all again for the first time in thirty-odd years before writing this book, but I didn't, not least because, as in the case of *Rich Man, Poor Man*, I was worried that it might not live up to my memories. So I am indebted to a fellow called Heath Blair (what misfortune, by the way, to be named after not just one much-lampooned Prime Minister, but two), who sat through the DVD collection and posted the following review on the internet:

> For all its supposed sexual candour (hints of incest and the endless confessions of sado-masochism) it's a deeply conservative piece at heart. The naughty girls and naughty boys get what they deserve in the end – misery and death. That'll teach 'em. It pretends not to pass judgement on the characters, but, really, their comeuppance is judgement enough.
>
> The serial's sexual politics would rightly enrage even a mild feminist then and now. For example, a major character (pregnant) is beaten half to death by her violent husband and the police are NEVER mentioned, not even by the doctors who treat her! The assault is put down to everyday domestic strife. And besides, the couple have a sado-masochistic relationship, so that's OK then.

So, what's good about it? Its ludicrousness. Viewed by contemporary audiences, a lot of it is enjoyable on a trash basis. There are moments of unintended hilarity only appreciable thirty years hence. For example, the leading lady's off-screen lover (a very lusty chap) is called Sven Erickson. I kid you not. And of course there's Frank Finlay's wardrobe – a nightmare torrent of Burtons menswear. Frank's ties are . . . well, *A Bouquet of Barbed Wire* features the first known instance of a tie wearing a man.

I hope this book contains more than a few entertaining nuggets of trivia, but if there's one that stands head and shoulders above the others (albeit with the help of stacked heels) it is surely the fact that, according to Mr Heath Blair, the script of *A Bouquet of Barbed Wire* referred to an oversexed character called Sven Erickson. Despite his suspect name, I'd like to think we can trust Mr Heath Blair on this. In which case, then, for anyone who enjoyed as much as I did the in-depth accounts of the former England football manager's sexual adventures, which included the marvellous detail that he left his built-up shoes neatly outside Ulrika Jonsson's bedroom, it is truly a nugget to cherish.

And yet despite that, and despite other even more memorable dimensions to *A Bouquet of Barbed Wire*, there were other dramas even in that same year of 1976 deserving of a more illustrious place in TV history. The pick of them was *I, Claudius*, the BBC's thirteen-part adaptation of Robert Graves's epic historical novel, which would doubtless have been just as good, if somewhat different, if instead of Derek Jacobi an earlier choice to play the stuttering, limping, twitching Claudius had taken the part. That was Ronald William George Barker, better known to the nation as Ronnie, and I hope Jacobi won't be offended if I state here that the Ronnie Barker Claudius seems like one of the great missed opportunities of our time.

That said, *I, Claudius* (which in the absence of Barker did at least star Christopher Biggins as the Emperor Nero) could hardly have been any better. The thirteen episodes ran right through the autumn, from 20 September to 6 December, and my mum and I, watching in Lynton Road, were riveted from the moment a snake slithered over a mosaic floor in the opening credits. We were, however, forced to overcome a degree of mutual discomfort during scenes such as the one in which Caligula (played by John Hurt as a hybrid of Quentin Crisp and Charles Manson) disembowelled his pregnant sister and ate the embryo, and another in which he bought his Uncle Tiberius (George Baker) a book of gay porn. Those may have been the moments when my mum went to the kitchen to make herself a glass of lemon tea. She wasn't nearly as buttoned-up as she might have been on the subject of sex, and of course had cheekily put my modest collection of girlie magazines with the *Look & Learns*, but she recognized that there were some viewing experiences that were best not shared by a teenage boy sitting alone with his mother.

It is also worth sparing a belated thought for those who had to make *I, Claudius*, with its flashes of nudity and bonking, acceptable to an American TV audience. It was shown there on the Public Broadcasting System, on a Sunday-evening programme presented by the venerable Alistair Cooke called *Masterpiece Theatre*. PBS carried no commercials and almost by definition was believed by educated Americans to be an oasis of quality in a cultural TV desert. Yet the very first episode of *I, Claudius* opened with a chorus of African dancing girls, naked from the waist up, helping the Emperor Augustus celebrate the seventh anniversary of the Battle of Actium. This was obviously unacceptable in a country that considered the baring of a female breast so morally degenerate that a fleeting glimpse of Janet Jackson's nipple during transmission of the half-time show at the 2004 Super Bowl twenty-eight years later practically caused a collective nervous breakdown. The opening sequence of *I, Claudius* was therefore deemed too racy for American sensibilities, and was cut by the censors. I, by contrast, thought it the best possible start.

Similarly gripped, it turned out, were Alfred and Daisy Jacobi, Derek's parents, an elderly couple from Leytonstone who had both worked for most of their lives in a department store on Walthamstow High Street and weren't at all sure what to make of their only child's career as an actor, until he pitched up in the title role in *I, Claudius*. 'For my parents, although I had been with the National Theatre, it really could have been the National Coal Board,' Jacobi told me years later, in an interview for the *Independent*. 'But to be on the telly . . . Derek's made it! They'd tried everybody for Claudius before they tried me, though. Charlton Heston, even Ronnie Barker.'

I did not share with Jacobi my regret at never having seen Ronnie Barker play Claudius. Instead, I asked him whether Robert Graves, then in his early eighties, was ever a presence on the set. 'He did come to the studio, but he was more than a bit gaga by then. I sat next to him at lunch, and at one point he turned to me and said, "I've always had a great deal of trouble with the Scots, I suppose because I've reached the grand old age of 130." Later, he sent the Beeb a telegram saying, "Claudius is very pleased." He thought he had a hotline to Claudius.'

Like so many actors who sprang to prominence in the 1970s, Jacobi is destined to be remembered more for the role that made him a household name than for any of the other great dramatic parts that earned him a knighthood in 1994.

But unlike Bernard Hill, for example, he doesn't seem to mind. Indeed, to his eternal credit, he has some fun with the association. Close to where we live in deepest Herefordshire there is a vineyard with a wonderful cafe attached, called Broadfield Court. The place is run by a splendid woman called Alex James, who was an actress in a former life and became extremely friendly with Derek Jacobi, who is godfather to one of her children. From time to time the great man escapes to Broadfield for a little R&R, and sometimes mucks in at the cafe, waiting on tables. On one occasion he noticed a couple having an intense discussion about him. It looks like him, they were clearly saying, and yet how can it be, coming over to take our order for tea and scones in a Herefordshire garden? Jacobi put them out of their misery in the best possible way, twitching violently and saying, 'Are you r—r—r—ready t—t—to order?'

When you see *I, Claudius* now, only the stillness of the camera and the stagey production values make it look dated. With the odd swooping helicopter shot and some slightly more extravagant crowd scenes (i.e. containing more than seven people), it could easily hold its head up in the twenty-first century. Whether too many TV dramas made nowadays would have enhanced the 1970s is a different matter. Back then, the writing and acting mattered more than anything else; now there are other things to consider, like where to put Robson Green.

As first witness in this defence of the 1970s I cite the courtroom drama *Crown Court*, which started in 1972 and ran on weekday lunchtimes. It can still be seen today on an obscure channel called Legal TV, and looks positively calcified in many ways, but it's fun seeing actors destined to become household names (Richard Wilson, Maureen Lipman, Ben Kingsley etc.) playing the QCs, and, more to the point, I would defy almost anyone to watch it for more than twenty minutes and not get hooked.

Even by the standards of the 1970s the action was a little on the static side, which one or two of the more avant garde directors tried to counteract by giving the cameraman licence to circle the witness box and occasionally shoot the defendant from a rakish angle. But here was a drama that fundamentally stood or fell by nothing other than its writing and acting, and it stood, triumphantly. According to my 1974 and 1975 diaries I was on two occasions kept off school with a cold and then blagged the following day off, even though I was right as rain, just to see what happened on *Crown Court*. Of course, Noel Gallagher's law of news – that regional news headlines in the 1970s concerned cats getting stuck up trees, and now concern people getting beheaded in post offices – applies equally to the *Crown Court* story-lines. A similar project these days would require mass murder or serial rape as topics; defendants in the 1970s were answering mugging or petty embezzlement charges. Yet it was compulsive stuff.

No less compulsive were those dramas as implausible as *Crown Court* was plausible, those from Lew Grade's Incorporated Television Company stable such as *Randall and Hopkirk (Deceased)*, *The Champions*, *Department S*, *Jason King* and *The Persuaders*. I loved every one of these shows, especially *The Persuaders*, which as already chronicled in these pages teamed Roger Moore with Tony Curtis as Lord Brett Sinclair and Danny Wilde, a pair of jet-setting playboys whose life stories cleverly unfolded alongside each other in what, to my mind circa 1974, were opening credits of unparalleled brilliance.

Even at the time I think I knew that *The Persuaders* was schlock – Jez Sykes and I often deconstructed the frequent fist fights, which always ended with either Sinclair or Wilde rubbing their knuckles, even though scarcely a punch had landed within even three inches of its target – but it at least carried the pretence of class. Not that in some of its dubbed European manifestations they even pretended. There was a decidedly tongue-in-cheek tone to the German dubbing, with references to Lord Brett Sinclair becoming 007 (as Roger Moore did in 1973) and Wilde saying to Sinclair, 'Du musst jetzt etwas schneller werden, sonst bist Du nicht synchron' (talk faster, you aren't in sync any more).

The reason Grade hired Curtis to play the millionaire oilman Danny Wilde was because he was perennially trying to break into the lucrative American TV market; indeed he had already approached Rock Hudson, who was unavailable. Had the discreetly gay Hudson signed on the dotted line, it would have meant that two stars of Lew Grade's ITC shows turned out to be far from the irrepressible ladies' men they portrayed on screen.

In 1975, Peter Wyngarde, who in *Department S* had played the fop-
pish but unequivocally heterosexual sleuth Jason King, a character so
popular that he subsequently got his own eponymous spin-off series,
was convicted of an act of gross indecency with a truck driver in the
toilets at Gloucester bus station. When word got out there was a
flurry of bad jokes at my school – most of them, as I recall, centring
on what the letter S might conceivably have stood for in *Department
S*. Whatever, Wyngarde was fined £75 and his career never recovered, which is a crying shame. In 1970, at the height of his popularity,
he had recorded an album with possibly the worst title of any album
in history – *When Sex Leers its Inquisitive Head* – and while that
might be a pretty good reason for an acting career to implode, a private quickie with a consenting truck driver surely isn't. After all,
thirty-odd years later George Michael was on *Parkinson* talking about
something rather similar and getting rapturous applause.

Another of Lew Grade's shows that gratuitously starred an
American – in this case the decidedly dishy Stuart Damon – was
The Champions, a preposterous piece of nonsense that I enjoyed
immensely, not least because it also starred, as widowed biologist
Sharron Macready, the uber-glamorous Alexandra Bastedo, who
seemed to me the most exquisite woman in the world by some distance. There are some already celebrated in these pages who were
sexier, but none more beautiful, and I was delighted to find when
writing this book that she is alive and well and even writes her own
internet blog. I called it up with almost breathless excitement, hoping
that she might be discussing old episodes of *The Champions*, each of
which began with a grave and somewhat long-winded voice-over:
'Craig Stirling, Sharron Macready and Richard Barrett . . . The
Champions. Endowed with the qualities and skill of superhumans . . .
qualities and skills, both physical and mental, to the peak of human
performance. Gifts given to them by the unknown race of people
from a lost city in Tibet. Gifts that are a secret to be closely

guarded . . . a secret that enables them to use their powers to their best advantage . . . as the Champions of Law, Order and Justice. Operators of the International Agency of Nemesis!'

But Bastedo's blog had nothing to do with *The Champions*. 'This month unfortunately has seen quite a few problems,' it began. 'Eddie the recently castrated Shetland has had problems with his back left hoof. The frog part is having to be bathed and disinfected daily with either Purple Spray or Pevidine and Jack the other little bay Shetland has been treated for a high temperature.' It turned out that she now runs an animal sanctuary in Sussex and is president of her local branch of the RSPCA. I'm glad she's still doing her bit for the world, albeit no longer for the Geneva-based International Agency of Nemesis, which lives on only in the memory. It remains obligatory for folk of my generation who find themselves in Geneva to pose in front of the famous Jet d'Eau fountain, as Craig, Sharron and Richard did.

By the time you read these words, incidentally, it could well be that a movie remake of *The Champions* is well into production, or even in the cinemas. In 2007 it was announced that the Mexican director Guillermo del Toro, who made the fantastical *Pan's Labyrinth*, had been hired to update the story for the delectation of a twenty-first century audience.

It was also announced, in 2006, that a big-screen version of *The Persuaders* was in the pipeline. Steve Coogan and Ben Stiller were mentioned. So, a little later, were Hugh Grant and George Clooney. *Randall and Hopkirk (Deceased)* has already been exhumed and re-cast for television with Reeves and Mortimer, and a great big pile of poop it was, too. Nor did I watch, on principle, the return of Penelope Keith and Peter Bowles for a one-off *To the Manor Born* screened over Christmas 2007. I don't know why these people can't leave our memories unsullied. As I've already incredulously reported in these pages, even the original 1970s mummy's-boy comedy *Some Mothers Do 'Ave*

'*Em* is supposedly to be remade by Fox TV, the American network owned by Rupert Murdoch. To which, mindful that Rupert entered his seventy-sixth year with his nonagenarian mother Dame Elisabeth still very much alive, there's really only one thing to say: Ooh Betty!

30

'You're a Star, You're a Star, Big Fat Bum and a Playtex Bra': Quiz Games and Talent Shows

Dame Elisabeth Murdoch and her boy Rupert bring me seamlessly to the theme of mother and younger child only, and thus to *Ask the Family*, on which quizmaster Robert Robinson used to target family combinations for particular questions. My mum and I always sat up a little straighter for the 'mother and younger child only' questions. Even though I had no siblings, they seemed meant for us.

Ask the Family ran throughout the 1970s, had an extremely jaunty theme tune of sitar music and, very excitingly for me, once featured a family from Southport, the Pollocks, whom I knew. In fact, in 1975 I escorted Elyssa Pollock to the Odeon to watch *The Man Who Would be King*, part of a double-date engineered by my friend Gary, who had his eyes – and, by the time Sean Connery and Michael Caine had reached Kafiristan, his hands too – on Elyssa's friend Louise. Gary was much more precocious in these matters than I was. I had never been on any kind of date before and wasn't at all sure what was expected of me, although I eventually dared to feign a stretch, and left my arm draped awkwardly around Elyssa's shoulders.

Watching *The Man Who Would be King* next to Elyssa Pollock at the Odeon, like Proust eating his childhood madeleines, has had enduring consequences. Every time I have seen all or part of it on TV I have been transported back to that cinema, where I sat through much of the film rigid with uncertainty while Gary and Louise necked energetically a couple of seats long.

I can't remember much about the Pollocks' run on *Ask the Family*, although they certainly got through the first round and I seem to recall them doing pretty well – it could even be that they reached the final. Robinson handled the quiz-mastering expertly, yet his expertise, and his impressive longevity as a broadcaster (it was he who chaired the discussion on *BBC3* in 1965 in which the critic Ken Tynan uttered the word 'fuck' – and even then he was something of a TV veteran, having started out presenting the film programme *Picture Parade* in 1956), never quite resulted in him being embraced to the nation's bosom. This may be because he always seemed rather condescending (*Private Eye* nicknamed him 'Smuggins'), but I've always liked him, if only because the familiar tones and gleaming pate have been a presence in my living-room for about as long as I can remember.

Robinson also chaired the obscure-word game *Call My Bluff*, which in the 1970s was one of the few programmes that I watched on the dedicatedly esoteric BBC2. I loved *Call My Bluff*, especially in the years when Frank Muir and Patrick Campbell were the team captains. Campbell was the sort of figure who would never feature regularly on television now, and television is much the worse for it. An Irish aristocrat – he was the third Baron Glenavy, no less – he also suffered from a dreadful, Emperor Claudius-like stammer, which Frank Muir described beautifully in his autobiography *A Kentish Lad*: 'Paddy was wonderful. His stammer was a bother to him – he was a natural talker – but when he unthinkingly embarked on a word beginning with an S and got stuck, he would rear up in his seat like an ostrich which had sat in something, eyes close together like a cuff link, and he would struggle until he had got the word out, banging the desk and muttering to himself "Come on! Come ON!"'

Muir told another lovely story about Campbell in *A Kentish Lad*. During the run of *Call My Bluff* a publisher took them both out for lunch, to an Italian restaurant in Soho, to discuss putting together a book based on the series. Campbell ordered one of most expensive dishes on the menu, quenelles of pike, but was disappointed, when his plate arrived, to find only four pieces of fish. Muir engaged his famous wit. 'Four quenelles for fifteen quid!' he exclaimed, and then, aping Campbell's slight Irish accent, added ambiguously: 'Four quenelles!'

'Paddy always said it was the best pun he had ever heard,' wrote Muir, with becoming immodesty. 'As he lived in the South of France where quenelles were often on the menu, he tried to appropriate my pun and dazzle his friends, but, alas, life is not as compliant as that. Whenever Paddy entertained in a Nice restaurant he would hopefully order quenelles and they were duly laid in front of him; sometimes there were three quenelles on the plate, frequently there was a more generous helping of five, six or seven quenelles, but never, ever, was Paddy served four quenelles.'

Panel shows have a long and honourable heritage on British television. *What's My Line?*, chaired by Eamonn Andrews, began in 1951, *Call My Bluff* in 1965. But I am duty-bound to concede, yet again, that America got there first. Even *What's My Line?*, generally considered the quintessential TV panel game of the monochrome era, was a US import, having begun on CBS the previous year. *Call My Bluff*, too, came from the States.

Whether America also got there first in terms of inventing television itself, incidentally, seems to depend on which side of the Atlantic you were raised. I was once walking through Soho with an American friend, who stopped abruptly, all the colour draining from his face as if he'd seen the ghost of his dead grandmother, the moment he happened to glance upward at a blue plaque that said something about this being the house where John Logie Baird invented television. 'But Philo T. Farnsworth invented television,' he yelped, outraged. I have since found that if you mention the name of almost any great British inventor or pioneer to Americans, they will either have their own alternative, or they will assume said pioneer or inventor to have been one of their own. 'Alexander Graham Bell? Wasn't he from Cincinnati? That guy Fleming who invented penicillin, I heard he was the tennis player Peter Fleming's grandfather, and was born and bred in New Jersey.' Americans claim as their own even things as quintessentially British as Yorkshire puddings, which they call 'popovers'. The only answer to all this is to fight fire with fire: pardon us but Thomas Edison didn't invent the electric light bulb, W.G. Grace did. Don't tell us that hotdogs originated in Coney Island – they come from the Isle of Wight.

But credit where credit's due: the TV panel game began in America, and so did the TV talent show. The first talent show on television was called *Original Amateur Hour* and started in the States in 1948, having already acquired a huge following on radio, where it had uncovered some genuine talent: it was on *Amateur Hour* in September 1935 that Frank Sinatra, singing with his group The Hoboken Four, made his first radio broadcast. Somewhat less illustriously, a rumour surfaced during World War Two that someone associated with the programme was a Nazi spy, because on several occasions, an American naval vessel was sunk by German U-boats shortly after

Amateur Hour had been transmitted. It was thought that map co-ordinates and the order to strike were somehow being conveyed in code, which was an exciting theory if almost certainly the product of an overactive imagination.

In its later television incarnation, *Amateur Hour* started the singers Pat Boone and Gladys Knight on the road to fame, and that, I suppose, is the measure of any talent contest, from *Amateur Hour* and *Stars in Their Eyes* to *The X Factor* and *Britain's Got Talent*: such shows should themselves be judged by the ability and longevity of those who win them.

By that criterion, *New Faces*, in Britain at least, is one of the most successful talent contests of all time. It began in 1973 and made a star of Victoria Wood, which would be sufficient justification for its existence even if it had discovered nobody else, and yet its other alumni include Lenny Henry, Michael Barrymore, Patti Boulaye, Jim Davidson, Showaddywaddy, Marti Caine and (OK, I might be scraping the barrel a bit here) Gary Wilmot. It also made small-screen stars of the judges, among them Mickey Most and Tony Hatch, the Sharon Osbourne and Simon Cowell of their day, not that Cowell has made a contribution to popular culture as weighty as Hatch, who composed the theme tune for *Crossroads* and later, with his wife Jackie Trent, *Neighbours* as well (not to mention *The Champions*, *The Doctors* and *Hadleigh*, just to throw in some other dramas that loomed large in the television of my childhood).

I loved *New Faces*, which for a year or two helped ITV mount a credible alternative to the BBC's Saturday tea-time viewing experience, as part of a light entertainment double-header with *Sale of the Century* (another US-inspired format, picked up here by Anglia). I loved *Sale of the Century* too, and if you know anyone who comes from the 1970s and boasts a keen memory for TV trivia then ask them who played the organ on *Sale of the Century*. If they don't say Peter Fenn immediately, then they should be ashamed of themselves.

As for the fellow who described the ineffably crap prizes, that was of course John Benson, whose disembodied voice – almost as familiar as that of Len Martin, who read the football results on *Grandstand* – introduced the show with those almost unbearably exciting words: 'From Norwich . . . it's the quiz of the week . . .'

New Faces had an even more stirring curtain-raiser: over an animated sequence of a geeky-looking chap being whisked off the street to stardom, Carl Wayne of The Move sang the catchy theme:

> Yesterday I was happy to play
> For a penny or two a song
> Till a fellah in a black sedan
> Took a shine to my one-man-band
> He said, 'We got plans for you, you'd never dream
> You're a star, you're a star
> A lamé suit and a new guitar
> And I know that you'll go far
> 'Cause you're a star.'

In the nation's primary schools, this was duly bastardized to 'You're a star, you're a star / Big fat bum and a Playtex bra,' although as someone making the transition from primary school to grammar school in the autumn of 1973, I considered this rather gauche, and on the whole desisted.

The only edition of *New Faces* I can remember now is the programme in 1974 in which a sixteen-year-old Lenny Henry made an immediate impact with an impression, his back to the audience, of Frank Spencer; when he turned round to reveal that he was a black kid, oh my, how everyone roared. I'm sure Tony Hatch gave him good marks but in general Hatch could be wonderfully caustic, which I enjoyed enormously, just as my own kids now enjoy Simon Cowell letting rip on *Britain's Got Talent*.

Hatch, it's worth adding for those in search of trivia gold, was not the only man who connected *New Faces* with *Crossroads*: in 1974 Carl Wayne married Susan Hanson, the motel's long-suffering waitress Miss Diane, whose long suffering came to an abrupt end in 1987 when she dropped dead with a brain haemorrhage, shortly after telling the show's new producer William Smethurst that she wanted to be paid as much as co-star Gabrielle Drake. In the world of soaps, salary demands, then as now, can be catastrophically bad for the health.

New Faces was briefly revived in the 1980s, with one of the show's original discoveries, Marti Caine, replacing Derek Hobson as host, but its first and most notable run lasted for almost five years, from July 1973 until April 1978. As it happened, 1978 was a bad year for talent shows, because that was also the year in which ITV pulled the plug on the much more venerable *Opportunity Knocks*, which had endured since 1961 and had helped to propel Les Dawson to stardom, as well as Freddie Starr, Paul Daniels, Mary Hopkin, Frank Carson, Stan Boardman, Max Boyce, Pam Ayres, Freddie 'Parrot Face' Davies, Peters and Lee, Lena Zavaroni, Cannon and Ball, Little and Large, and a floppy-haired prepubescent Scottish boy called Neil Reid, whose saccharin song 'Mother of Mine' reached number two in the charts on New Year's Day 1972, earning him the devotion of the nation's grannies and the undying hatred of its prepubescent boys, of whom I was one.

Another performer who got his big break on *Opportunity Knocks* was a ribald comedian from Yorkshire called Royston Vasey, who would later adopt the stage name Roy 'Chubby' Brown, but whose original name gained a curious fame all of its own when the *League of Gentlemen* comedy troupe appropriated Royston Vasey as the name of their weirdo-filled fictional town. There was another graduate of *Opportunity Knocks* whose name entered the nation's lexicon. Bernie Flint remained Cockney rhyming slang for skint long after Flint's record-breaking run of twelve consecutive *Opportunity Knocks*-winning weeks had been forgotten.

Forgotten, that is, everywhere but Southport, for Flint was one of our own, and practically everyone in the town felt the reflected warmth from his sojourn in the limelight. Moreover, his hit song 'I Don't Want to Put a Hold on You' rose to the heady heights of number three in the charts on 19 March 1977, and less than a fortnight later Southport's other favourite son, Red Rum, won the Grand National down the road at Aintree for an unprecedented third time. It seemed, in that spring of 1977, as if Southport were a truly gilded place, its streets paved with gold, not to mention copious amounts of horseshit if you lived, as I did, on the route Red Rum and his stablemates used to take to the beach for their early morning training runs.

In October that year I turned sixteen, and started spending occasional evenings at various Southport pubs, where there was every chance of catching sight of one or more of the town's famous residents. Not that Red Rum was ever likely to pop into the Fishermen's Rest, even for a quick slug of White Horse whisky, but several Everton and Liverpool footballers did. And regular sightings of Bernie Flint and another local, Tom O'Connor, compounded the feeling that if BOC was the Earls Court of the North, then Southport was the Soho of the north-west.

Tom O'Connor, a former maths teacher at St Joan of Arc School in Bootle, was another *Opportunity Knocks* alumnus, who in Southport's golden year of 1977 was accorded the ultimate honour of a tap on the shoulder from Eamonn Andrews, and told, 'This Is Your Life.' O'Connor was a pretty big star in those days. Years later, I was one of a posse of media folk invited to a drinks party by the then Director General of the BBC, John Birt, which took place in his sumptuous office at Broadcasting House. Knowing that Birt was from Merseyside, I told him that I came from Southport. 'Oh, I know Southport very well,' he told me, explaining that his grandmother had lived there, and that one day on a bus she had got chatting to the woman next to her, and that they'd enjoyed quite an animated conversation until the other woman had to get off, but before she did so she fished in her purse and pulled out a business card, which had a phone number at the bottom and above it, printed in bold letters, the legend 'Tom O'Connor's mother'. I love that.

Tom O'Connor still pops up on telly but I don't know what became of Bernie Flint. My friend Mike assures me that he's now a painter-decorator in Southport, although he appears still to be signed to a showbiz agency, which sings his praises lustily on the internet, telling us that Bernie 'owes his original success to *Opportunity Knocks* but the truth is that if his talents had been as diverse then as they are now, even greater fame and success would inevitably have ensued. And, just as a postscript – we are talking a super voice here. Rich in tonality and range and used to best effect in a marvellously eclectic programme to suit all tastes. Bernie Flint really is a "mustn't miss" attraction.' Wow!

31

From Bernie Flint to Bernie the Bolt, the Sunday-Afternoon Phenomenon

His continued status as a mustn't-miss attraction notwithstanding, Bernie's drift out of the public consciousness over the past three decades makes me wonder what on earth happened to the acts on *Opportunity Knocks* that didn't win twelve times, and indeed those that didn't win at all. These included the Mavis Whiting Junior Accordion Band, a clog dancer called Michael Snailham, a paper sculptor called Norman Beardsley, the Primrose Hill Gymnasts, the Reading Barbershop Harmony Club, and the Corcrain Flute Ensemble, which perhaps makes it easier to understand why Little and Large came storming through, if not why a guy from Leicester called Gerry Dorsey, later to change his name to Engelbert Humperdinck, failed even to make it past the audition stage.

Whatever, overseeing all this, and measuring the audience's

response to each act on his faithful clapometer, was the irrepressible Hughie Green, born in London but raised in Canada, which added an exotic transatlantic twang to the way in which he said, 'I mean that most sincerely, folks.'

Actually, he didn't say, 'I mean that most sincerely, folks.' It was part of impressionist Mike Yarwood's act, not Green's. Just as nobody on the Starship Enterprise ever said 'Beam me up Scotty', and indeed as Sherlock Holmes never said 'Elementary, my dear Watson', and Humphrey Bogart never said 'Play it again, Sam', it is a catch-phrase with a disappointing catch. Still, there is plenty to remember Hughie Green for without an invented catchphrase, not least the late Paula Yates, who in 1997 was revealed – at his funeral, no less – to have been his biological daughter, and not the offspring of *Stars on Sunday* presenter Jess Yates, as she, and we, had always supposed. Understandably, she wasn't happy. Nor was Hughie Green's legiti-mate daughter Linda Plentl, who described him as a 'monster' and suggested that there were more half-brothers and half-sisters she did not know about. 'My father has damaged so many people so viciously,' she said. 'He has hurt us all from the grave. He has humiliated us.'

It was all a far cry from *Opportunity Knocks* – more *A Bouquet of Barbed Wire*, perhaps. On the other hand, by the mid-1970s there were signs that Hughie Green, who liked to gaze into the camera and call us 'friends', was not quite as friendly as he seemed. On a show in December 1976 he sang an angry little ditty about the state of the country under Jim Callaghan's Labour government, called 'Stand Up and Be Counted', in which he yearned to live in a Britain 'where the managers manage and the workers don't go on strike'. His bosses at Thames Television were aghast, and rebuked him publicly, but he kept on letting slip his right-wing views on air, which is why *Opportunity Knocks* – despite being one of ITV's behemoths, regu-larly delivering 18 million viewers – was eventually binned, and rather radically replaced with *The Kenny Everett Video Show*.

Either knowing nothing of the reasons why, or caring nothing, I was sorry to see the back of *Opportunity Knocks*, which had been a fixture on the telly all my life. But actually I had warmer recollections of another show hosted by Hughie Green, a quiz with fabulous prizes called *The Sky's the Limit*, which ran for only three years from 1972 to 1975 and boasted a catchy theme tune: its lyrics, 'The sky's the limit / the limit's the sky', was another example of 1970s ingenuity with words, alongside 'Nice to see you, to see you nice!'

The reason I remembered *The Sky's the Limit* so fondly was that, almost unbelievably, it had conspired in the humbling of one of the boys who had made my early life at grammar school if by no means a misery, then at times decidedly challenging. His name was Parry. I have no idea now what his first name was, and probably had no idea then. At King George V, everyone knew everyone else by surnames; you addressed only your close friends by their given first names or their nicknames, and dared to use the first names of boys in the years above you only if you were closely related to them, and sometimes not even then. So Parry was Parry, a sixth-former when I was in my first year, and also a prefect, which accounted for his delusions of grandeur.

In fairness, they weren't mere delusions. Prefects at my school were treated as a superior breed even by some of the teachers, and to insignificant new boys they were remote, glamorous and somewhat intimidating figures, who were allowed to wear rakish waistcoats and even had their own common room, which in the rare glimpses we newts got of it, looked like a fun palace, with a ceiling covered – oh, the alpha maleness of it! – with beer mats. I would hate to give the impression that I did not enjoy my time at an old-fashioned boys' grammar school in the north of England, yet the analogy that springs inescapably to mind is that, if the teaching staff were the Waffen SS, the prefects were the Gestapo. And to extend that imagery, the one with the little round glasses and the cruel piercing eyes was Parry.

I should add here, before the fiftysomething Parry consults his solic-
itor, that I'm sure he grew into a delightful fellow. I am moderately
friendly these days with a TV star, a household name and a man of celebrated good cheer (not named anywhere in this book, I should add,
before anyone adds two and two and makes five), yet I have heard from
several unimpeachable sources that at school he was a particularly dastardly bully. It happens. With manhood come responsibilities and a
softening of schoolboy prejudices. Besides, I'm not even saying that
Parry was a bully. But he plainly didn't like me very much – perhaps, I
am prepared to admit, because I was especially obnoxious as an eleven-
year-old – and used all his prefectly authority to give me a hard time,
dishing out lines and even the odd prefect's detention.

Revenge, oddly, came at the hands of Hughie Green. Whether I
knew in advance I can't recall, but I switched on an edition of *The
Sky's the Limit* one evening and there as one of the contestants was
Parry, suddenly looking very young and vulnerable, which was almost
as disorientating for me as it doubtless was for him.

The subject Parry chose to answer questions on was Association
Football, and such is the power of Schadenfreude that I can still, more
than thirty years later, remember the one he got wrong. He was going
quite well but, as I remember the rules, there was always the option to
stop and count your winnings, rather like *Who Wants to be a
Millionaire?* now, instead of ploughing forward to the next question.
Parry ploughed forward, and when Green asked him to name the
president of the Football League, he said Alan Hardaker, who was in
fact (oh, what rapture in Lynton Road!) the Football League's secretary. So Parry lost all his money and I went to bed happy, with a soft
spot for Hughie Green that would survive even the revelation that he
was a randy old goat, although I do rather irreverently like to assume
that at some stage in the course of his promiscuous life he contracted
a sexually transmitted disease and was asked by a doctor with a sense
of humour if he wanted to consult the clapometer.

This brings me neatly to *The Golden Shot*, which I was troubled to find, on visiting a brothel in Melbourne, Australia, a few years ago, is a euphemism for an act of degradation involving urine: I'll spare you the precise details.

I was not, I hasten to add, visiting the brothel as a customer. I was in Melbourne on a sports-writing assignment, and when I found out that prostitution in the state of Victoria was legal, and that an Australian friend knew a brothel and was on pretty good terms with the madam there, I sniffed a decent story. My friend took me along to the brothel and I pretended to be a potential punter. I asked to meet a couple of the girls, one of whom turned out to be a well-bred young woman from Cheltenham whose mother thought she was in Australia teaching in a special-needs school, which in a sense, we both agreed, she was. The other girl took me to one of the bedrooms, and showed me a halogen bulb set into the wall at crotch level, strategically located so that she and her colleagues could make a pre-coital inspection of their clients' tackle to make sure there was no disease, a device fondly known in the trade as a 'dickie light'. She also showed me the menu of services on offer, and it was there that I saw the Golden Shot (A\$80 extra), and realized that I would never again think of Bernie the Bolt in quite the same way.

For some of us, Bernie the Bolt remains as synonymous with the late 1960s and early 1970s as intractable industrial disputes and Spangles, and I know that my rose-tinted memories are shared by the estimable *Guardian* columnist Martin Kelner, because he once wrote the following:

Even in the so-called Swinging Sixties, Sundays could be joyless affairs in Britain. No long Sunday lunches in country pubs in those days, children playing happily at your feet, no interactive Premiership football live on Sky, no bulging car-parks at out-of-town shopping centres. What we had instead was Bernie the Bolt.

You only ever saw the back of silent Bernie as he loaded a crossbow on host Bob Monkhouse's instructions. Then, in a not very sophisticated variation of a fairground rifle range, a contestant would shoot at targets in an attempt to win the main prize, a treasure chest of gold coins. In another game, the contestant was blindfolded, and guided by a telephone partner ('up a bit, left a bit, down a bit, FIRE!').

Norman Vaughan and Charlie Williams had spells as host, but the show's mystifyingly huge ratings must mostly be ascribed to Monkhouse, who was not only just as oleaginous as you expect a quiz show host to be, but also had an impressive armoury of gags, many of them at the expense of 'Golden Girl' Anne Aston, who struggled to tot up the scores. The show aired at teatime, after which all the weekend had to offer was a bath and your homework.

That tallies almost exactly with my memory: *The Golden Shot* – based on the German show *Der Goldene Schuss*, which in turn was inspired by the fifteenth-century legend of William Tell – started in 1967 and was moved from Saturdays to Sunday tea-times the following year, apparently because Michael Grade, then a theatrical agent, happened to remark to his uncle Lew, the ATV boss, that he had been to see the Bond film *You Only Live Twice* the previous Sunday afternoon, and couldn't believe the length of the queue. The reason cinemas were full on Sunday afternoons, he asserted, was because there was nothing worth watching on the telly. Uncle Lew had just the answer.

Whether or not that is why *The Golden Shot* was switched to Sundays, the ploy worked triumphantly. The show in its various forms on continental television had been a tremendous success – there was even a celebrity version, in which Gina Lollobrigida and Princess Grace of Monaco had cheerfully taken part – but in Britain it was slow to capture the public imagination. That all changed with the move to Sundays. The ratings rose to around 15 million, three of whom were my mum, my dad and me in Lynton Road, just back from visiting my father's mother and sister, my grandma Julia and my auntie Leah, who lived together in Liverpool.

I don't know whether those Sunday-afternoon visits to Liverpool were timed so that we would get back just in time to see *The Golden Shot*, but that's how it usually worked out. Not everyone approved of the change in scheduling, however. A fire-and-brimstone lay preacher from Redditch complained vehemently about 'weapons of the devil', meaning crossbows, being celebrated on the Lord's Day in the name of frivolous light entertainment. So in a valiant attempt to disarm him, the producers of *The Golden Shot* invited him along to the studio in Birmingham to watch the show going out live, and to persuade him that it really was just good simple fun. And yet by some cosmic misfortune there was a contestant that week operating the crossbow who not only had a glass eye but also suffered from a terrible twitch. When she fired, the bolt flew upward, rebounded off the lighting system and landed on the preacher's head, which at least stopped him praying loudly in Latin, as he had been doing since the start of the transmission. The preacher won few friends that day, even after he had been banjaxed by the erring bolt. Bob Monkhouse, in his 1993 autobiography *Crying With Laughter*, described him as 'a supercilious old bore'.

At the height of its popularity *The Golden Shot*, unimaginably by today's standards, went out live fifty-two weeks a year. Transmission had to be live because some of the contestants were at home on the end of a telephone, and had to watch the telly to give Bernie the Bolt (originally Heinz the Bolt, which didn't have quite the same ring) his directions. But even at the time it was highly unusual for a game show to go out live every week of the year, and it meant that *The Golden Shot* became associated with all sorts of embarrassing hitches and accidents, not least the business with the preacher, which did the ratings no harm at all.

On one bizarre occasion, a pair of contestants who had been successful over the phone the previous week, and had therefore been invited to come into the studio to fire the crossbow in person, went missing in the studio during transmission. This was Mr Henry Doak from Rawtenstall and Mrs Flo DeMange from Didcot, who both won the so-called bronze combat to qualify for the silver stage of the show, but in doing so formed an instant mutual attachment and apparently decided that Cupid's arrow was of more interest than Bernie's bolt. Unaware that the floor manager had been frantically searching for them all over the building, Monkhouse announced Mr Doak and Mrs DeMange for the second half of the show, and was understandably astonished when a pair of complete strangers walked onto the set. In desperation, and with seconds to spare, the floor manager had simply grabbed a couple of people from the audience and pushed them on.

Immaculate old pro that he was, Monkhouse concealed his surprise, addressed the pair throughout as Henry and Flo, and watched as one of them won a washing machine and the other £300. Nobody in the audience noticed that they were two completely different people, nor were there any baffled phone calls from even one of the 15 million viewers. 'Of Mr Doak and Mrs DeMange I can tell you nothing more,' Monkhouse wrote in *Crying With Laughter*. 'They vanished and we never even saw the going of them. We received no enquiries from distraught families and our staff were too busy to make any of their own. I like to think they were two lonely people who experienced love at first sight and eloped. In [his co-writer] Wally Malston's less romantic view, "They lost their bottle and pissed off."'

The live nature of *The Golden Shot* also meant that the show was an obvious target for IRA bomb threats, whether genuine or not, and they duly arrived almost every week. To start with, the people in the ATV studios in Birmingham told the audience that a threat had been issued and left them to make up their own minds whether to leave or not. But after a while they stopped bothering, although the police asked them to record all incoming calls. Thus it was that practically everyone at ATV ended up with a precious cassette copy of the following memorable exchange, which took place at ten past four one Sunday afternoon.

An ATV switchboard operator took the call, and heard a man with an unmistakable Dublin accent, evidently reading from a prepared script, say: 'Sir, I have to inform you of the presence of a two-pound gelignite bomb hidden in the studio where *The Golden Shot* is due to begin shortly. Take note that the device has been well concealed and timed to explode during the early part of the programme, causing maximum damage to anyone foolish enough to remain in the vicinity. Failure to take immediate action to abandon the area must be the responsibility of those in charge of the studios. You will now confirm that you have understood all that I have said.'

Whereupon the switchboard person asked wearily, 'Is this a hoax?'

There was a stunned silence, lasting several seconds. 'How the fuck,' said the Irishman eventually, 'did you know that?'

32

'Meet Mike, He Swims Like a Fish': The Heyday of the Public Information Film

In many ways we live in a far more dangerous world now than we did in the 1970s, yet at least it is not a world in which popular television shows get weekly bomb threats. Moreover, there was a sense in the 1970s that everyday life was fraught with danger, and that one of the government's responsibilities was to save us from ourselves. There was even a public information film stressing the importance of using a handkerchief should one be unfortunate enough to sneeze in company, and another highlighting the dangers of polished floors. 'Polish a floor and put a rug on it . . . you might as well set a mantrap,' intoned a grave voice-over, quite naturally assuming that only men would be stupid enough to be sent flying in this manner, and that only women would have the time on their hands to polish the floor in the first place.

It being the 1970s, nobody challenged this assumption for a second. The Women's Libbers who disrupted the 1970 Miss World contest with their flour bombs had a long way to go to overturn pre-conceptions based on gender; indeed I am reminded of a classic children's book published in 1968, which my own children loved when they were little. It is *The Tiger Who Came to Tea*, by Judith Kerr, and it features a mother and her daughter Sophie understand-ably taken aback by the surprising arrival in their house of a large tiger, who 'drank all the milk, and all the orange juice, and all Daddy's beer, and all the water in the tap'.

Then the tiger leaves, and Sophie's mummy is aghast, because she has nothing to give Daddy for his supper. Happily, Daddy then arrives home, hears what has happened, and saves the day by resourcefully suggesting a visit to a cafe. Kerr's very charming accom-panying illustrations have him striding in masterly fashion along a high street, with Sophie and her mummy on either side. In a twenty-first century version, Sophie would be at home with her daddy, wondering what to cook that night for Daddy's partner when he came home from work. And Sophie would be mixed-race, of course. And someone would make the salient point that the tiger, while eating all the buns on the plate, all the biscuits, and all the cake, and therefore risking obesity, is an endangered species.

As for public information films, they had been running on tele-vision since the beginning of the TV era, but they found a new vigour in the late 1960s and 1970s, when there was a rash of them to help us through the forthcoming trauma of decimalisation. There were doubtless some old soldiers who winced at the decision to call 15 February 1971 D-Day, but it seemed to me, aged nine, as if scarcely anything more exciting could happen to my country. I was sad that the threepenny bit was about to become extinct, because I had a collection of them in a jar on my bedroom window-sill, but my mum nobly promised to give me the equivalent in decimal money, or 'new' money as it was called for years after-wards.

So seismic was the change that public information films contin-ued for months before D-Day. 'The pound will be divided up into a hundred new pence, and we'll do our decimal shopping in pounds and new pence only,' said one of those frightfully pukka disem-bodied voices that right through the 1970s and well into the 1980s were considered, simply by virtue of speaking the Queen's English, to be authoritative. It clearly didn't dawn on anyone back then that the nation could take instructions in a regional accent. Maybe it couldn't.

This began to change slightly when celebrities – or 'personalities' as they were then known – were engaged to give us much-needed guidance. From January 1971 Jimmy Savile started telling us to wear seat-belts in the 'Clunk Click, Every Trip' campaign, while Jimmy Hill reminded motorists to look out for motorbikes – 'Think once, think twice, think bike!' Then there was Rolf Harris – the Australian Junior Backstroke Champion of 1946 – standing in a municipal swimming-pool expounding on the need for all children to be able to swim.

My friend Chris Barry can to this day remember Rolf's exhortation by heart. 'Kids and water, they love it. Rivers, canals, even the lily pond in the garden, you can't keep them away from it. Water has a fascination for children, and I should know. When I was three years old I fell in the river at our place . . . couldn't swim. Somehow man-aged to scramble my way to the bank. Frightened the wits out of my mum and dad, and you can bet they had me taught to swim not long after that.

'But some children aren't quite so lucky, and if they can't swim and go off to play by themselves by the side of some water somewhere, you know only too well what might happen. That's why I had my little girl taught to swim as soon as possible. So have your children taught to swim. They're never too young to start, and if they get that confidence in the water, they love it. Ask at your local swimming-pool. All right? Or if you can swim yourself, why not teach them yourself. It's fun. See ya.'

Chris then completes the impression by leaning back and wiggling his toe, a party piece that holds absolutely no interest for anyone under the age of forty, and might leave some people over the age of forty smiling fixedly, while surreptitiously looking over his shoulder for someone else to talk to. But it's worth asking why the government no longer considers it worth its while to stress the importance of being able to swim. In the 1970s it was deemed roughly as important as the national debt, and while Rolf Harris was used to appeal to parents, a cartoon of a teenage girl went directly for the impressionable adolescent market, suggesting that even the dishiest-looking lad would struggle to exude sex appeal if he was all at sea in the water.

'Dave is super, Dave can do anything,' she said. But then she invited Dave into the sea. 'It's just not my scene, man,' he said. 'What he really meant was,' she disdainfully informed us, 'he couldn't swim.' At which her fairy godmother appeared and conjured up a weedier-looking fellow called Mike. 'Meet Mike, he swims like a fish,' said the girl proudly, and the implication was clearly that within a few minutes of getting out of the water they would be enjoying hot sex in the sand dunes. Dave, meanwhile, was disconsolate. 'I wish . . . I wish I didn't keep losing me birds,' he said. 'Well, learn to swim, young man,' the fairy godmother admonished him. 'Learn to swim.'

Where Rolf Harris had failed to stir me, cartoon Mike succeeded. Having reached the age of ten unable to swim, despite my parents' best efforts on holiday, not to mention those of a formidably stern swimming instructor called Mrs Lee at the Victoria Baths in Southport (for whom I harboured an intense and entirely mutual loathing), I finally made it my business to get my feet off the bottom, and the notion that it might somehow make me more attractive to the opposite sex was undoubtedly an incentive. Not that it did, of course. I had to wait until my late teens before I acquired a girlfriend, and when I finally did it was certainly nothing to do with my breaststroke, which remained somewhat tentative.

Whether anyone was able to compute the success of these animated public information films I don't know, but for a few years in the early 1970s there was certainly a vogue for them, making household names of a singularly stupid couple called Joe and Petunia, who had made their TV debut in 1968, sunbathing on a cliff top and mistaking the signs from a sailor in distress: 'Oh, he's decided to have a swim. Now he's going to climb back again. I expect that water's a bit cold, don't you? Oh, oh, he's changed his mind. Now he's waving to us. Coooeeee! I can't say I recognize him, though.'

The object of the exercise was to teach us all to phone the coastguard should we ever spot a boat in difficulties, which frankly wasn't likely to happen to 99.9 per cent of the population, but I suppose if even one person ambling along on a cliff top saw a boat in trouble and remembered Joe and Petunia, then it was all worthwhile.

Nonetheless, the 1971 film in which Joe and Petunia left chaos in their wake on a country walk seemed like a worthier vehicle for their talents. First of all they left a gate open and all the cows escaped into the lane, then Joe threw a rock at a bottle and smashed it, then they allowed their dog Bingo to chase the sheep. Meanwhile, a cartoon farmer went literally hopping mad.

Joe: 'You know, there's a farmer there with a purple face.'
Petunia: 'I expect it's all that sun and the open-air life, Joe.'
Joe: 'Now he's doing one of those country dances.'
Petunia: 'I don't think he looks very friendly.'
Joe: 'Maybe you're right. It can't be anything we've done.'

Petunia: 'No! But I won't stay where I'm not wanted. Come on, Joe!'
Farmer: 'When folk come out to the country, why oh why won't
    they follow the Country Code?'

At home the nation concurred heartily, even though some of us wondered why such a pair of retards had to be from the North – the immensely buxom, scarlet-lipsticked Petunia sounded like someone from Cheshire trying to be posh, while Joe, who liked to wear a handkerchief on his head, sounded like someone from Rawtenstall after a semi-lobotomy. We consoled ourselves with the idea that they were meant to be funny, and everyone knew that the funniest double-acts came from the north of England. In the 1970s we in the North could boast Morecambe and Wise, as well as, a little less loudly, Cannon and Ball and Little and Large. What did the South have to offer? Mike and Bernie Winters? Ray Allen and Lord Charles?

Back then, the North/South divide was much more sharply defined than it is now. Among my schoolfriends I was considered something of a novelty for having been to London so often; most of them had never been at all. Meanwhile, my cousins in London thought it was hilarious when I said bath or path, rather than barth or parth, and I was too much in their thrall to protest that my way of speaking was no less valid than theirs. It wasn't until the late 1990s that I stood up for the cadences of what remained of my northern accent, when a Londoner with whom I regularly played tennis mocked the way I pronounced 'one'. What gave him the right, I asked him, to assume that his pronunciation of 'one' was correct, and mine wrong? He was a little taken aback by my vehemence, but behind it was a childhood of gentle yet sustained cousinly ribbing.

Besides, it is not because northern accents are inherently funnier, but because they are more expressive, that the best stand-up comedians have invariably come from the north of England: the Home

Counties could never have spawned Les Dawson, Ken Dodd, Victoria Wood or Peter Kay. Nor was it purely an accident of birth that the two men who bestrode the world of 1970s TV entertainment like colossi came from Morecambe in Lancashire and Leeds in Yorkshire. Even if one of them was a colossus with short, fat, hairy legs.

33

Eric and Ernie

It is not over-egging the point, or even stretching the pudding, to say that in the 1970s, for many people, myself included, the entire festive season was judged by the quality of the *Morecambe & Wise Christmas Special*. If it was a classic, then we all had a classic Christmas. If it was ever so slightly disappointing, then Yuletide as a whole received the same thumbs-down verdict.

But before I sound the obligatory paean, I should balance it with the views of A.A. Gill, the waspishly brilliant TV critic of the *Sunday Times*, who in his last column of 2007 wrote the following:

The one Christmas programme everyone over the age of 40 remembers with uncritical nostalgia is *Morecambe and Wise*. Nativities should have little Morecambes and Wises next to the sheep and the donkey. Sadly, I'm not allowed to do uncritical. Watching *Morecambe and Wise: The Greatest Moment* (Christmas

Eve, UKTV Gold) reminded me of how low our entertainment needs used to be, how simple Christmas was: four doubles entendres, three catch phrases and one humiliated newsreader.

There was a time when half the country watched Eric and Ernie's Christmas Special, and you wonder what excuse the other half came up with. A lot of us watched because the alternative was *Christmas with the Vienna Boys' Choir*, cartoon fairy tales from Czechoslovakia or playing Boggle with your grandmother and the lonely man from next door. *Morecambe and Wise* was the best on offer, and we were grateful, but it was thin pickings. I'll be perfectly happy never to have to watch the breakfast stripper sketch, or Angela Rippon's legs, ever again. I ask my children who André Previn was: never heard of him. And who could now name all the presenters who did the *South Pacific* sketch? But, oh, how we laughed. This ridiculing of celebrity was the first budding of a light-entertainment idea that ended up with *I'm a Celebrity, Get Me Out of Here!* This was a limp programme: a lot of talking heads telling us how brilliant Eric Morecambe's timing was, which is unarguable – he died right on cue at fifty-eight, before he could turn into John Cleese or suffer the sad comedic dementia that is Bill Oddie.

Gill knew when he wrote those words that slagging off Morecambe and Wise is still the nearest thing in British popular culture to the offence caused by Salman Rushdie in *The Satanic Verses*; if Middle England were collectively of a mind to issue a fatwa, or in this case perhaps a short, fatwa hairy legs, then he would even now be in hiding, being accompanied to occasional public events by Special Branch officers. But to a certain extent he was right: we did have simple entertainment needs in the 1970s, and they were fairly easily met. Moreover, I kind of agree with him about the breakfast stripper sketch in the 1976 *Morecambe & Wise Christmas Special*, albeit for the worryingly pedantic reason that when Eric chopped the four grapefruit in half, he hit the third of them far too far to the right of centre, which has always offended my sense of symmetry. Even at the time I think it slightly bothered me, although I'm sure I realized that it was the kind of routine that had to be done in one take. Maybe my enjoyment was also slightly curbed by the absence of my dad. He'd been dead for ten months, and it wasn't as much fun watching my mum laugh.

All that said, there has arguably never been a greater British TV phenomenon than the *Morecambe & Wise Christmas Special* at its height, and it's an insult to nigh-on 30 million of us to suggest that we only watched because there was bugger-all else on. Besides, Eric Morecambe had a mastery of comic timing that remains unsurpassed on British television, and unlike almost all of his fellow comedians he did not rely on gurning, cack-handedness or vulgarity, or props, or, to be frank, on Ernie Wise. More than any other comedian of that or any other era, he just seemed to be himself. After all, nobody else, with the possible exception of Tommy Cooper, could have made us roar with laughter simply by watching an ambulance speed by, siren blaring, and muttering, 'He's not going to sell much ice-cream going at that speed.' That wasn't funny because we were easily amused. It was just funny.

It was André Previn's famous guest appearance in 1971 that established the Christmas show as unmissable, as well as priming us for the rest of the decade to expect the unexpected. Eric and Ernie, and their producer John Ammonds, then had to meet these public expectations, but to their surprise and delight they found that the most dignified of performers were all too willing to poke fun at themselves. Yehudi Menuhin duly turned up with a banjo, Rudolf Nureyev was told that he owed his big break on the show to Lionel Blair's sudden indisposition, and Shirley Bassey sang 'Smoke Gets in Your Eyes' wearing one of Eric's boots. None of this was achieved without diligent preparation. Morecambe and Wise liked to spend five weeks rehearsing their Christmas special and expected similar commitment from their guests. Yet when Ammonds rang Previn's agent, the exquisitely named Jasper Parrott, to request that the great conductor make himself available for five days, Parrott nearly fell off his perch, or at any rate his chair.

Eventually they compromised with three days, much to the chagrin of Eric the perfectionist, but then, after the first day's rehearsal, Parrott told Ammonds that Previn was very sorry but he had to fly to America to be with his sick mother and wouldn't be back until the evening before the show was due to be recorded. Eric's response to this was withering: 'Well sod him, then, we'll do without him. We'll use Ernie as the conductor instead.' But Ammonds promised him that he would send a car to meet Previn at the airport, and whisk him straight to Television Centre for four hours of rehearsals. This duly happened and Previn, who had learnt his script by torchlight on the way in from the airport, turned out himself to have a great, and previously untapped, sense of comic timing. Eric, however, still fully expected the sketch to flop.

According to Michael Grade, who was close to Eric and Ernie, it is possible to see on screen the point at which the apprehension left them. Previn – 'Mr Preview' – agreed that he would conduct Grieg's piano concerto and would go and get his baton, to which Ernie said, 'Please do that,' and Previn acidly added, 'It's in Chicago.'

'You can see the tension evaporate in that moment,' Grade told Morecambe and Wise's biographer, Graham McCann. 'Eric's face lights up as if to say, "Oh yes! This is going to be great!" They'd both been pretty nervous, I think, because they knew that if Previn had lost his nerve, or fumbled his lines, the entire thing would've fallen flat on its face. But Previn was superb – rock-solid – and so you can see Eric mentally rubbing his hands together and thinking "Can't wait to get to the piano now. This is going to be a ride!" Wonderful, wonderful moment.'

For more than a decade Morecambe and Wise contributed many such wonderful moments to the collective Christmas experience, peaking – at least in terms of ratings – with the 1977 Christmas special in which a troupe of newsreaders and assorted others 'performed' their acrobatic dance routine while singing that old favourite of the Black and White Minstrels, 'There is Nothing Like a Dame'. An estimated 28,835,000 tuned in at 8.55 p.m. to watch that show, and a worrying number of them thought that it really was Richard Whitmore, Richard Baker, Frank Bough, Michael Aspel, Barry Norman and co turning the cartwheels and somersaults. Baker was subsequently inundated with requests to open garden fêtes with a short tumbling routine, and to the many people who for months afterwards said, 'I didn't know you could do that!' Norman mischievously used to explain that it wasn't so hard if you used a hidden springboard.

That 28,835,000 figure puts the 1977 *Morecambe & Wise Christmas Special* narrowly behind the 1966 World Cup final, the 1986 Christmas Day episode of *EastEnders* and the funeral of Princess Diana as the most-watched programme in the history of British television. It was getting on for 7 million more than had sat through the Queen's Speech earlier in the day, although you might think it even more astounding that in 1977 – albeit the year of the Queen's Silver Jubilee, when monarchist fervour swept the nation – more than 21 million dutifully listened to what she had to say. Times have changed.

In fact, writing this book has been one big reminder to me that times have changed in myriad ways since I was a boy. For example, within a few weeks of that show, the London *Evening Standard* broke the shattering news that Eric and Ernie were leaving the BBC for ITV, where they had started their television careers. These days, I can't think of any transfer between broadcasting companies that would have anything like as seismic an impact as that one did. Ant and Dec to the BBC? *Celebrity Big Brother* to ITV? Sir Trevor McDonald to Channel 4? I think we'd all raise an eyebrow, perhaps even utter a profane exclamation of surprise, and then get on with our day.

Wise would always claim that it was a straightforward commercial decision, that Thames simply offered more money, but Graham McCann found evidence to refute this. Bill Cotton, the BBC's head of light entertainment, knew that Thames were trying to pinch his crown jewels, and told Morecambe and Wise that he would match whatever the opposition were offering. What he couldn't offer them, however, was the opportunity through the Thames subsidiary Euston Films to make another movie. And Eric and Ernie yearned to conquer the big screen as they had the little one. So they turned their backs on the BBC, just as in 1968 they had turned their backs on ITV following a bust-up with Michael Grade's Uncle Lew, who felt they were getting uppity by asking for their shows to be made in colour.

It was the BBC, though, that had turned them into the national treasures that by 1977 they had indubitably become. As I write this book, the most recent switches of loyalty that are in any way comparable are Michael Parkinson's move from the BBC to ITV, and the same move a little earlier by Des Lynam. But neither of those rocked the nation like the news that Morecambe and Wise were switching channels, at a time, don't forget, when the BBC was still considered to represent all that remained great about Great Britain. Jonny Cook's ITV-despising father must have been gutted.

The worry that Eric and Ernie wouldn't be as funny on ITV was soon shown to be justified. Apart from anything else, their brilliant writer, Eddie Braben, had decided not to leave the BBC with them, and it showed. Accordingly, Christmases were never quite the same again, although for me they wouldn't have been anyway, because by Christmas 1978 I was seventeen, and far more interested in spending as much of the festive period as I could manage getting pissed with my mates in Southport's many pubs than watching telly. That December, I was positively blasé about the arrival at Holder's newsagents of the bumper Christmas editions of *Radio Times* and *TV Times*, where previously it had been an event of almost unimaginable excitement, enabling me to plan my Christmas viewing with forensic precision, or as forensic as one can be in purple felt-tipped pen.

I will make only one more reference in this book to the cultural deprivation suffered by my children and their generation and here it is: they will never know, in this age of digital TV and cupboards-full of DVDs, the thrill of leafing through two fat listings magazines to find out what big films were going to be on the telly over the festive period. For my friends and me, there was hardly any conversation all year more enjoyable than the one in which we told each other which Christmas films we were looking forward to and why.

Nowadays, just about everyone over forty remembers one definitive Christmas film from their childhood, the one that seemed to be on every year. For some it's *The Sound of Music*, for others *The Wizard of Oz*, *The Great Escape* or *It's a Wonderful Life*. For me it's *Jason and the Argonauts*, the 1963 film showcasing the genius of special-effects wizard Ray Harryhausen, and even if by the mid-1970s we could begin to see the joins in Harryhausen's wizardry, I was never less than riveted. The sequence in which seven skeleton warriors rose from the earth to give Todd Armstrong's Jason yet another run for his money looks primitive now in the era of the Harry Potter and *Pirates of the Caribbean* pyrotechnics, but as a kid – right up to my mid-teens – hardly anything unnerved me so much as those skeletons.

I hope that my memory has been reliable for most of this book, but it might at the last be letting me down, because *Jason and the Argonauts* can't have been on TV every Christmas for twelve consecutive years, yet I can't remember a Christmas when I didn't, at some point, sit down to watch it.

Maybe, in the final analysis, that's the whole point about nostalgia.

It's an emotional impulse, not an intellectual one, and as such it is vulnerable to inaccuracy and even delusion. I dare say that a regular refrain of mine in the 1970s was that there was nothing worth watching on the telly, but if it was I don't remember ever uttering it. Television loomed almost as large over my childhood as my mother and father did, and if they made me the person I am today, telly had a hand in the process, too. Opinions vary dramatically between those who consider the 1970s to have been a golden age for television and those who insist that there was far more trash than gold. I don't know whether this book has settled the argument. All I can subjectively, and indeed Bruciely, say of telly in the 1970s is that, all things considered, and with the glaringly obvious exception of *Yus, My Dear*, it was nice to see it . . . to see it nice.

Epilog

This book has to have an epilog and it has to be styled the American way, as a tribute to *The Streets of San Francisco* and all those other imports that did wonders for our evenings, if not our spelling.

For homicide detectives Mike Stone and Steve Keller, of course, the epilog was there to tie up loose ends. Here it serves a different purpose, to acknowledge some of the many programmes, a few of them hugely significant, and in some cases positively ground-breaking, that for whatever reason have not yet been explored in these pages.

One is *The Good Life*, which began in 1975, ran until 1978, and by 1980 was overwhelmingly the major factor in a record 51,000 small-holdings sprouting up in Britain. I don't know whether a vegetable patch was dug in the back garden of Buckingham Palace but the Queen was a huge fan: in 1978, asked what programme she would most like to watch being made, she opted for John Esmonde and Bob Larbey's gently amusing sitcom about self-sufficiency in Surbiton.

Like all the best 1970s sitcoms, *The Good Life* created characters who thirty years later still feature prominently in the nation's conscious-ness. In 2005, when I wrote a book called *Tales of the Country* about my family's move from north London to north Herefordshire, I wanted to convey the image of an essentially urban couple trying to embrace country ways. I chose to write that Jane and I were Margo and Jerry trying to be Tom and Barbara: no surnames or any further elaboration were needed.

I loved *The Good Life*, but the reason in most cases for not mentioning programmes until this epilog is that, prosaically, I don't really remember watching them. This applies, alas, to two of the most epic documentary series ever shown on British television: *The World at War* and *The Ascent of Man*. The former, four years in the making at the then-staggering cost of £4 million, and eventually screened in no fewer than twenty-six parts in 1973, was narrated by Laurence Olivier, which even to the 11-year-old that I then was indicated the enormity and gravity of the project. I had heard my parents talking about this fellow Olivier with veneration. Moreover, it is worth reflecting that 1973 was a fair bit closer to the Second World War than we now are to 1973, and that a documentary series made then – as opposed to anything that could be made in the twenty-first century, even with much more sophisticated technology – had the incalculable advantage of access to many of those who had been wartime movers and shakers, including high-ranking former Nazis such as Albert Speer, Hitler's chief architect and Armaments Minister, and Heinrich Himmler's adjutant Karl Wolff.

Just as *The World at War* chronicled the foibles and frailties of humankind, so Jacob Bronowski's *The Ascent of Man* celebrated its ingenuity. That too could not be made now, at least not with that title, with its suggestions of male supremacy, and I doubt whether anyone like Bronowski, a short, Polish-accented Jew in his sixties, could become a TV star these days. Not without rising impressively to a Bushtucker challenge on *I'm a Celebrity, Get Me Out of Here!*, anyway. Yet Michael Parkinson to this day, when asked to name his most memorable interview, selects the one he did in 1973 with Bronowski.

Another monumental documentary series of the early 1970s was Alistair Cooke's *America*, in 1972, and though I don't remember watching it, I do remember it being obligatory for all households that considered themselves even vaguely middle class and literate to make the book of the series conspicuous to all visitors, preferably by placing it insouciantly on a coffee-table, where in homes up and down the land it would remain until at least 1979, if by then principally as a mat for mugs of coffee.

While I don't recall watching *America* (which was produced by Michael Gill, father of A.A. of Morecambe and Wise-knocking fame), I do recall the excitement it generated, for it was transmitted simultaneously on both sides of the Atlantic. That seemed like a thrillingly modern concept, especially as we were so used in this country to lagging months if not years behind the United States when it came to the latest film releases. What it also did, however, was show how far ahead of the United States we were in terms of grown-up attitudes to sex and nudity. I have touched on this already by explaining how the US transmission of *I, Claudius* was not permitted to begin, as it did here, with the spectacle of African women jiggling their bare breasts to help the Emperor Augustus celebrate the seventh anniversary of the Battle of Actium. Similarly, in Alistair Cooke's *America*, footage of naked bathers solemnly observing certain therapeutic rituals in a Californian commune was cut before it could offend the ghosts of the Founding Fathers. Over here in the Old Country, happily, we got the full tit-and-bum treatment.

Cooke was used to the fragile sensibilities of his adopted countryfolk. On public television's *Masterpiece Theatre* he also introduced *Poldark*, and was rewarded with a slew of angry letters and phone calls, one of them denouncing a sordid exercise 'in bouncing from bed to bed'. It was precisely that bed-bouncing that made *Poldark* – an adaptation of Winston Graham's saga of tin-mining and bodice-ripping in eighteenth-century Cornwall – such a hit here in 1975.

By the early 1970s it was clear that colour television and historical drama were perfect bedfellows. *The Onedin Line*, about a family-owned shipping line based in Victorian-era Liverpool, almost spanned the decade, beginning in 1971 and running until 1980. Writer Cyril Abraham had been commissioned by the BBC before he had thought of a title for his seafaring tale, but then he heard about a mythological water nymph called Ondine, and had the brainwave of moving the E. Almost more memorable than the name of *The Onedin Line*, however, was the theme tune: 'Spartacus', from the ballet by Aram Khachaturian. Once again, I am prepared to admit subjectivity, but it seems to me that television in the 1970s produced the greatest of all TV theme music, from stirring, symphonic stuff like 'Spartacus', to popular folk songs like 'Dance Ti' Thy Daddy', whence came the title of *When the Boat Comes In*.

Then there was the orchestral arrangement that announced more oily goings-on in *Dallas*, still one of the most evocative of TV themes. *Dallas* began in 1978, and was soon a fabulous hit all over the world, even behind the Iron Curtain in Romania, where Communist leader Nicolae Ceauşescu allowed his people to watch it not because he thought they might enjoy it, but because he felt certain that it would convince them of the iniquitous decadence of capitalism. Instead, they simply felt miffed at what they were missing, and when Ceauşescu was toppled, a Romanian businessman created a *Dallas* theme park, to celebrate the show's role in bringing down Communism.

Chicanery at Southfork continued until 1991, and while it might seem perverse to conclude a book about television in the 1970s with something that happened in the 1990s, I feel I should share with you a short paragraph I read in the London *Evening Standard* shortly after the world waved goodbye to J.R. Ewing and associates. It was reported in the *Standard* that a Bedouin tribe had delayed its annual migration across the Sahara because its elders were not prepared to miss the last episode of *Dallas*.

I'm still not sure whether that is an uplifting or dispiriting example of television's impact on the behavioural habits of the planet's population, but either way I remember my mother telling me repeatedly in my formative years that I was getting square-eyed, and letting television rule my life. She wasn't altogether wrong. Had I not been quite so devoted to the box in the corner of the room I would have done better in my O-levels, and perhaps even increased my repertoire on the recorder beyond 'Three Blind Mice'. I would have had a better stamp collection. I would have read more. I might have helped my mum more around the house. But I take great comfort from the knowledge that I was far, far from alone.

Acknowledgements

This book was a collaborative exercise in nostalgia, and I am enormously grateful to those who shared with me their memories of telly in the 1970s. They include Jonny Cook, Chris Taylor, Steph and Craig Cash, Mike King, Lou Dalgleish, Babs Powell, Colin Sinclair, David Morrissey and Avril Hill, who still can't believe that I wasn't a fan of *The Tomorrow People*. If at any stage I have inadvertently made their memories mine, I apologise.

I also made use of a number of excellent books, all of which I think I have credited in the text. My thanks again to the authors concerned.

I am grateful too to my father's old business associate Roy Dickens, and to my esteemed colleague on the *Independent*, Jim Lawton, for letting me use his Manny Klein joke.

At Simon & Schuster, my editor Mike Jones offered excellent advice, and this book is a much better one for his input. Without his predecessor Andrew Gordon, the project might not have got off the ground. And thank you to Rory Scarfe for his desk-editing. I must also thank my agent, Camilla Hornby, who is far too young to remember most of what I've written about, but was nevertheless a great source of encouragement.

Finally, I am indebted to my beloved wife, Jane, and our wonderful children Eleanor, Joe and Jacob. I hope that when I finally emerged from my study, blinking in the sunlight, it was nice to see me, to see me nice.

Brian Viner
Herefordshire, autumn 2008